Southern Black Women

in the Modern Civil Rights Movement

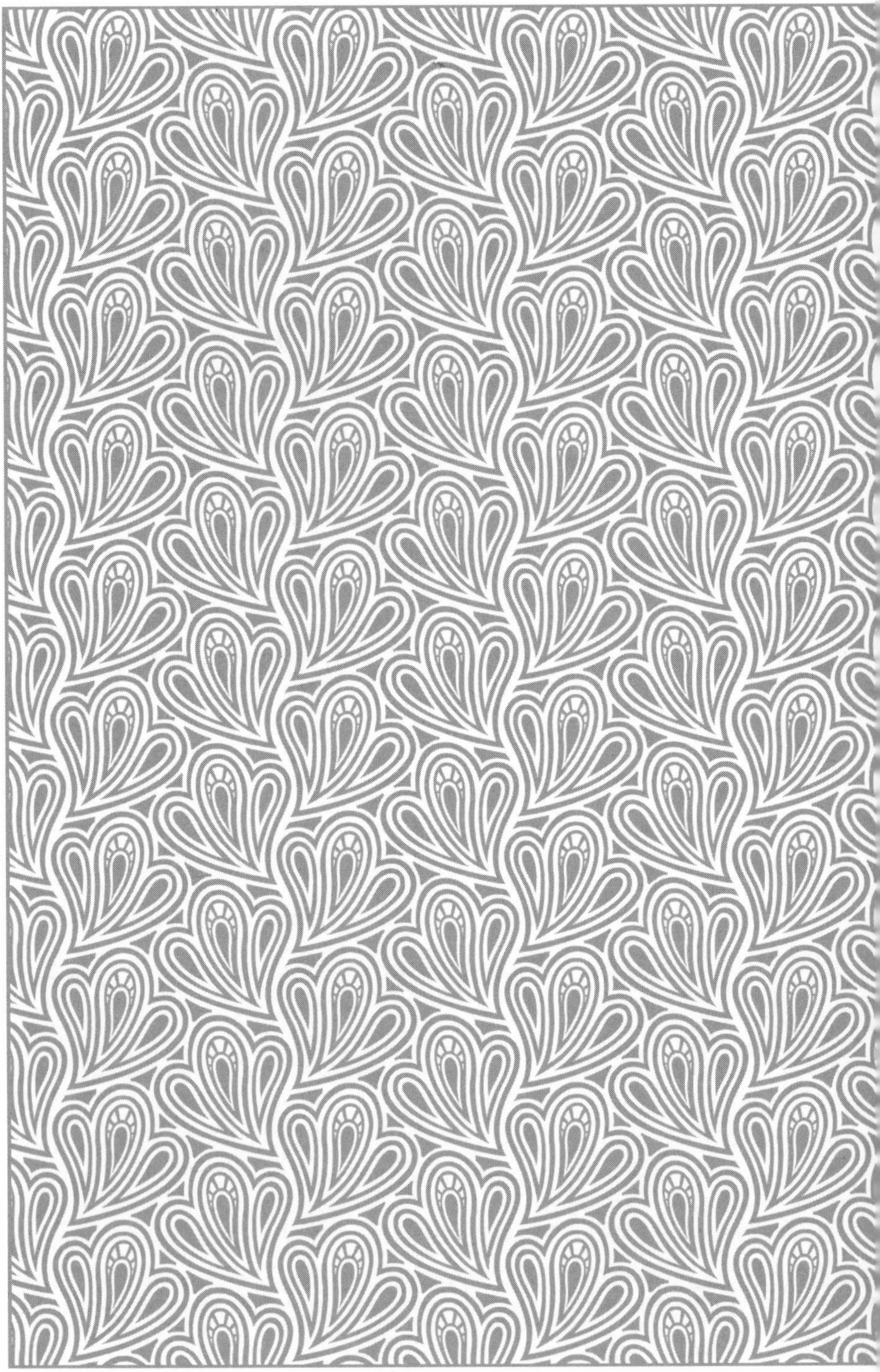

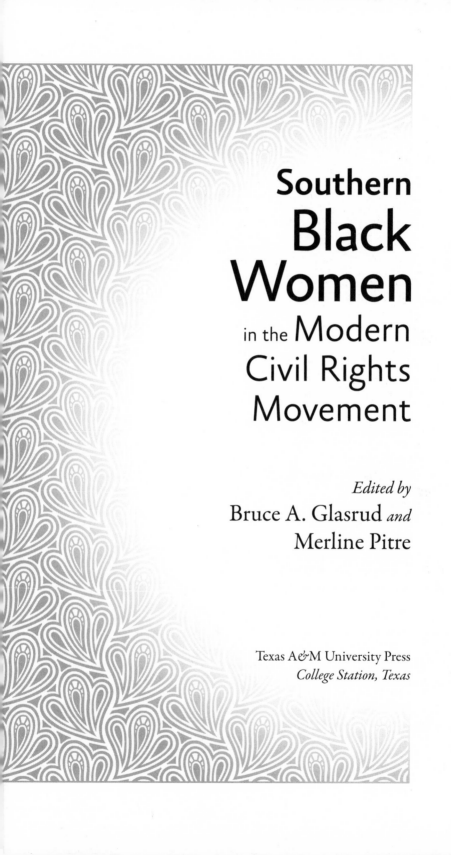

Southern Black Women in the Modern Civil Rights Movement

Edited by
Bruce A. Glasrud *and*
Merline Pitre

Texas A&M University Press
College Station, Texas

First edition

This paper meets the requirements of
ANSI/NISO Z39.48-1992 (Permanence of Paper).
Binding materials have been chosen for durability.
♾ ♻

Library of Congress Cataloging-in-Publication Data

Southern Black women in the modern civil rights movement / edited by Bruce A. Glasrud and Merline Pitre.—1st ed.

p. cm.

Includes bibliographical references and index.

ISBN-13: 978-1-60344-946-5 (cloth : alk. paper)

ISBN-10: 1-60344-946-9 (cloth : alk. paper)

ISBN-13: 978-1-60344-947-2 (pbk. : alk. paper)

ISBN-10: 1-60344-947-7 (pbk. : alk. paper)

[etc.]

1. African American women civil rights workers—Southern States—History—20th century. 2. African American women civil rights workers—Southern States—Biography. 3. Civil rights workers—Southern States—Biography. 4. African American women—Civil rights—Southern States—History—20th century. 5. Southern States—Social conditions—History—20th century. 6. Southern States—Race relations—History—20th century. 7. Civil rights movements—United States. I. Glasrud, Bruce A. II. Pitre, Merline, 1943

E185.92.S682 2013

323.1196'073075—dc23

2012044174

Contents

Acknowledgments

We received considerable help in preparing and publishing this book. For that assistance we wish to thank a number of people. Without the scholarship and ability of the authors, of course, the book would not have been feasible. We are grateful for the cooperation of the eleven authors whose original articles comprise this book. Two readers carefully reviewed the manuscript, asked pertinent questions, made suggestions, and greatly improved the publication. They helped us consider a better approach to studying southern black women in the modern civil rights movement. Mary Lenn Dixon, editor-in-chief at Texas A&M University Press, provided initial acceptance and encouragement for our proposal. The staff at TAMU Press took our manuscript and produced a book, thanks.

More than in other works, we needed and received insight and help from scholars around the nation. We undoubtedly will miss someone, but among those scholars and colleagues are Julianna Barr, University of Florida; Randall Woods, University of Arkansas; Gail S. Murray, Rhodes College; Robert Cassanello, University of Central Florida; Stephanie Cole, University of Texas-Arlington; David Colburn, University of Florida; Beverly G. Bond, University of Memphis; Jack E. Davis, University of Florida; Judson Jeffries, Ohio State University; John Dittmer, DePauw University; Vicki L. Crawford, Clark Atlanta University; Angela Boswell, Henderson State University; Jacqueline Anne Rouse, Georgia State University; Barbara Ransby, University of Illinois at Chicago; Rebecca Sharpless, Texas Christian University; Stephanie Shaw, Ohio State University; Valinda Littlefield, University of South Carolina; and Cary D. Wintz, Texas Southern University. For the rest we remain responsible.

Bruce A. Glasrud
Merline Pitre

Southern Black Women
in the Modern Civil Rights Movement

Introduction

Contributions of African American Women in the Modern Civil Rights Movement

Bruce A. Glasrud and Merline Pitre

African American women have played a significant role in the ongoing struggle for freedom and equality since the inception of this nation. Nowhere is this better illustrated than in the former Confederate states during the modern civil rights era, from 1954 to 1974. During the height of civil rights struggles, black women, like black men, were foot soldiers in sit-in, pray-in, and stand-in campaigns. They were crucial as grassroots and organizational leaders, stimulating mass participation in the movement. Women also served as chief sources for mobilization of people and capital within local communities. They organized black consumers, supported labor unions, and worked in politics and journalism. They particularly helped attack school segregation, coordinate lunch counter sit-ins, boycott buses, mobilize voter-registration drives, and establish communication networks. Yet during the era under study, black women were not typically quoted in the media or consulted by white politicians. Even in historians' accounts, the contribution of women remained obscure for a long time. As Charles Payne has argued, this historical invisibility did not match the historical reality.[1] What is now needed as a match for historical reality is a study that identifies, explores, and evaluates the roles and contributions of African American women in the modern civil rights movement throughout the South. *Southern Black Women in the Modern Civil Rights Movement* attempts to meet this need.

Even though black women performed prominent duties in the civil rights movement—bridge-building, organizing, protesting, participating, mobilizing, creating, energizing, and leading particular efforts—they seldom received credit either for their involvement or for their contributions. For example, no woman was a speaker during the 1963 March on Washington celebration, and only a few women were invited to sit nearby as Mahalia Jackson sang. But, despite the lack of public recognition, African American women set the stage for that moment—and for decades to follow—by their notable part in the eradication of the white-dominated, segregated Southern society. As Stephen Tuck phrases it so well, "the activities of women were so obvious in Georgia protest that it would be a gross oversight to overlook them."[2] This observation was true not only of Georgia but of all the Southern states.

Studies of what happened at the state level are critical not only because of what black women accomplished but also because their activism, leadership, and courage demonstrated the militancy needed for a mass movement. Historians and sociologists have illuminated the ways in which blacks in urban centers, as well as in rural areas, interacted with major civil rights organizations and leaders. Yet we are still some distance from a convincing synthesis of national, or even regional, strategies and factors embodied in the history of the civil rights movement in this country. Our book is a major step toward that goal. Like Paula Giddings's *When and Where I Entered,* it makes clear that not all black women in the South entered the movement in the same way.[3] Some led demonstrations; others remained behind the scene. Most wanted integration; some promoted separate but equal. Many provided money; many, nurturing. Some gave up a career; others made a career of protests and demonstrations. The participants included high-profile women and women who acted without fanfare, even downplaying the importance of their personal leadership, focusing instead on the success of a collective effort.

Southern Black Women in the Modern Civil Rights Movement focuses on the civil rights efforts of black females in the former Confederacy, devoting one chapter to each state. This approach is based on the assumption that white supremacy was most entrenched in those states. Local and state movement studies published in 1988 and 1990 transformed the field of civil rights by constructing narratives about a variety of women rather than focusing on a single national icon such as Rosa Parks. These studies pointed out that the transformation of America's black-white relations occurred differently in different locales. For example the strategies and methods used by Lulu B. White to eradicate Jim Crow in Texas were different from those used by Fannie Lou Hamer to end apartheid in Mississippi. Similarly, the factors in a city run by businessmen differed from those in a rural area dominated by people with farming interests.

It is generally agreed that the modern civil right movement spanned the years 1954 and 1974. We start with 1954, the year in which the US Supreme Court, in *Brown v. Board of Education of Topeka,* struck down segregated education, triggering years of struggle to integrate K-12 and university classrooms. The movement continued to grow. In 1955 a flurry of activity and agitation followed the lynching of fourteen-year-old Emmett Till in Mississippi and the unanimous acquittal of two white men charged in his death. And in December of that same year, Rosa Parks's refusal to yield her seat on a bus in Montgomery, Alabama, ignited a massive civil rights protest. We end two years following Barbara Jordan's 1972 election to the US House of Representatives. The year 1974 witnessed what Genna Rae McNeil refers to as a "nonrevolutionary social movement" on behalf of Joan Little. Sexually attacked by an ice-pick-wielding guard in a North Carolina prison, Little killed him. When she was tried, a massive "Free Joan Little" movement began, and in 1975 she was acquitted by a jury.[4] In 1974, Floridians unveiled a statue honoring a key state and national black leader, Mary McLeod Bethune.

We do not assert that the years 1954–74 were the only years to witness the civil rights revolution or that black women did not participate in earlier and later efforts to change and challenge white supremacy. We note only that these two decades were pivotal in the modern civil rights and black-power movements. In *Freedom's Daughters: The Unsung Heroines of the Civil Rights Movement from 1830 to 1970,* Lynne Olson thoroughly delineates the myriad efforts of women in the civil rights movement through one hundred forty years. She is not alone. Numerous authors have depicted black women's pre-1954 efforts to improve their status and that of their race vis-á-vis white supremacy in the South. One such collection, *Time Longer Than Rope: A Century of African American Activism, 1850–1950,* edited by Charles M. Payne and Adam Green, comprises a thoughtful group of articles.[5] However, we know of no study of the roles of black women in the modern civil rights and black-power movements during the key years 1954–74. *Southern Black Women in the Modern Civil Rights Movement* is written to fill this gap.

The story of women in the modern civil rights movement emerged as an area of concentration for research and teaching following the international conference "Women in the Civil Rights Movement: Trailblazers and Torchbearers, 1941–1965," hosted in 1988 by the Martin Luther King, Jr., Center for Nonviolent Social Change and by Georgia State University. At this event, scholars and activists spent a week reconstructing the activism of women. The papers presented at this conference, edited by Vicki L. Crawford, Jacqueline A. Rouse, and Barbara Woods and published by Indiana University Press in 1990 as *Women in the Civil Rights Movement: Trailblazers and Torchbearers, 1941–1965,* sparked the publication of memoirs, community studies, biographies, organizational studies, and autobiographical essays from black and white women (and men) who picketed, demonstrated, and went to jail for the cause of freedom and justice. This new body of literature introduced the issues of race, class, and gender to the movement.

Book-length studies of black women in the civil rights movement are becoming numerous. Seven years following *Women in the Civil Rights Movement,* Belinda Robnett's *How Long? How Long? African-American Women in the Struggle for Civil Rights* appeared. A sociological study, Robnett's work emphasized the relationship of gender to the civil rights struggle and developed a theory of bridge-building to explain the central role of black women in the civil rights efforts. Peter J. Ling and Sharon Monteith continued the emphasis on gender in their 1999 anthology, *Gender and the Civil Rights Movement.* As Ling and Monteith emphasized, "the civil rights movement was primarily concerned with race, but it was also about personal identity."[6]

Two influential books published in 2001 continued the study of black women and the civil rights movement. Lynne Olson's previously mentioned *Freedom's Daughters* discussed the modern civil rights era in connection with a long history of black women's activism. *Sisters in the Struggle: African American Women in the Civil Rights–Black Power Movement,* edited by Bettye Collier-Thomas and V. P. Franklin, moved the discussion to the years beyond 1970 by including the black-power movement in a signal collection of articles. As some of the essays note, the position of black and white women in the movement changed as a result of the goals and aspirations of the black-power movement.[7] For studies of white women in the struggle see Constance Curry, *Deep in Our Hearts: Nine White Women in the Freedom Movement,* and Gail S. Murray's collection, *Throwing Off the Cloak of Privilege: White Southern Women Activists in the Civil Rights Era.*[8]

Publication continued. In 2005, Jeanne Theoharis and Komozi Woodard edited *Groundwork: Local Black Freedom Movements in America,* which considered a much broader geographic scope than the Southern states. The editors pointed out the centrality of women in local black-freedom movements across the nation.[9] One other pivotal work should be included: in 1978, Sharon Harley and Rosalyn Terborg-Penn published *The Afro-American Woman: Struggles and Images.* This pioneering collection of excellent essays encompassed the earlier stages of the freedom struggle and provided a much-needed work for classes in women's history. Darlene Clark Hine and Kathleen Thompson later prepared an analytical study, *A Shining Thread of Hope: The History of Black Women in America.* Two other broad-based studies, *When and Where I Enter: The Impact of Black Women on Race and Sex in America,* by Paula Giddings, and *Too Heavy a Load: Black Women in Defense of Themselves, 1894–1994,* by Deborah Gray White, brought varied, albeit highly original, concepts to the study of black female history and its relationship to the civil rights movement.[10]

More local studies significantly increased our understanding of the centrality of black women in the Southern civil rights struggles. Five monographs of special importance are Shannon L. Frystak, *Our Minds on Freedom: Women and the Struggle for Black Equality in Louisiana, 1924–1967,* a thorough investigation of Louisiana women and civil rights. *Undaunted by the Fight: Spelman College and the Civil Rights Movement, 1957–1967,* by Harry G. Lefever, carefully tracks the emergence of a protest tradition in Spelman College. Merline Pitre's *In Struggle against Jim Crow: Lulu B. White and the NAACP, 1900–1957,* portrays a woman too often overlooked in regional as well as national studies. She belongs in the pantheon of prominent women. Cynthia Griggs Fleming's *In the Shadow of Selma: The Continuing Struggle for Civil Rights in the Rural South* concentrates on the rural areas of Alabama and the civil rights efforts largely conducted by women. Christina Greene turned our attention to a locality in North Carolina in *Our Separate Ways: Women and the Black Freedom Movement in Durham, North Carolina.*[11]

Memoirs or autobiographies and biographies allow us to understand some black women leaders of the civil rights movement. Memoirs include Dorothy Height's *Open Wide the Freedom Gates: A Memoir;* Daisy Bates's, *The Long Shadow of Little Rock: A Memoir;* Septima P. Clark's *Echo in My Soul;* Cynthia S. Brown's *Ready from Within: Septima Clark and the Civil Rights Movement;* Charlayne Hunter-Gault's *In My Place;* and Lulu Westbrooks-Griffin's *Freedom Is Not Free: Forty-five Days in Leesburg Stockade, A Civil Rights Story,* the brutal story of thirty young women locked in a filthy setting for their civil rights efforts.[12]

The outpouring of studies in recent decades regarding the modern civil rights freedom struggle continues to provide information about the role and contribution of women. African American females, we learn, were indispensable to the success of the struggle for racial equality in each of the former Confederate states. Local and state movement studies published in the 1980s and 1990s transformed the field of civil rights by constructing narratives about a variety of women rather than about a single prominent individual. These studies pointed out that the transformation of America's black and white relations occurred differently in different localities.

The purpose of this book is to depict black female civil rights action across all former Confederate states, not (as in other books on the topic) only five or six states. Nor is this book about only the stars; it is about black women generally and their contributions to civil rights throughout the South. It is intended for use in undergraduate and graduate classes in such fields as women's history/studies, civil rights, black studies/history, Southern history, and United States surveys. It will appeal to general readers with an interest in the modern civil rights struggle in the United States. And because it is based on both secondary and primary courses, it will be useful for the scholar.

Contributors to this volume, who come from across the South, have published books and articles about their topics. Together they identify general patterns and factors that distinguished civil rights activism in each state. They have supplemented previous scholarly investigations and, at the same time, have drawn attention to the roles played by African American women in the sustained protest effort. By reclaiming and retelling the contributions of black women to the civil rights movement, the contributors and their colleagues can view the past through a different lens. In the words of Glenda Gilmore, the time has come to "re-vision the southern political narrative from other angles" to "take into account the plethora of sources on African American and women's history."[13]

The organizational framework of *Southern Black Women in the Modern Civil Rights Movement* was developed purposefully. Each of the eleven states of the former Confederacy is discussed by a leading historian, who profiles one woman or more. The book is divided into two parts. Part I is titled "Professional and Organizational Leaders." Belinda Robnett describes a professional leader as one who had significant civil rights experiences prior to the movement activities and whose concerns transcend local issues. The chapters on Texas, Virginia, and Arkansas focus on individuals who fit this category. Each black female leader in those states worked with the NAACP in her efforts to destroy the legal basis for Jim Crow. Texas and Virginia blacks faced moderate resistance from whites. Blacks in Arkansas faced violent resistance, but with NAACP support and with Daisy Bates at their head, they pressed forward.

Part II, "Bridge Leaders and Foot Soldiers in the Deep South," treats North Carolina, South Carolina, Florida, Georgia, Alabama, Mississippi, Louisiana, and Tennessee, the eight states where white resistance was extreme. This violence served as a catalyst for bridge leaders and foot soldiers in their quest to change the status quo. According to Robnett, a bridge leader served as a liaison between organizations such as the Southern Christian Leadership Conference and the community the bridge leader strove to serve, and foot soldiers were local activists who worked in concert with community leaders.[14] Given the fact that the national civil rights movement had its roots in local movements, female foot soldiers and bridge leaders contributed immensely in bringing about an end to the Jim Crow system in their individual states and in the nation. A glimpse of the activities of black women in each state will be instructive.

According to Caroline Emmons, black women in the Virginia civil rights movements frequently have been overlooked because Virginia featured a supposedly "genteel" resistance, because key black women activists fought for civil rights accomplishments earlier than traditional dates, and (as elsewhere in the South) because men seemed to be leading and accomplishing advances. Virginia's black female leaders fit well the category of professional and organizational leaders, but black women in Virginia also effectively challenged segregation in public transportation, education, and other arenas. Generally the civil rights struggle in Virginia produced peaceful protests and resistance, but violence erupted in Danville. In every effort to halt the segregation of society, black women played a vital role. Virginia was at the center of early civil rights battles over educational access, teacher-pay equity, and integration in public transport. Important legal victories in Virginia, often with women as the plaintiffs, laid the groundwork for later struggles in the Deep South. Black females such as Irene Morgan and Barbara Johns, who were actively pursuing civil rights before the Montgomery bus boycott, help us understand not only how and why African Americans began to protest for greater equality but also the critical role played by women (and girls). This chapter, which examines the experience of African American women in the Virginia civil rights movement, offers further evidence that historians need to broaden their longitudinal (and geographical) boundaries when evaluating the history of the civil rights movement.

Yvonne Frear posits that African American women of Texas have been at the forefront of the civil rights movement since the 1940s. Lulu B. White, who would become the first female executive secretary of the NAACP in the South, was at the helm of the Houston chapter in 1944, when, in *Smith v. Allwright,* the US Supreme Court declared the Texas white Democratic primary unconstitutional. Nor was White instrumental in this endeavor only; she also encouraged blacks to vote and seek office. Among those heeding her advice was Hattie M. White, the second black and first black female to be elected to office in Texas since Reconstruction. Standing on Hattie White's shoulders would be Barbara C. Jordan, the first black from Texas to be elected to the US Congress since Reconstruction. Other black women throughout the Lone Star State, such as Juanita Craft, were organizers, mobilizers, and foot soldiers in the struggle against Jim Crow. They helped integrate universities and public facilities, and eventually they changed the landscape in Texas.

As Jeannie Whayne points out, black women contributed significantly to the civil rights struggle in Arkansas between 1940 and 1974, particularly in the struggle to achieve equal educational opportunities. They were at the forefront of the battle to equalize teacher salaries and to integrate professional schools. A professional leader and the most famous African American civil rights activist in Arkansas, Daisy Bates presided over the state chapter of the NAACP and counseled the "Little Rock Nine" as they integrated Central High School in 1957. In the early 1960s a group of black women played notable roles during SNCC's effort to end segregation practices and secure voting rights for African Americans in the Arkansas Delta.

In the Deep South—Florida, Alabama, Georgia, South Carolina, Mississippi, North Carolina, Louisiana, and Tennessee—civil rights activists faced intense prejudice and even violence. But in spite of confrontations and threats, black women participated extensively, as bridge leaders and as foot soldiers, in efforts to throw off Jim Crow.

Initially, Maxine Jones tells us, African American women in Florida supported black community efforts to eliminate such wrongs as lynching, injustice in the courts, and police brutality and to obtain the right to vote. Among these women, Mary McLeod Bethune was a leader. During the 1960s, black Florida women, serving as foot soldiers, still confronted Jim Crow, especially in the cities of Tallahassee, Jacksonville, and St. Augustine. Striving for improvements in education, transportation, politics, and economic opportunity, they moved closer to full citizenship—but not as close as others in those years of civil rights agitation.

In Alabama, Stefanie Decker notes, Rosa Parks's decision to sit in the front of a bus started the Montgomery struggle, but black women had long been preparing for such a challenge. Black men received media attention, but black women were a moving force during the march to Selma and in civil rights activities throughout southwestern Alabama. It was the women who led the integration of the University of Alabama, who supported the "Children's Crusade" in Birmingham, and who encouraged voter registration and protests. The women met vicious white opposition and retaliation, but they held the civil rights movement together. Women acted both as bridge leaders and as foot soldiers. In the late sixties and early seventies, black women also turned their attention to economic opportunity and achieved gains for themselves as well as their race. As Decker phrased it, they "dismantled the system of Jim Crow."

In negotiating the treacherous landscapes of segregation and racism in urban and rural Georgia, Clarissa Myrick-Harris discovered, African American women made profound contributions to the civil rights movement locally and nationally. United by a common purpose, these women—young and old—hailed from a range of socioeconomic backgrounds. Many worked behind the scenes as foot soldiers. Several, circumventing the undercurrent of sexism in the movement, became founders and leaders of organizations and institutions in the forefront of the fight for equality. This chapter explores the tradition and contexts of activism among black women in Georgia during four key phases of the struggle for social change in the state—beginning with the laying of the foundation in the 1940s.

W. Marvin Dulaney's judgment is that black women played a very important role in the civil rights movement in South Carolina. To win social and political justice, they participated in major lawsuits, such as *Elmore v. Rice* and *Briggs v. Elliott,* and in direct-action campaigns. In addition they served as bridge builders, and they established innovative programs to improve the lives of African Americans in the state. Women such as Septima Poinsette Clark, Modjeska Monteith Simkins, and Elizabeth Waring challenged the status quo, worked with the NAACP and other organizations, and advanced the causes of social and political justice nationally.

In the early twentieth century, Mississippi, a rural Southern state, was dominated by poverty and a virulent white-supremacist mind-set. Beginning in the 1950s, both in spite of and because of the lynching of Emmett Till, the assassination of Medgar Evers, and the murder of at least three northern civil rights workers, the state produced an active group of civil rights participants. Black women, Tiyi M. Morris argues, engaged heavily in this effort. Black Mississippian bridge leader Fannie Lou Hamer epitomized their strength and leadership. She encouraged women not only to register to vote but also to take active roles in their communities. Black women did so, and they even challenged the national Democratic Party.

In North Carolina, as Dwonna Naomi Goldstone iterates, the physical and psychological strength of African American women, "served them both in leadership and behind-the-scenes roles in a civil rights movement that would not have been successful without them." In many organizations and events, the majority of participants were black women. In Greensboro many came from Bennett College (at one time more than half the student body had been jailed), and in Durham women assumed pivotal roles, serving as protesters, marchers, and canvassers. Black women fought job discrimination, work overloads, and racial harassment. They battled for school desegregation. North Carolina women produced a national civil rights leader, Ella Baker, and a leader for gender equality, Pauli Murray.

Shannon Frystak focuses on the significant role black women played in Louisiana's "long civil rights movement." Beginning in the 1920s, African American women foot soldiers not only fought for equality and citizenship in myriad ways; they also attained formal leadership positions in a movement largely overshadowed and dominated by men. They served as bridge builders. In the aftermath of the civil rights movement "proper," these same women continued their fight on behalf of Louisiana's black citizenry: in neighborhood associations, in War on Poverty initiatives, and in the world of politics.

Tennessee's civil rights movement, Bobby L. Lovett notes, involved women extensively. Long before the 1950s and 60s, and continuing into the twenty-first century, black women used social and civic clubs, benevolent societies, church auxiliaries, and professional training to promote black social and cultural uplift, agitate for racial equality, and gain woman's suffrage. Others assisted in the modern version of the civil rights movement, and provided support for black men. Through national and world exposure, athletes such as the Tennessee State University Tigerbelles helped sideline Tennessee's racial problems. A black woman led the effort to desegregate the higher education system. Women helped lead the political rights revolution. By 2006, women constituted 47 percent of blacks in the state legislature.

In this wide-ranging collection of essays, more than one truth stands out: African American women, many of whom had been marginalized within the large body of civil rights literature, were part of the defining national trajectory of the black liberation movement. Sources for mining African American women's history during the civil rights era have become more accessible. The use of gender as a system of analysis found its way into the emerging studies in the field of Southern history. And written histories have begun to shift toward a more balanced representation of black female reformers. It is also important to note that black women were not monolithic. They fought Jim Crow and segregation as professional and organizational leaders, as bridge leaders, and as foot soldiers. Without their efforts, the modern civil rights movement very likely would not have been as successful. Or successful at all.

Notes

1. Charles Payne, "Men Led, but Women Organized: Movement Participation of Women in the Mississippi Delta," in Vicki L. Crawford, Jacqueline Anne Rouse, and Barbara Woods, eds., *Women in the Civil Rights Movement: Trailblazers and Torchbearers, 1941–1965* (Bloomington: Indiana University Press, 1993), 1–12.

2. Stephen G. N. Tuck, *Beyond Atlanta: The Struggle for Racial Equality in Georgia, 1940–1980* (Athens: University of Georgia Press, 2001), 248.

3. Paula Giddings, *When and Where I Enter: The Impact of Black Women on Race and Sex in America* (New York: William Morrow, 1984).

4. Genna Rae McNeil, "'Joanne Is You and Joanne Is Me': A Consideration of African American Women and the 'Free Joan Little' Movement, 1974–75," in Bettye Collier-Thomas and V. P. Franklin, eds., *Sisters in the Struggle: African American Women in the Civil Rights–Black Power Movement* (New York: New York University Press, 2001), 276, n. 6.

5. Lynne Olson, *Freedom's Daughters: The Unsung Heroines of the Civil Rights Movement from 1830 to 1970* (New York: Simon and Schuster, 2001); Charles M. Payne and Adam Green, eds., *Time Longer Than Rope: A Century of African American Activism, 1850–1950* (New York: New York University Press, 2003).

6. Crawford, Rouse, and Woods, eds., *Women in the Civil Rights Movement;* Belinda Robnett, *How Long? How Long? African-American Women in the Struggle for Civil Rights* (New York: Oxford University Press, 1997); Peter J. Ling and Sharon Monteith, eds., *Gender and the Civil Rights Movement* (New York: Garland Publishing, 1999), 1.

7. Olson, *Freedom's Daughters;* Collier-Thomas and Franklin, eds., *Sisters in the Struggle.*

8. Constance Curry, ed., *Deep in Our Hearts: Nine White Women In the Freedom Movement* (Athens: University of Georgia Press, 2000); Gail S. Murray, ed., *Throwing Off the Cloak of Privilege: White Southern Women Activists in the Civil Rights Era* (Gainesville: University Press of Florida, 2004).

9. Jeanne Theoharis and Komozi Woodard, eds., *Groundwork: Local Black Freedom Movements in America* (New York: New York University Press, 2005).

10. Sharon Harley and Rosalyn Terborg-Penn, eds., *The Afro-American Woman: Struggles and Images* (Port Washington, N.Y.: Kennikat Press, 1978; reprint, 1997); Darlene Clark Hine and Kathleen Thompson, *A Shining Thread of Hope: The History of Black Women in* America (New York: Broadway Books, 1998); Giddings, *When and Where I Enter;* Deborah Gray White, *Too Heavy a Load: Black Women in Defense of Themselves, 1894–1994* (New York: W. W. Norton, 1999).

11. Shannon L. Frystak, *Our Minds on Freedom: Women and the Struggle for Black Equality in Louisiana, 1924–1967* (Baton Rouge: Louisiana State University Press, 2009); Harry G. Lefever, *Undaunted by the Fight: Spelman College and the Civil Rights Movement, 1957–1967* (Macon, Ga.: Mercer University Press, 2005); Merline Pitre, *In Struggle against Jim Crow: Lulu B. White and the NAACP, 1900–1957* (College Station: Texas A&M University Press, 1999); Cynthia Griggs Fleming, *In the Shadow of Selma: The Continuing Struggle for Civil Rights in the Rural South* (Lanham, Md.: Rowman & Littlefield, 2004); Christina Greene, *Our Separate Ways: Women and the Black Freedom Movement in Durham, North Carolina* (Chapel Hill: University of North Carolina Press, 2005).

12. Dorothy Height, *Open Wide the Freedom Gates: A Memoir* (New York: PublicAffairs, 2003); Daisy Bates, *The Long Shadow of Little Rock: A Memoir* (Fayetteville: University of Arkansas Press, 1987); Septima Poinsette Clark, *Echo in My Soul* (New York: Dutton, 1962); Cynthia S. Brown, ed., *Ready from Within: Septima Clark and the Civil Rights Movement* (Navarro, Calif.: Wild Tree Press, 1986); Charlayne Hunter-Gault, *In My Place* (New York: Knopf, 1993); Lulu Westbrooks-Griffin, *Freedom Is Not Free: Forty-Five Days in Leesburg Stockade, A Civil Rights Story* (Hamlin, N.Y.: Heirloom, 1998).

13. Glenda Gilmore, "But She Can't Find Her [V.O.] Key," *Feminist Studies* 25, no. 1 (Spring 1999): 137.

14. Robnett, *How Long? How Long?* 19–23, 150.

PART I

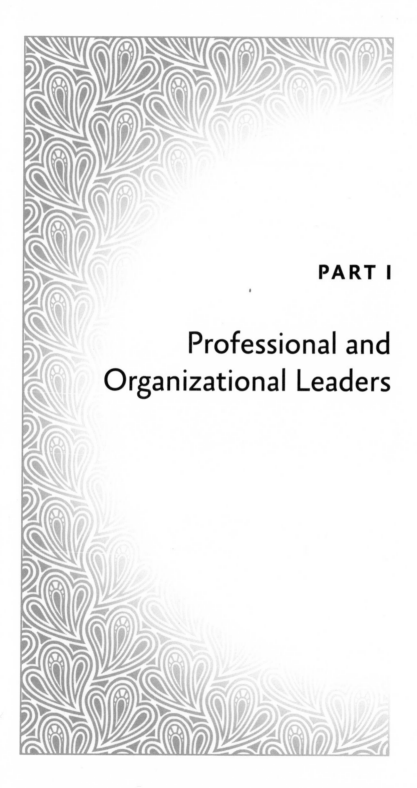

Professional and Organizational Leaders

1 "A Tremendous Job To Be Done"

African American Women in the Virginia Civil Rights Movement

Caroline S. Emmons

The names of Irene Morgan and Barbara Johns are unfamiliar to many students of the civil rights movement. Because historians have focused on more visible male leaders and on a handful of pivotal battlegrounds in the South, these women, like so many others who played important roles in the movement, have been sidelined. As a consequence, few students of the movement understand how African American activism developed and intensified in the mid-twentieth century. In response, historians of the movement increasingly argue that, rather than examine this complex and diffuse movement from the top down (as studies of Martin Luther King, Jr., and the Southern Christian Leadership Conference tend to do), they can better understand it by looking at it from multiple perspectives.

Many civil rights studies also have distorted the timeline of the movement. Early studies in particular promoted the years 1954 and 1968 as its bookends. Pivotal events certainly occurred during that period, but such an emphasis seems to suggest that the Montgomery Bus Boycott sprang out of a vacuum. Furthermore, this division of history into periods suggests that the movement ended with King's assassination. Such assumptions might be convenient for the purposes of historical organization, but they do not reflect reality. When the movement began and when (or if) it ended are issues that engender ongoing messy, contentious debate.[1]

Given these problems with historical presentations of the civil rights movement, it is not surprising that Irene Morgan's and Barbara Johns's names are unfamiliar to many. Morgan's act of resistance took place in 1944 and Johns's in 1951, placing them well ahead of the traditional "beginning" of the movement. In addition, both are women and neither was active in existing civil rights organizations. Their challenge to Jim Crow was initiated as a personal act of courage. That might make them more remarkable, but it also makes them more likely to be forgotten.

To complicate matters further, Morgan's and Johns's civil rights movement began in Virginia, a state not typically seen as pivotal in the struggle from the mid-1950s onward for African American political and social equality. Thurgood Marshall and others noted that, as an Upper South state, Virginia was judged more likely than the Deep South to be relatively moderate. The doctrine of Massive Resistance was first developed in Richmond, but the state did not experience the violence and terrorism that marked civil rights protests in the Deep South. White Virginians worked to preserve the racial status quo but discouraged overt violence as a means of doing so. Proud of Virginia's "genteel" image, white politicians in Virginia were committed to protecting Jim Crow but recoiled from the tactics of figures such as Bull Connor.

African American women in Virginia played important roles in the challenge to segregation in public transportation and education. This is not especially surprising. Like white women, they often were excluded from political roles during the mid-twentieth century. Black women were very dependent on public transportation. And like white mothers, they were concerned about the education of their children.

In challenging Jim Crow practices on public transportation, black women in Virginia played critical, but overlooked, roles. In 1940, for example, more than a decade before Rosa Parks was arrested in Montgomery, Alabama, for refusing to give up her seat to a white man, Pauli Murray and Adelene McBean were arrested in Petersburg, Virginia.[2] The two women were en route from New York to North Carolina when, as their bus drove through central Virginia south of Richmond, they were instructed to move to the rear. McBean, never having traveled in the South, refused to do so, and the women were jailed over the weekend. NAACP leaders in Petersburg contacted Charles Houston of the NAACP legal office, who arranged local representation for them. More than two hundred fifty people, black and white, came to the courtroom to watch a most unusual spectacle, two young African American women defying Jim Crow conventions. They were found guilty of disorderly conduct and public disturbance. When they lost their subsequent appeal, the women refused bail and went to jail—an extraordinarily courageous action that presaged future civil rights leaders' strategies.[3]

In 1944, Irene Morgan was arrested while traveling from Gloucester, Virginia, to Baltimore. When she refused to give up her seat and physically resisted being removed from the bus, she was jailed. While being held, Morgan called out the window to a passing African American child, who told a local black minister of her arrest. He in turn contacted Morgan's mother to let her know what had happened. The Gloucester courtroom where Morgan was tried bore the seal of the Ku Klux Klan on the door. Morgan was represented by NAACP-affiliated attorney Spottswood Robinson, and with his encouragement, she refused to plead guilty. With fellow NAACP lawyers Thurgood Marshall and William Hastie, Robinson argued that Virginia segregation laws interfered with interstate commerce. Eventually they took the case on appeal to the US Supreme Court. In a 6–1 vote, the court overturned Morgan's conviction.[4]

The Morgan case is especially significant because the Supreme Court ruling that segregation on interstate buses was unconstitutional led to a change in Interstate Commerce Commission policy. In 1947, members of the Fellowship of Reconciliation, a pacifist civil rights group based in New York, embarked on a Journey of Reconciliation throughout the Upper South in which riders would test the ICC policy. Of course this strategy was employed even more famously by members of the Congress of Racial Equality in 1961, when they organized Freedom Rides throughout the Upper and Lower South. Although Morgan's name is not well known among students of the civil rights movement, her bold and lonely action in 1944 set a number of important events in motion.

Education was the focus of the earliest civil rights battle. Black women were underrepresented in this field, but they would be at the forefront of the struggle to end school segregation. In Virginia they had long been outspoken critics of the substandard educational facilities provided for their children. Groups such as the Martha E. Forrester Council of Women in Prince Edward County, Virginia, had worked for decades to establish a public high school for African American students. The women in the council—schoolteachers, homemakers, and clubwomen—were committed to the program of racial uplift popular among middle-class African Americans. The council is not even a footnote in most studies of *Brown v. Board of Education,* but (as will be discussed later in this essay) the activism of these women had effects far beyond what even they probably imagined.

The NAACP began its attack on segregated education by challenging segregation in graduate and professional schools and pay inequities between white and black teachers. In 1935, NAACP lawyer Charles Houston met with African American educators to discuss plans to challenge segregation in graduate education at the University of Virginia. Alice Jackson wanted to be considered as a plaintiff in the planned case. A graduate of historically black Virginia Union University, Jackson had enrolled in the graduate program at Smith College. The expense of attending Smith became prohibitive for Jackson, however, and the reduced cost of attending the University of Virginia was appealing. As a consequence, in 1935, Jackson applied to the University of Virginia. The NAACP offered quiet support, but major newspapers in the state, especially the *Richmond Times-Dispatch,* were immediately critical, and the university rejected her application without providing a reason. When it became apparent that Jackson's work at Smith had not been especially strong, the NAACP backed away from its earlier encouragement. In 1936 the Virginia Assembly established a scholarship fund for black students to pursue graduate work out of state, and Jackson continued her studies at Columbia.[5]

While efforts to desegregate graduate schools proceeded, the NAACP legal team also began challenging teacher-pay inequities. Houston and Marshall believed that such challenges were best mounted first in the Upper South, and the first successful suit originated in Maryland. In 1938 the NAACP took up the case of Aline Black, a schoolteacher in Norfolk, with Thurgood Marshall heading up her legal team. African American teachers in Norfolk received a $699 minimum salary and a maximum of $1105; white teachers were paid $970 minimum and $1900 maximum. In a strategy frequently used by Southern school boards to prevent salary challenges, Black's contract was not renewed and the NAACP was forced to drop her case.[6]

Beginning in the 1930s, NAACP lawyers pursued a policy of forcing Southern K–12 school districts to meet the standard set in 1896 by *Plessy v. Ferguson,* which said that separate but equal was constitutionally permissible. Of course, black and white schools in the South were not equal in facilities. This strategy put pressure on white politicians in the South, but it was expensive and seemed likely to exhaust NAACP resources before it could produce meaningful change. Consequently, in the late 1940s, NAACP lawyers began a direct legal challenge of the constitutionality of segregated education.

For decades, blacks in Prince Edward County had sought to secure better educational opportunities for their children. And then, in the 1930s, African American students initiated a challenge of their own. The unusual role played by black students in the lawsuit and the county's extreme reaction to the decision—closing the entire public school system for an astonishing five years—have drawn historians, journalists, documentarians, educators, and others to this story. In fact, most studies of the impact of the *Brown* decision in the South have focused on Prince Edward County.[7]

Observers characteristically have overlooked the role of black women in the struggle for educational equality in Prince Edward County. Often the women worked behind the scenes, without fanfare, without dramatic public presentations. But through at least two generations, their work profoundly shaped the contours of the Prince Edward story. The efforts of the Martha E. Forrester Council of Women to secure better school facilities for black children was particularly important.[8] In 1927 the first Robert R. Moton School was built for African American students in Farmville, Prince Edward County, but its facilities were quickly overwhelmed by large enrollments. The school was built to hold 325 students, but within a few years 469 were enrolled, forcing students to attend in shifts.[9] In 1939, following further demands for improved conditions, the Robert R. Moton High School was built across the street.[10] But this facility, too, was rapidly overcrowded.

In addition to lobbying for new and improved school buildings, the council worked diligently to address shortfalls in materials and equipment, which were common in African American schools during the Jim Crow era. The council helped furnish the school auditorium, paying some of the cost of a piano, helping purchase school supplies, and donating candy for holiday celebrations.[11] Despite the efforts of the council and other African American organizations, however, black schools in Prince Edward County, as in most of the South, lagged far behind those of whites. Blacks, disproportionately poor and mostly disenfranchised, had to bear a double tax burden: supporting white schools to which their children were not admitted and finding the means to support chronically underfunded black schools. But no matter how hard African Americans worked to bring their schools up to the level of white schools, it was simply too expensive without aid from federal and state governments. Of course these inequities led to the NAACP legal campaign to end discriminatory practices.

The moment that black women in Prince Edward County united in an effort to secure better facilities, the NAACP lawyers chose that county for an important commitment of resources. In response the white power structure, swearing absolute opposition to the efforts of the black women and the NAACP, initiated what would be known as Massive Resistance. The confrontation was initiated in the spring of 1951 by sixteen-year-old Barbara Johns, a student at Moton High School who became fed up with its inadequate and overcrowded conditions. Angered by the contrast with the newly built white school less than a mile from Moton, in a remarkable act of self-assertion, Johns persuaded fellow students to join her in a student strike of Moton High School. She and some of her fellow students marched on the Prince Edward County Courthouse, where they demanded that something be done about the discrepancy.

When white school officials, taken aback by this demand, began a program of intimidation against the students' parents, Johns contacted NAACP-affiliated attorneys Oliver W. Hill and Spottswood Robinson. The NAACP had not considered Prince Edward County a likely focal point for legal action, but the attorneys who visited Farmville were astonished by the broad support for the students' actions expressed by parents and others in the African American community. Consequently, when the local black community agreed to accept the NAACP's new focus on desegregation rather than equalization of school facilities, the organization took on the Prince Edward County case. Ultimately it became one of five suits heard by the US Supreme Court as *Brown v. Board of Education.* Johns, however, paid a price for her victory. She began receiving death threats and was sent away for her safety. She went to live with her uncle Vernon Johns, in Montgomery, Alabama. (As pastor of Dexter Avenue Baptist Church, Johns was well known for his fiery denunciations of Jim Crow. Eventually the church leaders asked him to leave Dexter because of his confrontational style. Then, seeking a more mild-tempered replacement, they hired young Martin Luther King, Jr.)[12]

Despite the excitement generated by the *Brown* decision, Prince Edward County became the site of the most significant application of Massive Resistance in the Upper South and arguably in the entire South. In 1959, after repeatedly resisting the Supreme Court order, Prince Edward County officials were ordered to desegregate without further delay. Rather than comply, they cut off all funding for local schools, shutting down the entire school system. Incredible as it seems, no public schools operated in Prince Edward County for five years. The courageous actions of a sixteen-year-old girl had reverberated far beyond what she could have imagined.

During this shutout, African American women played important roles in the effort to provide educational opportunities for the black children of Prince Edward County. The American Friends Service Committee, in particular, was active in placing Prince Edward County schoolchildren in homes in the North and West so that they could attend school. The Martha E. Forrester Council of Women served as a means by which black women in Prince Edward County could assert their demands for better educational opportunities. And black women from outside the county also lent support.

Helen Baker, whose lively, funny personality comes through vividly in her letters, was an African American Quaker born in Suffolk, Virginia. She reports that during the Depression she had been forced to spend a brief period working eleven-hours days in a tobacco plant for sixty-two cents a day. The experience politicized her and led her to become active in a variety of causes.[13] By 1960 she was working in Prince Edward County as the community-relations consultant for the American Friends Service Committee's Emergency School Project. Baker's job was to help place Prince Edward County's African American schoolchildren in the homes of volunteers elsewhere in the country where they could continue their schooling. The group placed about fifty children, and although this number represented a significant organizational effort, Baker lamented that fifty was but a small percentage of the approximately fifteen hundred shut out.[14]

Baker also helped oversee the creation of ten "training centers" in Prince Edward County to provide some education and especially to give kids somewhere to spend supervised time while parents and other caregivers had to work. Nine of these centers were overseen by women, several of whom had taught in the PEC school system before the closings. They could not replace the public education system, but they made an important contribution in a very difficult situation.[15]

By 1960, NAACP efforts to implement the *Brown* decision were having limited success in most parts of Virginia. Prince Edward County is probably the most extreme example of Massive Resistance, but a few other Virginia schools, notably in Charlottesville and Norfolk, also closed. In the spring of that year, while the school cases were moving through the courts, the civil rights movement took an unexpected turn. Inspired by the actions of four students at the Agricultural and Technical College of North Carolina, black college students across the South, including Virginia, began holding sit-ins in their cities. Richmond, with two historically black colleges in the larger metro area, had plenty of potential activists to draw upon.

Unlike some states in which the national NAACP office struggled to maintain good working relations with local black attorneys, Richmond had a leading civil rights lawyer in Oliver W. Hill, who attended law school and later worked closely with Thurgood Marshall. Hill's partner, Spottswood W. Robinson III, also played an important role as part of the NAACP team preparing for the *Brown* arguments. Many studies of the movement in Richmond have focused on the efforts of these two lawyers and of the student protestors from Virginia Union, including Charles Sherrod, who became a well-known leader of the Student Nonviolent Coordinating Committee. But as two scholars of the Richmond civil rights movement, Lewis Randolph and Gayle Tate, have written, African American women in Richmond, as in so many other places, played important but typically unsung roles as activists: "The participation of women, working class people and poor people . . . was limited [in the Richmond movement] to the role of foot soldiers and/or sub-leaders."[16]

Aside from the NAACP, whose branch in Richmond was not in continuous operation, the Richmond Crusade for Voters became the most significant civil rights group in the city. Although the original founders of the group included two black women, Ethyl T. Overby and Lola H. Hamilton, their names were not included in documents describing the origins of the group.[17] Overby played a major role by helping keep the organization financially solvent. She served as chair of the finance committee from 1961 to 1975 but was never promoted to serve as treasurer. One member said "One of the best fundraisers we have had was Mrs. Ethyl Overby, who asked everyone she saw in the neighborhood and every Crusader to save newspapers [which were sold to raise money]." The member said that those newspaper drives were frequently the primary source of income for the group.[18]

Overby was the first black woman to serve as principal of a Richmond public school. She was known to challenge Jim Crow when she encountered it in her daily life. On one occasion, for example, she refused to wait at the back door for a white friend she was meeting at the train station. She risked her position as a school official when she covertly discouraged black parents from signing Pupil Placement Act sign-up sheets.[19] (In the wake of the *Brown* decision, pupil-placement laws were used to maintain racial segregation by making school assignments on some basis other than race. Students were supposed to be assigned to schools according to a variety of criteria, but of course race was the primary consideration.) Earlier, in the 1950s, Overby also had fought for equal pay for black teachers.

In addition, Overby was an important leader in the Richmond Urban League. When the Ku Klux Klan tried to undermine the League by denying it access to community funds, Overby organized teachers and other African Americans to contribute money to keep the organization afloat. Lewis Randolph and Gayle Tate note that Overby was an excellent example of a 'bridge leader' as described by Belinda Robnett.[20] Robnett says a bridge leader is an individual, often a woman, who helps bring different populations together within a community in order to pursue a common goal.[21] As critical as this function is, bridge leaders are often found in support positions, not necessarily in highly visible leadership roles. As a leading educator and as a member of many important civil rights groups, Overby was ideally positioned to serve as such a leader.

Another important but unheralded black woman active in the Richmond movement was Janet Jones Ballard. She was a founding member of the Richmond Council on Human Rights and was the first female executive officer of the Richmond Urban League. One of her courageous acts of resistance against the white power structure in Richmond occurred in 1959, a year before major sit-ins began in the city. Ballard had gone to Thalhimers, Richmond's leading department store, to get her hair done and was told she could be served in a separate room of the salon. Ballard insisted that she would not be served in a segregated room and persuaded the salon employees to disregard the policy. During the course of her argument with the employees, they named other black women who were content to be served in the separate room. Ballard subsequently contacted the women and made them promise to insist on integrated service—which they did.[22]

Dr. Laverne Byrd Smith was another activist in the Richmond civil rights movement. She was a member both of the Richmond Crusade for Voters and of the Virginia Council on Human Relations, an organization for which she served as president while teaching at Virginia State University and Virginia Union University. As a young woman she wrote for the *Richmond Afro-American* and had an opportunity to interview Martin Luther King, Jr., during one of his visits to the city. By the late 1960s and 1970s, Smith credited the RCHR with helping prevent Richmond from "blowing up" as other areas did with race rioting. She said Richmond always had a fair degree of interracial cooperation, which helped lessen the likelihood of violence.[23]

Ora Lomax, an activist with the SCLC in Richmond, helped bring King to speak at the First African Baptist Church, but her particular contribution to the Richmond civil rights movement was not directly related to her work with the SCLC. Because Lomax had a varied work background, she became valuable to the movement as a "tester," challenging employment discrimination at several Richmond area stores. She would apply for jobs for which she was well qualified but would be passed over for hiring, presumably because of her race. Sometimes when she was hired, she was passed over for promotions. One employer tried to frame her for theft by placing in her purse an item she had not purchased.[24] Eventually Lomax sued both Thalhimers and Miller & Rhoads (another of Richmond's leading department stores) because of alleged discrimination.[25]

The best-known event of the civil rights movement in Richmond occurred in 1960 and 1961, with the boycott of several downtown department stores. The protests began in February 1960 when students at Virginia Union University, inspired by the actions of students at North Carolina A&T, initiated sit-ins at lunch counters in several downtown Richmond stores.[26] A few days later, Charles Sherrod, Wendell Foster, and Frank Pinkston decided to boycott Thalhimers. Picket lines went up on February 23, but protests generally were peaceful.

Elizabeth Johnson Rice, a student at Virginia Union, had heard about plans to picket Thalhimers. On the morning of February 23 she told her parents that she intended to go downtown and observe the protests. They were apprehensive but agreed she could go. At some point she decided to enter the store and demand service and, without planning to do so, found herself sitting in at the lunch counter. Despite harassment from onlookers, the students remained nonviolent. Eventually, she said, they were arrested, and they were in jail for only a couple of hours when the NAACP and other local citizens bailed them out. An impromptu party was organized at a nearby hotel, and Rice was relieved to see her father there. He was, she said, very proud of the actions of the students that day.[27]

The protests in Richmond remained, for the most part, peaceful. White reprisals took the form of economic intimidation rather than overt violence. But one moment from the boycott was photographed and published in *Life* magazine. This image became a symbol of the Richmond demonstrations. Ruth Tinsley, an older African American woman who had served as advisor to the Richmond NAACP Youth Council and who was married to a former NAACP branch president, was waiting downtown for her ride to pick her up. When the police ordered her to move, assuming incorrectly that she was involved in the protests, she refused to do so and was photographed being dragged away by the police. In their analysis of Richmond's political evolution, scholars Lewis Randolph and Gayle Tate state that "Tinsley's arrest is important because of her age and class advantage; she was a respected elder in Richmond's black community."[28] Local blacks were outraged over the treatment to which Tinsley was subjected.

Although Tinsley was not participating in the boycott at the time of her arrest, many African American women did participate. Throughout the South, black women served as the foot soldiers of the movement. Because they acted as a collective, historians tend to overlook or minimize their role. According to activists in the Richmond movement, "The picket line was organized and manned for the most part by African American women six days a week."[29] Many women spent their lunch hour on the picket line despite their employers' efforts to make them stop.[30] Given the disproportionate number of black women who worked full time, the sacrifices involved in this sort of daily commitment become all the more impressive.

White Virginians claimed that the Jim Crow practiced in their state was more benign than in the rest of the South. The exception was Danville. That small city in the southwestern section of the state—where traditional mores had long proved difficult to uproot—became the scene of the most violent civil rights protests in Virginia during this era. Protests there began to escalate in 1963, drawing many black and white residents of this small city into the broader national debates about race and rights. Dr. Joyce Glaise, who grew up in Danville and later became a member of the Danville City Council, remembered the strict segregation that had been enforced there when she was a child. Nevertheless, she attended North Carolina A&T, in part because she was inspired by the students who had initiated the sit-in movement. When Glaise returned to Danville, she joined the Danville Voters League and became active in the movement. Martin Luther King's visit at the height of the protests brought national attention to this rural community. But the intransigence of the white community was a major challenge for the activists. When teenage protestors were arrested and their parents came to bail them out of jail, Danville police also arrested the parents, for contributing to the delinquency of a minor. Entire families ended up in jail.[31]

Although female attorneys did work with the NAACP at the national and local level, their numbers are fairly small. Ruth Harvey Charity was one of the principal attorneys working to defend African American protestors in Danville. As a SNCC protestor, Nikki Giovanni recalls Charity as "a beautiful young black woman with presence . . . the first woman lawyer in the city."[32] Charity's career ended in charges of embezzlement, but in the early 1960s she was an important resource for civil rights activists. In an interview conducted years after the protests in Danville, Dr. Glaise remembered Ms. Harvey as a major inspiration.

Glaise's commitment to improving the lives of African Americans in her community did not end with the decline of civil rights protests. She went on to write her master's thesis on the movement in Danville and then moved into political work herself, serving for twelve years on the Danville City Council. Among other projects, she sought to improve educational and recreational facilities for blacks in the area. In particular, Glaise struggled to fund a city pool. Because black children had no swimming options besides the Dan River, a disproportionate number drowned each summer. Her failure to obtain that funding, she thinks, was a product of lingering racism, the wish to prevent black and white kids from swimming together. When an interviewer asked Glaise if she had any dealings with the Ku Klux Klan, she reluctantly reported that they had ridden around her house for six weeks during one tense period.[33]

By the 1970s, African American women were beginning to move into leadership positions in Virginia politics. Jessie Rattley became the first woman, and first African American, elected to the Newport News City Council. Later she served as mayor, and in 1979 she became the first black woman elected president of the National League of Cities.[34] In Richmond, Willie Dell was one of the first black women to enter local politics, serving on the city council in the late 1970s and early 1980s. Considered a "radical" for her championing of the poor, in 1982 she was defeated by a coalition of moderate black and white male politicians.[35]

The civil rights and voting-rights legislation of the 1960s opened political and economic opportunities for black Virginians that would have been unimaginable in earlier decades. And large demographic shifts affected all Virginians. Significant growth in urban areas such as Hampton Roads, Richmond, and the northern Virginia suburbs of Washington, DC, afforded opportunities. Affirmative-action programs led to a major increase in the number of African Americans in federal jobs. The rise in the number of middle-class blacks was especially notable in the DC suburbs. This demographic shift also served to erode the remnants of the Byrd machine, the powerful group of Democrats who had developed and implemented Massive Resistance doctrines. With growing electoral strength, supported by new, often more moderate, white residents, African Americans in Virginia were able to challenge the stranglehold that Byrd supporters had maintained in Virginia politics. The 1989 election of L. Douglas Wilder—the first African American governor of a Southern state—represented a major transformation of Virginia politics.

For many black women, however, the experience of Patience Gromes resonated more closely with their own lives. Gromes moved to Richmond as a young married woman, where she and her husband struggled to achieve working-class respectability in the Fulton neighborhood. By the mid-twentieth century, having worked hard, they were able to purchase some property and become part of a thriving African American community.[36] But the urban-renewal programs of the 1960s, along with other broad economic changes, benefited neither the Gromeses nor many other residents of Fulton.[37] The neighborhood declined, suffering from high rates of unemployment and all the usual ills, such as rising rates of substance abuse and crime, that accompany economic distress. Gromes could vote, but she was deeply alienated from the political process. She could eat in downtown restaurants, but she had no money. How, or whether, the civil rights movement benefited her and her neighbors remains a troubling question. According to Christopher Silver and John V. Moeser, by the 1980s, Richmond's "black community was substantially more segregated at the neighborhood level than it had been in the 1960s."[38]

The example of the Fulton neighborhood and the continuing struggles of Richmond's inner-city African American population is not intended to diminish the successes of the civil rights movement in Virginia. No student of the movement could seriously argue against the important, meaningful changes brought about as a result of the remarkable courage of many African American men and women in Virginia. But as the heyday of the movement recedes into memory, complex questions about its legacy remain. Many black Virginians' lives were transformed by the victories of the civil rights movement, and as time passes, the achievements of Irene Morgan and Barbara Johns likely will find their way into more textbooks. For many black Virginians, however, the pursuit of equality is challenged by a growing class divide within the African American community.

Notes

1. Jacquelyn Dowd Hall, "The Long Civil Rights Movement and the Political Uses of the Past," *Journal of American History* 91 (March 2005): 1233–63, http://www.historycooperative.org/journals/jah/91.4/hall.html. This article is one of many recent studies visiting the mid-1990s in an effort to expand the traditional timeline of the movement.

2. It is worth noting that at the turn of the twentieth century, Richmond was the site of a successful streetcar boycott by African American residents.

3. Larissa Smith, "Where the South Begins: Black Politics and Civil Rights Activism in Virginia, 1930–1951" (PhD diss., Emory University, 2001), 140.

4. Jessie Carney Smith, ed., *Notable Black American Women.* (Detroit: Gale Research Group, 2002), 3: 445–46.

5. Smith, *Notable Black American Women,* 3: 91.

6. Smith, *Notable Black American Women,* 3: 140. The NAACP next turned to Melvin O. Alston as a plaintiff. His case resulted in a settlement in 1941.

7. Bob Smith, *They Closed Their Schools: Prince Edward County, Virginia, 1951–1964* (Farmville, Va.: Martha E. Forrester Council, 1996). Donald P. Baker, "Closed," *Washington Post Magazine,* 4 (March 2001), 8.

8. Roxann Prazniak, "Race and Gender in the Limits of Place-Based Politics," *SID On-Line Dialogue* 45(1): 121–25, 122.

9. Kara Miles Turner, "It Is Not at Present a Very Successful School: Prince Edward County and the Black Educational Struggle" (PhD diss., Duke University, 2001), 125.

10. Prazniak, "Race and Gender," 123.

11. Turner, "It Is Not at Present a Very Successful School," 130.

12. Smith, *Notable Black American Women,* 3: 79.

13. Anonymous, undated profile. Helen Baker Papers. M182, Special Collections Room, Virginia Commonwealth University Library, Richmond, Va. (hereinafter Baker Papers).

14. Undated letter, Helen Baker to Don Griffin. Baker Papers. In Don Baker's article, he says that seventy children were placed in homes across the country. Baker, "Closed," 8.

15. "Special Report" of the Prince Edward County Christian Association. Baker papers.

16. Lewis Randolph and Gayle T. Tate, *Rights for a Season: The Politics of Race, Class and Gender in Richmond, Virginia* (Knoxville: University of Tennessee Press, 2003), 153.

17. Randolph and Tate, *Rights for a Season,* 153.

18. Anonymous, undated document. Richmond Crusade for Voters Archives, M306. Special Collections, Virginia Commonwealth University, Richmond, Va.

19. Randolph and Tate, *Rights for a Season,* 154.

20. Randolph and Tate, *Rights for a Season,* 174.

21. Belinda Robnett. *How Long? How Long? African American Women in the Struggle for Civil Rights* (New York: Oxford University Press, 1997), 20.

22. Randolph and Tate, *Rights for a Season,* 169. The authors note that although Thalhimers maintained segregation in other areas of the store, there was an increase in black patronage of its salon, which reduced business in black-owned salons.

23. Laverne Byrd Smith, interview by Ronald E. Carrington, March 21, 1903. Voices of Freedom Oral History Project, Virginia Commonwealth University Library Special Collections, www.library.vcu.edu/jbc/speccoll/civilrights/smith01.html.

24. Ora Lomax presentation, panel discussion, "Richmond Women in the Civil Rights Movement," Virginia Commonwealth University, Richmond, Va, February 12, 2008.

25. Randolph and Tate, *Rights for a Season,* 177–78.

26. Randolph and Tate, *Rights for a Season,* 180.

27. Elizabeth Johnson Rice presentation, panel discussion, "Richmond Women in the Civil Rights Movement."

28. Randolph and Tate, *Rights for a Season,* 182.

29. Randolph and Tate, *Rights for a Season,* 190.

30. Hilda Warden presentation, panel discussion, "Richmond Women in the Civil Rights Movement."

31. Ronald E. Carrington, interview by Dr. Joyce E. Glaise, March 20, 1903. Voices of Freedom Oral History Project.

32. Nikki Giovanni, *Grandmothers: Poems, Reminiscences, and Short Stories about the Keepers of Our Traditions* (New York: Henry Holt, 1996), 120.

33. Giovanni, *Grandmothers,* 120.

34. Smith, *Notable Black American Women,* 3: 489–90.

35. Randolph and Tate, *Rights for a Season,* 36–38.

36. Scott C. Davis, *The World of Patience Gromes: Making and Unmaking a Black Community* (Lexington: University Press of Kentucky, 1988), 27–32.

37. Davis, *The World of Patience Gromes,* 52.

38. Christopher Silver and John V. Moeser. *The Separate City: Black Communities in the Urban South, 1940–1968* (Lexington: University Press of Kentucky, 1995), 167.

2 Making the Invisible Visible

African American Women in the Texas Civil Rights Movement

Yvonne Davis Frear

During a sermon one Sunday during Black History Month in 2007, the pastor at a predominantly urban African American church in Houston, Texas, told his congregation that "overcoming inequality was not a one-man operation."[1] At that I could not help but change my church lady's hat to my professor's hat as I thought, once again, "What about the women?" I considered approaching the pastor about my quandary, but knowing that he was aware of this fact and was merely employing rhetorical technique, I made a mental note to address the disturbing issue later in a more appropriate setting. After all, I did not want to miss the blessing in the sermon. The idea that many women go unnoticed as active participants in the fight for civil rights appears to be the norm in historical analysis and even in sermons on Sunday morning. After all, the modern African American civil rights movement is generally recognized as a male-dominated movement with the key leader of the movement identified as Martin Luther King, Jr., not his wife, Coretta. Unfortunately many individuals have not readily accepted that African American women in the South were more than silent followers or that they contributed to the movement by serving in roles comparable in many ways to those of African American male leaders.[2]

There are two principal explanations for the exclusion of African American women from discussions of the modern civil rights movement in the South. First, because they are excluded from scholarly and general literature, there is no evidence of their participation. Second, age-old racial subjectivity identifies them as insignificant because of their race. Because this hypothetical two-edged sword cut them off from the mainstream of society, the contributions of African

American women to the modern civil rights movement in the South were unaccounted for or invisible.

In the last decade of the twentieth century, however, historical studies suggested that even though African American women were not at the helm of the modern civil rights movement in the South, they were largely responsible for keeping activism brewing at local and state levels.[3] Charles Payne explained that males judged women's grassroots activities—establishing and organizing good working relations within their communities—as respectable and nonthreatening because the women could fulfill those activities while still functioning as followers or assistants who accompanied, organized, mediated, and served the male leadership. More-detailed research about African American women in Texas suggests, however, that often it was they who initiated protest efforts and developed strategies on how change might and should occur.[4]

This essay explains the roles, strategies, and contributions of African American women in Texas. It asserts that these women are important to the modern civil rights movement and to its ongoing efforts to establish and maintain a racially equitable society. It highlights their involvement and demonstrates that they actually served as agents and intermediaries in larger and more prominent protests and US Supreme Court rulings. It also explains that, as African American women became key trailblazers in the fight for equal rights throughout Texas, they also strove to improve their own social, educational, and political position.

On May 18, 1954, a headline in the *Dallas Morning News* read, "Segregation Ruling Ends an Era." The headline and accompanying editorial referred to the US Supreme Court decision in *Brown v. Board of Education.* For more than fifty years, African American residents in the Lone Star State and the rest of the South were governed by the doctrine that "separate but equal" is constitutional. On May 17, 1954, however, the law that had mandated de jure segregation in Southern states was ruled unconstitutional and the civil rights struggle received new life.[5] The case not only reversed the racist separate but equal doctrine; it signaled the beginning of the modern civil rights movement.[6]

In Texas, a firmly entrenched, segregated, Southern state, the modern movement appears to have begun a few years before the Supreme Court decision in *Brown.* During the earliest part of the 1950s, African Americans were aggressively challenging the absence of civil rights in the state. African American women became more prominent in these struggles. Bernice McNair Barnett reports that some moved from their traditional positions behind the male leaders and became what Belinda Robnett identified as "grassroots organizers" or "bridge leaders."[7]

The involvement of black women in the modern civil rights movement in the Lone Star State began with black Houstonians' twenty-two-year struggle to eliminate the white Democratic primary, a statute permitting only white males to vote in primaries. At first, black females were in the background of the movement, but by the 1930s they were visible. One such individual was Lulu Belle Madison White, the mentor of Juanita Jewell Shanks Craft and Christia Adair, both of whom continued the struggle in the 1950s and 1960s. Born in 1900 in Elmo, Texas, White received her early education in the public schools of Elmo and Terrell, Texas. Following her high school graduation, she attended Butler College for one year before transferring to Prairie View College, where she earned a bachelor's degree in English in 1928. After her marriage to Julius White and teaching school for nine years, White resigned her post to devote full-time service to the NAACP. In 1937 she became the Director of Youth Council and field worker and, in 1939, acting president of the Houston branch of the NAACP. In 1943 she was elevated to full-time executive secretary of the Houston branch, making her the first woman in the South to hold such a post.[8]

Before and after Lulu White became executive secretary, she traveled from town to town, covering most of the state, garnering contributions, organizing new branches and reactivating old ones. Her job description as executive secretary included managing the office, conducting branch activities, helping to organize other branches, and most especially directing membership and fund-raising drives. The organization depended entirely upon these sources of income and support, and Lulu White became a successful recruiter and fund-raiser. Under her direction the Houston branch grew from 5,674 members in 1943 to 12,700 in 1948. This increase reflected White's aggressive fieldwork in recruiting new members and her charisma among black Texans, especially black Houstonians. As a result, in 1946 she became director of State Branches.[9]

When she was appointed executive secretary of the Houston chapter of the NAACP, Lulu White became a traditional leader. Because she was familiar with black Texans' struggle to retrieve the ballot, she became directly involved in the *Smith v. Allwright* case, contacting the national headquarters daily and serving as liaison among the national office, the local chapter, and the black press. She also mounted a "pay your poll tax" campaign two months prior to the Supreme Court's April 1944 decision in *Smith v. Allwright.* When the court declared the white primary statute unconstitutional, White hailed the decision as a "Second

Emancipation" and looked forward to the day when African Americans would realize the full impact of that decision.[10]

One of White's greatest concerns from 1944 to 1948 was how to get blacks into the political system that opened as a result of *Smith v. Allwright*. White not only urged blacks to vote and seek office; she also conducted voter-registration seminars, helped select candidates and draft platforms, and used black churches to address public issues. She even campaigned for some candidates—contrary to NAACP policy. As a result of her effort, in the 1940s black voter registration increased and several blacks became candidates for office.

Lulu White's vision did not end with blacks gaining the right to vote; she also was convinced of the need to expand economic opportunities. And her energetic pursuit of equal opportunities took her, more often than not, along a stormy path. Some white business managers refused to see her, others slammed doors in her face, and still others were evasive. But the persistent Lulu White refused to accept "no" as an answer. She staged solo as well as group demonstrations one of which resulted in having the "colored and white" sign removed from the soda fountain at a Houston department store in 1948.[11]

Lulu White was not one to walk away from any form of discrimination. It is no surprise, then, that she was at the forefront of the movement to integrate the University of Texas Law School. In fact, historian Merline Pitre reports that when the NAACP decided to bring a segregation lawsuit against the University of Texas that would become the Supreme Court case *Sweatt v. Painter*, 339 US 629 (1950), it was Lulu White who persuaded Heman Marion Sweatt, a mail carrier from Houston, to become the plaintiff. She facilitated local, state, and national efforts to fund the case and the cadre of attorneys needed on Sweatt's behalf. And it was she who encouraged Sweatt during the trial and advised him to reject the accommodationist offers made by the university and the state of Texas. In June 1950 the Supreme Court ruled that the University of Texas would have to admit Sweatt, thus establishing a legal precedent for *Brown v. Board of Education*, 347 US 483 (1954). Lulu White's commitment to establishing equality in education allowed the state of Texas to play a major role in integration of higher education institutions during the civil rights movement in the 1950s.

Juanita Craft was a major activist in the civil rights movement in Dallas, Texas. She served the NAACP, first as a branch organizer and later as Youth Council advisor for the Dallas branch. In the late 1940s, when she and another field organizer, Lulu White, worked to reactivate and rebuild NAACP chapters throughout Texas, some people said her visits were "like a blood transfusion to a very weak patient."[12] In 1950, Craft quickly organized Youth Council members to participate in social-mobilization protests geared to integrate institutions of higher education.[13] Craft organized the Dallas NAACP Youth Council and the youth on the University of Texas campus to picket and raise money for Heman M. Sweatt, the Houston postman handpicked by Lulu White to apply for admission to the University of Texas law school but denied because of his race.[14] In June 1950 the Supreme Court ruled unanimously "that [Sweatt] be admitted to the University of Texas Law School."[15] Both Lulu White and Juanita Craft believed that all students should have equal access to a first-class education. The youth's involvement may have appeared minimal to many observers, but to White and Craft their involvement helped pave the way for additional education desegregation cases and eventually *Brown v. Board of Education.*[16]

Brown, however, was not the end. African American women in Texas continued to strive for desegregation in higher education. In 1955, Juanita Craft participated in the desegregation of North Texas State University (now the University of North Texas). Joe L. Atkins, a member of the Youth Council led by Craft and an honor student, applied for admission to North Texas State University. Atkins, his mother, and Craft traveled to Denton to meet the school president and vice president about his admission. According to Craft, a week later, Atkins received a letter from the president refusing to admit him because of his race.[17] Craft encouraged Atkins to respond by filing a lawsuit against North Texas State University. The NAACP legal team represented Atkins in the case, and by the middle of the fall semester, the Eastern District court had ruled that North Texas had to admit Atkins.[18] For Atkins the court decision was bittersweet: he was attending the integrated Texas Western University and did not wish to transfer. For Craft, however, the victory was sweet justice: she had been instrumental in ending segregation in education and opening North Texas State University doors to African American students.

African American women participated directly in the desegregation of universities in Texas. Their presence was often criticized, but they were considered less physically dangerous to the university climate. Dorothy Robinson, an oral historian, was one of the first African American females to take advantage of the desegregated admissions policy at the University of Texas. In the summer of 1955 she entered the university as a graduate student in education.[19]

The years following the Supreme Court ruling in the *Brown* decision forced African Americans in Texas to take a more direct approach to the civil rights struggle in the state. According to Martin Kuhlman, "The Brown decision motivated many more African Americans to become directly involved in the civil rights struggle."[20] Armed with Supreme Court decisions reversing antiquated

Jim Crow mandates and backed by the NAACP, they began aggressively attacking segregated public accommodations.

An African American youth in Dallas under the leadership of Juanita Craft endured the first test of courage. For years, African Americans had been barred from the State Fair of Texas, except on the second Monday in October, Negro Achievement Day. The State Fair of Texas billed itself as the "nation's biggest state fair" because it was largest state fair that provided entertainment and recreational public accomodation.[21] Some conservative African American leaders in Dallas who were affiliated with the Negro Chamber of Commerce believed that the gradual desegregation of the State Fair was accommodation enough for the African American community. But Juanita Craft and other members of the Dallas NAACP disagreed. Blacks, they complained, spent approximately "three dollars to perpetuate segregation" while the NAACP had "to beg for two dollars per year to fight Jim Crow."[22]

The Youth Council of the NAACP Dallas Chapter responded to the white political oligarchs and the conservative African American leaders by traveling to the state fair on Monday, October 17, 1955, to picket the fair. A sea of Negro Achievement Day parade visitors were greeted by protest signs carried by Youth Council members that read: "This is Negro Aggrievement Day—Keep Out" and "Don't Sell Your Pride for a Segregated Ride—Keep Out." The youth members also handed leaflets to prospective African American visitors encouraging them to stay out because they would experience "humiliation and disgrace." Some visitors turned away, leaving the fair; others joined the protestors.[23] Craft and the Youth Council showed the Dallas leaders that African Americans were committed to ripping down segregation not only in educational areas but also in public accommodations.

Direct-action protests against public accommodations continued into the 1960s, when African American students across the nation began participating in lunch-counter sit-in protests. Lunch-counter sit-ins spread uncontrollably throughout Southern states and the nation in general. Editors for *The Crisis,* the NAACP organ, wrote that black "students in the South are justifiably in revolt against lunch counter jim crow" and that "those Americans who genuinely believe in democracy for all should support these young people in every way possible."[24]

In Houston in early March 1960, thirteen students from Texas Southern University, including Holly Hogrosbrook, began Houston's first sit-in at a grocery store lunch counter.[25] The student protesters wanted to highlight the unfair treatment of African Americans under Jim Crow. Hogrosbrook recalled that the thirteen, together with other courageous students, filled the thirty lunch-counter stools in Weingarten's supermarket.[26] They encountered no violence or aggressive behavior, and patrons from the black community showed their support by abandoning their grocery carts in the middle of the store aisles.[27] Holly Hogrosbrook and many other African American female students, along with SNCC and the local community, had shown that interrupting economic and commercial sectors within the city was a viable form of civil rights action. Early sit-ins in Houston did encounter opposition from some white businessmen, such as Bob Dundas, vice-president of Foley Brothers, a major retailer in downtown Houston. Dundas convinced the local media that not reporting on the student sit-ins at grocery and retail stores in the city would circumvent violence and curtail economic losses. The student protestors, unaware of the "media blackout," continued boycotting such local stores as Henke & Pillot and Walgreens. Dundas recalled that by August 1960, several stores in Houston had quietly desegregated their lunch counters.

In April 1960, students from the University of Texas warned lunch-counter owners that they had one week to integrate those counters. Following in the footsteps of sit-ins in Wichita, Oklahoma City, and Greensboro, the students received support from such local activists as Eva McMillan, Juanita Craft, and Minnie Flanagan. The students believed that the pace of integration needed a jolt.[28] The collective work of women in the local NAACP chapters in San Antonio, Houston, and Dallas also provided funding, housing, and leadership. For example, Minnie Flanagan, president of the Dallas branch of NAACP, supported students who participated in the Wiley-Bishop sit-ins in 1960. Wiley College and Bishop College were two predominantly African American colleges in the East Texas town of Marshall. Many African American students from metropolitan cities, including Houston, San Antonio, and Dallas, attended the college and worked hard to desegregate public facilities and accommodations in Marshall.[29] Minnie Flanagan knew many of the students. As members of the Youth Council in Dallas they had learned how to stage protests. Although Flanagan was overshadowed by NAACP male leaders in the state and nationally, her legal and financial assistance to sit-in protestors in Marshall enabled them to continue fighting for the integration of public facilities and accommodations.[30]

Eva McMillan supported the work of SNCC members when her son Ernie, a former Morehouse College student and SNCC field worker in the Deep South, established a local chapter in Dallas. According to Stefanie Gilliam Decker, McMillan "found she would be desperately needed as a community leader and advisor for the organization."[31] She responded, and her guidance to young people in the community and in the SNCC organization earned her the moniker "Mama Mac." McMillan became a friend to the civil rights movement through all its high points and low.[32] African American students believed that their work was acceptable and noteworthy because it brought attention to the inequitable standards that African Americans faced in the city. Many businessmen, however, believed that SNCC was a radical organization that caused trouble, especially after the pickets and protests of the OK Supermarket. Varying accounts surrounding the incident suggested that aggressive behavior by Ernie McMillan (Eva's son) and Mathew Johnson cost the grocery chain more than $200 in damages.[33] Eva soon discovered that the struggle for civil rights was more difficult without the support of the NAACP. She sought legal aid for her son but was turned down because of a paperwork error. This refusal led McMillan and her son to seek legal assistance from a Caucasian lawyer. McMillan later charged that "justice in Dallas proved it was not color blind." The fight for civil rights in Dallas would no longer be headed up by SNCC.[34]

As the civil rights movement expanded into what students would identify as a "Black Power" movement in the late 1960s, the focus shifted from the integration of educational facilities to the complete desegregation of clubs, organizations, and programs. Students were actively seeking more than accommodation in education. Now they struggled and fought for social justice and recognition. In November 1968, members of the Afro-Americans for Black Liberation (AABL) at the University of Houston Central Campus sponsored and endorsed Lynn Eusan, an African American female student from San Antonio, for homecoming queen.[35] The homecoming queen position at the predominantly white school had been informally sanctioned as a position held by a white female from one of the segregated Greek organizations. However, in 1968 the AABL sought to change the so-called, informal legacy by endorsing an African American female candidate. On November 22, 1968, in the Astrodome, billed as the "eighth wonder of the world," the University of Houston crowned its first African American homecoming queen before a crowd of approximately fifty thousand. This action by Lynn Eusan and other student activists, such as Audrey Taylor, Dwight Allen (now Omawale Luthuli-Allen), and Gene Locke demonstrated a commitment to nonviolent student activism to bring about equality in a less-than-equal society.[36]

As the struggle for an egalitarian society continued in the South, African Americans pressed on in the battle against segregation. The attention received by sit-in protesters in Austin, Dallas, and Houston energized other women in the state. The elite social and cultural organization for African American youth, Jack and Jill, formed a Mothers Action Council in the Austin area.[37] The MAC was established as a means to integrate a local ice-skating rink that did not let African American youth enter. Mothers and children who were affiliated with Jack and Jill and MAC marched tirelessly for twelve months until, in 1963, the owners integrated the facility.[38] During the same year, African American club women in the coastal of city of Galveston petitioned the city manager and city council in a writing campaign to end discrimination in public accommodations throughout the city.[39] Black women in Texas had willingly picked up the gauntlet that was the Supreme Court ruling in *Brown* when it had been cast down before them almost ten years earlier.

Education and public accommodations were not the only areas in which African American struggled for civil rights. Many in the South experienced years of frustration when they attempted to participate in the political arena. Before the modern civil rights movement, African American women had tried many times to dismantle the antiquated system of political disfranchisement in Texas. One of the earliest challengers was Christia Adair. A black suffragist and civil rights activist, Adair began her battles for civil rights in Kingsville, about one hundred ninety miles south of San Antonio. She created a church-affiliated Sunday school program and joined an integrated group of women who were opposed to gambling in the city.[40] The women hoped to dissuade teenaged males, African American and white, from skipping school and frequenting a local gambling house.[41] Shortly after her involvement with the integrated group, Adair turned her attention to women's suffrage issues in Texas, particularly as they affected African Americans. In 1918, two years before the Nineteenth Amendment granted women the right to vote, and almost four decades before the *Brown* decision, Adair was collecting signatures on petitions demanding that the Texas State Legislature pass laws allowing women the right to vote in Texas.[42] Many whites, both supporters and critics of women's suffrage, feared that granting suffrage to women would enfranchise black women and that if African Americans received the right to vote, they would control state politics and would disfranchise whites.[43] Thus in 1918, Adair came to realize that her race would prevent her from participating in the very process for which she had petitioned the legislature.

Texas granted women the right to vote in primary elections in 1918, but Christia Adair and other African American women were denied that right. Although Adair and the other women were understandably upset, they continued to press for full equality in the democratic process. Adair even severed her membership with the Republican Party after being slighted by Republican presidential nominee Warren G. Harding in 1920. She had taken several African American youth to see the presidential candidate during his stopover in Kingsville. However, when it came time to shake the hands of the young constituents, Harding deliberately reached over the African American youth and shook the hands of the white kids standing behind them. After that incident, Adair said that she "was offended and insulted and I made up my mind I wouldn't be a Republican ever," and she joined the Democratic Party.[44] Adair would finally be able to participate in the voting process in 1944 after the US Supreme Court ruled, in *Smith v. Allwright,* that the all-white primary in Texas was unconstitutional This landmark court decision removed the barriers to voting that African Americans in Texas had experienced since Reconstruction and helped establish what would become a first-class electoral system.[45]

Adair continued to resist political discrimination well into the 1950s, when she demonstrated her commitment to the NAACP and privacy. In 1950, Texas Attorney General John Ben Sheppard attempted to close down NAACP offices throughout the state. Alleging that the branches were "inciting racial prejudice," he demanded that Christia Adair give him the membership lists of the members associated with the Houston branch.[46] When Adair refused to submit the lists, she and the NAACP underwent a grueling seventeen-day trial in Tyler.[47] The State of Texas lost the case, and Adair reopened the Houston branch, but she said that the intimidation and violence, like bomb threats, had taken a toll on her.[48]

In the 1970s another dedicated African American woman took a stand for political and civil rights for African Americans. Barbara Charline Jordan, who was eighteen years old when the Supreme Court handed down its ruling in *Brown,* was dedicated to fairness and justice in an egalitarian society as defined in the US Constitution. Jordan realized that "some black people could make it in this white man's world, and that those who could, had to do it."[49] Jordan began her political involvement in civil rights when she joined the Kennedy-Johnson campaign ticket in 1960. She was a card-carrying member of the NAACP, but she had not participated in any major protests or sit-in demonstrations, so her position on the campaign was not threatening.[50] Jordan caught the political fever of the election of 1960 and ran for state political office in 1962 and 1964. An African American female had never run for an elected seat in the Texas House of Representatives, and her loss was no surprise.[51] However in 1966, two years after President Lyndon Baines Johnson had signed the Civil Rights Act of 1964, which afforded African Americans more distinct voting opportunities, Jordan ran for a seat in the Texas State Senate and won. This was a landmark win. Barbara Jordan became the first African American to serve in the Senate since Reconstruction, in 1883.[52]

Like Christia Adair before her, Barbara Jordan fought for voting rights. If there was a difference between Jordan and her predecessor, it was in the fact that Jordan was committed to equal rights and not merely the civil rights of African Americans. Jordan believed that all "minorities" should join the political system rather than challenge it.[53] While other African American leaders clamored over civil rights issues, she believed that she had "her own role to play."[54] William Broyles, the founding editor of *Texas Monthly* magazine, said of Jordan: "She considered the Voting Rights expansion her most significant legislative accomplishment. The franchise is her sort of issue; its exercise is decorous, restrained, impersonal—but effective. It is the cornerstone of the system she believes in."[55]

It can be inferred that, as the modern civil rights movement waned, Jordan expanded the nation's observation of civil rights into an understanding of human and equal rights. She motivated people to look beyond race and gender and to embrace the greater needs of society, such as fair employment, wage laws, tax credits for low-income workers, and workers' compensation. As Jordan ascended the political ranks in state and national politics, she did not participate in violence or radicalism, but she never forgot that others had paved the way for her.[56] In 1972, Jordan was elected to the US House of Representatives, becoming the first African American woman from the South elected to Congress. Curtis Graves, a formidable political opponent and local civil rights activist, accused her of being a pawn of moneyed blacks and whites, but Jordan refused to be distracted. She remained firm in her resolve that people would "vote for the person who can get things done."[57]

Former President Lyndon Johnson supported Jordan's appointment to the House Committee on the Judiciary, one of the most significant congressional committees in the national legislature. In her capacity as a member of this committee, and during the televised impeachment hearings for President Richard Nixon, Jordan delivered what is acknowledged as the most egalitarian statement about the Constitution. Speaking to the committee and millions of television viewers, she said: "When the Constitution of the United States was completed . . . I was not included in that 'We the People.' . . . I have finally been included. . . . My faith in the Constitution is whole. It is complete. It is total. I am not going to sit here and be an idle spectator to the diminution, the subversion, the destruction of the Constitution."[58]

The extant literature asserts that the modern civil rights movement was led and empowered by men. In Texas, however, African American women were conspicuous in their challenges to segregation and in their support of the movement. Grassroots activists, bridge leaders, and public servants, they served as agents and intermediaries in prominent protests, Supreme Court rulings, and legislative initiatives. The women were key trailblazers in the fight for equal rights.

Notes

1. Pastor Danny Davis, *"We Shall Overcome,"* Sunday Sermon at Jordan Grove Missionary Baptist Church, Houston, Texas, February 2007.

2. Bernice McNair Barnett, "Invisible Black Women Leaders in the Civil Rights Movement: The Triple Constraints of Gender, Race, and Class," *Gender and Society* 7 (1993): 162–63.

3. Charles Payne, "Men Led, but Women Organized: Movement Participation of Women in the Mississippi Delta," in Vicki L. Crawford, Jaqueline Anne Rouse, and Barbara Woods, eds., *Women in the Civil Rights Movement: Trailblazers and Torchbearers, 1941–1965* (Brooklyn: Carlson Publishing, 1990), 1–11.

4. Ruthe Winegarten, *Black Texas Women: 150 Years of Trial and Triumph* (Austin: University of Texas Press, 1995); Darlene Clark Hine, Elsa Barkley Brown, and Rosalyn Terborg Penn, eds., *Black Women in America: An Historical Encyclopedia* (Brooklyn: Carlson Publishing, 1993); Ruthe Winegarten and Sharon Kahn, *Brave Black Women: From Slavery to the Space Shuttle* (Austin: University of Texas Press, 1997); Ruth Edmonds Hill, ed., *The Black Women Oral History Project* (Westport, Conn.: Meckler Publishing, 1991).

5. The literature that focuses on other Southern states is extensive, and this reference serves to highlight only a few sources. See for example, John Dittmer, *Local People: The Struggle for Civil Rights in Mississippi* (Champaign: University of Illinois Press, 1994); William Chafe, *Civilities and Civil Rights: Greensboro North Carolina and the Black Struggle for Freedom* (New York: Oxford University Press, 1981); Charles Payne, *I've Got the Light of Freedom: The Organizing of Tradition and the Mississippi Freedom Struggle* (Berkeley: University of California Press, 1996); Diane McWhorter, *Carry Me Home: Birmingham, Alabama: The Climactic Battle of the Civil Rights Revolution* (New York: Simon & Schuster, 2001); Glen T. Eskew, *But for Birmingham: The Local and National Movements in the Civil Rights Struggle* (Chapel Hill: University of North Carolina Press, 1997).

6. Initially, in *Plessy v. Ferguson,* 163 US 537, 16 S. Ct. 1138 (1896), the US Supreme Court supported segregation. The jurists held that racial segregation of public train passengers in separate but equal facilities complied with the Equal Protection clause. States relied upon this doctrine for fifty-four years, until the jurists held, in *Brown v. Board of Education of Topeka, Shawnee County, Kansas,* 344 US 1, 73 S. Ct. 1 (1954), that mandatory racial separation contradicted the Fourteenth Amendment guarantee of equal protection.

7. Belinda Robnett, *How Long? How Long? African-American Women in the Struggle for Civil Rights* (New York: Oxford University Press, 1997), 15–20.

8. Merline Pitre, *In Struggle against Jim Crow: Lulu B. White and the NAACP, 1900–1957* (College Station: Texas A&M University Press, 1999), 1–13, 25–32; Winegarten, *Black Texas Women,* 242–43.

9. Pitre, *In Struggle against Jim Crow,* 38.

10. Pitre, *In Struggle against Jim Crow,* 43–44.

11. Pitre, *In Struggle against Jim Crow,* 60, 134–35.

12. Michael Lowery Gillette, *"The NAACP in Texas, 1937–1957"* (PhD diss., University of Texas at Austin, 1984), 29.

13. Dorothy Robinson, "Interview with Juanita Craft," January 10, 1977, The Black Women Oral History Project, 15.

14. The US Supreme Court ruled, in *Sweatt v. Painter et al.,* 339 US 629 (1950), that an African American law student must be admitted to the all-white University of Texas because separate facilities for blacks at the university were not equal. In 1947, prior to the court ruling, the University of Texas attempted to maintain a segregated law school by establishing separate facilities for Sweatt in the basement of a downtown Austin office building. Chandler Vaughn, ed., *A Child, the Earth, and a Tree of Many Seasons: The Voice of Juanita Craft* (Dallas: Halifax Publishing, 1982), 20.

15. Dwonna Goldstone, *Integrating the Forty Acres: The Fifty-Year Struggle for Racial Equality at the University of Texas* (Athens: University of Georgia Press, 2006), 27. Goldstone notes that, despite the US Supreme Court ruling to desegregate the university, many white students did not want to accept the mandate. Some transferred to other law schools, and white female students petitioned for "black only" restrooms even though no African American female students attended the law school in the fall of 1950.

16. Merline Pitre, "At the Crossroads: Black Texas Women, 1930–1954," in *Black Women in Texas History,* edited by Bruce A. Glasrud and Merline Pitre (College Station: Texas A&M University Press, 2008), 152.

17. Yvonne Davis Frear, "Juanita Craft and the Struggle to End Segregation in Dallas, 1945–1955," in *Major Problems in Texas History: Documents and Essays,* edited by Sam Haynes and Cary D. Wintz (Boston: Houghton Mifflin, 2002), 434–35; Robinson, 19.

18. In *Atkins v. Matthews,* Civil Action No. 1104 (E. D. Texas, 1955), the federal magistrate reversed the district court's temporary injunction and ruled that Joe Atkins be admitted by North Texas State University without delay.

19. Dorothy Robinson, *The Bell Rings at Four: A Black Teacher's Chronicle of Change* (Austin: Madrona Press, 1978), 42–43.

20. Martin Herman Kuhlman, "The Civil Rights Movement in Texas: Desegregation of Public Accommodations, 1950–1964" (PhD diss., Texas Tech University, 1994), 86.

21. Warren Leslie, *Dallas Public and Private: Aspects of an American City* (New York: Grossman Publishers, 1964), 62.

22. Letter from Juanita Craft to Walter White, October 25, 1951, NAACP files, Library of Congress.

23. *Dallas Express,* October 22, 1955; *Dallas Morning News,* October 18, 1955.

24. "Lunch Counter Jim Crow," *The Crisis,* March 1960, 162.

25. "A Sit-In to Face Down Jim/Jane Crow," *The Houston Chronicle,* March 3, 2008; *Houston Chronicle* writer Serbino Sandifer-Walker chronicled the forty-eighth anniversary

of the Houston lunch counter sit-in as a means to inform readers about the legacy of TSU 13 and their efforts to battle Jim Crow and initiate immediate social change in one of the state's largest metropolitan areas.

26. F. Kenneth Jensen, "The Houston Sit-In Movement of 1960–61," in Howard Beeth and Cary D. Wintz, eds., *Black Dixie: Afro-Texas History and Culture in Houston* (College Station: Texas A&M University Press, 1992), 213–15.

27. Jensen, "The Houston Sit-In Movement of 1960–61," 213–15.

28. Goldstone, 70–75; Stefanie Lee Gilliam, "Mama, Activist, and Friend: African American Women in the Civil Rights Movement in Dallas, Texas, 1945–1998" (Master's thesis, Oklahoma State University, 1998), 44–45.

29. Donald Seals, Jr., "The Wiley-Bishop Student Movement: A Case Study in the 1960 Civil Rights Sit-Ins," *Southwestern Historical Quarterly* 106 (January 2003): 419–40.

30. Yvonne Davis Frear, "Minnie A. Flanagan," in *African American National Biography,* edited by Henry Louis Gates, Jr., and Evelyn Higginbotham (New York: Oxford University Press, 2008), 285–86; Seals, Jr., "The Wiley-Bishop Student Movement," 419–40.

31. Gilliam, "Mama, Activist, and Friend," 44.

32. Gilliam, "Mama, Activist, and Friend," 48–49.

33. Gilliam, "Mama, Activist, and Friend," 48.

34. Gilliam, "Mama, Activist, and Friend," 49.

35. Lori Rodriguez, "Thirty Years Ago, African-Americans Forged a Presence at UH: Ex-Student Activists Tell How They Changed the School in the Late '60s," *Houston Chronicle,* January 18, 1998, A1. African-Americans for Black Liberation (AABL) grew out of an earlier multiracial organization, Committee on Better Race Relations (COBRR) at the University of Houston Central Campus in the sixties. The goal of AABL and of COBRR, was to "include African Americans and students of color into mainstream university life" and to embrace the doctrines outlined in the *Autobiography of Malcolm X,* as suggested by Stokely Carmichael, a visitor to campus that year. Lynn Eusan and Dwight Allen were co-founders of AABL.

36. Malika Reed, "Lynn Eusan Park a Tribute to All of UH: Houston's First African American Homecoming Queen Remembered," *The Daily Tiger,* November 9, 1995, vol. 61. Lynn Eusan is remembered as an activist for change of race relations during a period of black power in the late 1960s that had transitioned from the civil rights activities of her predecessors. Eusan and others dedicated themselves to improving race relations and assisting with community relations and youth education in the Third Ward area. She was brutally murdered in 1971, a year after her graduation from the University of Houston, but the African American causes that she defended are still embraced by many students on the University of Houston campus.

37. Winegarten, *Black Texas Women,* 258; Jack and Jill of America is a nonprofit organization geared toward empowering youth by bringing together children in a social and cultural environment.

38. Winegarten, *Black Texas Women,* 258.

39. Winegarten, *Black Texas Women,* 258.

40. Nancy Baker Jones, "Christia V. Daniels Adair," *Handbook of Texas Online,* http://www.tshaonline.org/handbook/online articles/AA/fad19.html, accessed June 8, 2012.

41. Dorothy Robinson, "Interview with Christia Adair," April 25, 1977, *The Black Women Oral History Project,* 58–59.

42. Ruthe Winegarten and Sharon Kahn, *Brave Black Women: From Slavery to the Space Shuttle* (Austin: University of Texas Press, 1997), 49–50.

43. Hine, Brown, and Penn, eds., *Black Women in America,* 44.

44. Winegarten and Kahn, *Brave Black Women,* 53.

45. Dr. Lonnie Smith, a dentist in Houston and an active member of the NAACP, brought suit against the election judge for denying him a ballot in the July 1940 primary and the runoff primary in August 1940. Under the legal direction of the national office of the NAACP and Thurgood Marshall, Smith brought suit against the Democratic Party in Texas. In 1944 in an 8 to 1 decision, the US Supreme Court ruled that the white primary was unconstitutional and that the Democratic Party was acting on behalf of the state and was not a private organization that could determine who would qualify to vote in state primary elections.

46. J. W. Peltason, *58 Lonely Men: Southern Judges and School Desegregation* (Champaign: University of Illinois Press, 1971), 69–70; Jean Flynn, "Christia V. Daniels Adair," *Texas Women Who Dared to Be First* (Austin: Eakin Press, 1999), 69.

47. *State of Texas v. NAACP et. al.,* in the District Court, 7th Judicial District, Smith County, Texas, filed September 21, 1956; *Dallas Morning News,* September 21, 1956.

48. Robinson, "Interview with Christia Adair," 63–65, 72, 92.

49. Nancy Baker Jones and Ruthe Winegarten, *Capitol Women: Texas Female Legislators, 1923–1999* (Austin: University of Texas Press, 2000), 145.

50. William Broyles, Jr., "The Making of Barbara Jordan," in *Texas Monthly on Texas Women* (Austin: University of Texas, 2006), 165; For a more extensive analysis of the life of Barbara Charline Jordan, see Mary Beth Rogers, *Barbara Jordan: American Hero* (New York: Bantam Books, 1998) and Barbara Jordan and Shelby Hearon, *Barbara Jordan: A Self Portrait* (Garden City: Doubleday and Company, 1979).

51. Jones and Winegarten, *Capitol Women,* 145.

52. Jones and Winegarten, *Capitol Women,* 146.

53. Jones and Winegarten, *Capitol Women,* 146.

54. Broyles, "The Making of Barbara Jordan," 166.

55. Broyles, "The Making of Barbara Jordan," 166

56. Broyles, "The Making of Barbara Jordan," 166

57. Jones and Winegarten, *Capitol Women,* 148.

58. Mary Beth Rogers, *Barbara Jordan,* 178–79; Jordan and Hearon, *Barbara Jordan,* 186–87.

3 Black Women in the Arkansas Civil Rights Movement

Jeannie M. Whayne

The Jim Crow system and poverty relegated the majority of black women in Arkansas to jobs as farm laborers or domestic servants for the first half of the twentieth century. Because Arkansas was overwhelmingly rural, its principal industry was agriculture, and its rural African American population had few opportunities to work other than on farms and plantations. It took revolutions both in agriculture and in civil rights to free them of poverty and to overturn disfranchisement and segregation. Given the fact that most of the black population lived in the plantation counties of eastern and southern Arkansas or along the Arkansas River valley, which stretches up through the middle of the state, it is no coincidence that the most notable black women in the civil rights struggle came from those areas. They shared other things in common: early family tragedies and a determination to make their lives better. Along the way, they also improved life for other African Americans in the state. They played a role in the equalization of salaries for African American teachers, in integrating professional schools, and in desegregating the school system. As the civil rights struggle turned more militant in the early 1960s, they also joined the Student Nonviolent Coordinating Committee and agitated for desegregating public facilities and for securing voting rights, particularly in the Arkansas Delta. By 1974 black women—like black men—had far more opportunities open to them.

Daisy Bates is the dominant figure among black women in the history of the civil rights movement in Arkansas. The only other iconic female among Arkansas African American women is Charlotte Stephens, an ex-slave who became a leader in black education in the post–Civil War period. Images of both Bates and Stephens are immediately recognizable to anyone familiar with the history of Arkansas. And they deserve the attention they have received, for their accomplishments were truly remarkable. Daisy Bates in particular demonstrated fortitude and courage in assuming the role of advisor to the nine students who integrated Central High School in 1957. And the event itself is pivotal in the civil rights struggle, occurring as it did in the face of white segregationists' "massive resistance."[1] But there were other significant milestones and other black women who risked and accomplished much between 1940 and 1974. Their struggles required similar personal courage and often necessitated great sacrifice.

One woman who paid the price for stepping forward to advocate for African American rights was Sue Cowan Morris. A teacher at Dunbar High School in Little Rock, she filed suit against the Little Rock School District in 1942 seeking the equalization of teacher salaries. Although she put herself forward as the point person in the suit, she was not alone. The NAACP had engaged in a long campaign against the injustices inherent in the Southern "separate-but-equal" school system. Blacks were educated in separate facilities, but little about the system was equal. The black infrastructure was inferior, the books provided to blacks were worn-out discards from white schools, and few black schools provided instruction beyond the primary grades. If a black child was fortunate enough to graduate from high school, higher education was difficult to secure, not only because of the cost but also because of the lack of facilities. Although Southern states typically had at least one college designated for African Americans, in-state graduate and professional schools usually were unavailable. Despite these obstacles, a small cadre of African Americans secured higher education, but they found few opportunities other than as teachers in black schools. Talented white college graduates enjoyed a number of options, but blacks could entertain no hope of securing employment in business or industry, at least not in jobs that would draw on their education and ability. However, as good as they were at their jobs as educators in the black school system, they were typically paid far less than whites. The NAACP understood this and, as historian John Kirk observed in *Redefining the Color Line,* the organization engaged in a two-pronged strategy to address the problems faced by black teachers and students: they litigated to secure equal pay for black teachers, and they pressed for the admission of qualified black applicants to graduate and professional schools. Both efforts had their day in Arkansas.[2]

In the early 1940s the Little Rock branch of the Colored Teachers Association, having seen NAACP efforts to secure equal pay for black teachers meet with some success in other Southern states, prepared to do battle. The NAACP relationship with black organizations in Arkansas had not been close since the

1919 Elaine Race Riot, when the national organization expressed its belief that Arkansas African Americans had failed to contribute significantly to the defense of twelve black men condemned to death. For that reason, it was said, in 1928 the NAACP declined to support Little Rock's Dr. John Robinson in his opposition to the Arkansas white primary.[3] By 1942, however, the landscape had changed. Thurgood Marshall and other national NAACP figures were impressed with Arkansas's CTA, so much so that Marshall would play a pivotal role in the battle taking shape in Little Rock.[4]

Sue Cowan Morris was the perfect person to bring the suit against the school board. As head of the English program at Dunbar High School, she was a recognized black educator. She had overcome a great many obstacles to rise to her position at Dunbar. Born to teacher-parents in the small Delta town of Eudora, she suffered the loss of her mother shortly after her birth. Her grandmother reared her in Texas until age four, when she was returned to her father. He sent her to Clinton, Mississippi, for primary education and then sacrificed to send her to high school at Spelman, in Atlanta, and then to Talladega College, in Alabama. During the summer of 1941, when she was head of the English Department at Dunbar, she secured graduate training at the University of Chicago. "I wanted to prove that I was capable of being the test case, and the summer before we went to trial, I went to the University of Chicago and took a course in methods of teaching English." The suit was filed early in 1942, and Scipio Jones, the most respected black attorney in the state, prepared his case. Jones had worked closely with the NAACP twenty years earlier in securing the freedom of twelve black men condemned to death in the Elaine Race Riot case. He was at the end of a long, distinguished career and, in fact, would die before the teacher-equalization case was resolved. A young NAACP lawyer, Thurgood Marshall, would bring the case to a satisfactory conclusion, but only after initial defeat.[5]

Despite Morris's accomplishments and credentials, the trial judge in Little Rock, Thomas C. Trimble, accepted the argument that the worst white teacher was superior to the best black educator, testimony provided by Annie Giffey, a white woman who supervised primary teachers in the Little Rock School District.[6] In ruling against Morris, Judge Trimble rejected Thurgood Marshall's legal argument that her Fourteenth Amendment rights had been violated by virtue of the lower salary she was receiving. Marshall appealed the verdict, and in 1945 the Eighth Circuit Court of Appeals in St. Louis overturned Judge Trimble in *Morris v. Williams*.[7] By then, however—at the end of the 1942–43 school year—Morris had been fired from her job. She moved to Pine Bluff, where she taught briefly at Branch Normal College (now the University of Arkansas at

Pine Bluff) before returning to Little Rock and working in a munitions factory.[8] Once the war was over and the munitions factory had no further need of her, she worked in a variety of jobs, some menial and far beneath her abilities. It was 1952 before Morris was able to return to a teaching position in the Little Rock school system and then only after apologizing for bringing the suit. Her suit could be regarded as successful, but she paid a high price, and, in any case, by the time the Eighth Circuit made its ruling, the Little Rock School Board had instituted a merit system designed to justify lower salaries for black teachers. Among other things, they established a ranking of colleges that relegated most black institutions to inferior status. Only a few black teachers were able to pass the rigorous merit system and achieve higher salaries.[9]

Success was more fully realized in another NAACP strategy: securing admission of blacks to graduate and professional schools. Edith Mae Irby's desegregation of the University of Arkansas College of Medical Sciences in the fall of 1948 was indirectly connected to series of successful suits filed by the NAACP. The first step toward providing graduate and professional training for blacks came with the US Supreme Court decision in *Missouri ex rel. Gaines v. Canada, Registrar of the University, et al.* In 1936, Lloyd Gaines had applied for admission to the law school of the University of Missouri. When rejected, he took his case to court, and when the state courts ruled against him, he appealed to the federal courts. In the Supreme Court decision in 1938, Chief Justice Charles Evans Hughes Sr., declared that it was the duty of the state to provide education for all its citizens and that the provision had to be made within the state. To provide legal education for white residents within a state and to fail to do so for blacks "is a denial of the equality of legal right to the enjoyment of the privileges which the state has set up, and the provision for payment of tuition fees in another state does not remove the discrimination."[10] The decision caused some Southern states to move tentatively toward integration, but most simply sought other ways to continue segregation. Missouri hastily created a school of law for African Americans, and Virginia increased the amount of money allocated for African American students to attend professional schools elsewhere.

Even as Edith Mae Irby was dreaming of a medical career, Ada Sipuel of Oklahoma was laying the groundwork for another significant victory at the US Supreme Court. Thurgood Marshall, who had played such an important role in Morris's efforts against the Little Rock School board just a few years earlier, led the NAACP-funded suit against the State of Oklahoma after the University of Oklahoma denied Sipuel admission to its school of law in 1946. When the state court ruled against her that year, she pursued the case in the federal courts, and in 1948 the US Supreme Court ordered the state to admit her to its law school. When Oklahoma created a black law school instead, she again took them to court and won in 1949.[11]

In 1948, in the midst of Sipuel's struggle, young Edith Mae Irby made her application to the University of Arkansas School of Medical Sciences. Irby was not alone among African Americans in Arkansas to aspire to graduate or professional education within the state that year. Even as she was contemplating her application to Arkansas's medical school, Silas Hunt, a World War II veteran and UAPB graduate, made the trip from Pine Bluff to Fayetteville. Accompanied by two civil rights activists and a photographer, he applied for admission to the University of Arkansas School of Law. He was not acting in concert with the dean of the law school, Robert Leflar, his application coincided with the dean's own behind-the-scenes effort to persuade the university president, Lewis Webster Jones, and the board of trustees that, given the decisions in Oklahoma and Missouri, the state should open its doors to qualified black applicants. Hunt's application was accepted without controversy. He endured some harassment on campus, but he completed his first semester without any violent incidents. He was, however, denied permission to eat in the cafeteria and required to attend lectures in the basement of the building, segregated from white students. Some white students joined him in the basement, however, and others studied with him. Tragically, he had to withdraw from the university because of ill health after only one semester, and in February 1949 he died of tuberculosis, apparently complicated by injuries he had received at the Battle of the Bulge. Jackie Shropshire, who was admitted to the law school in the fall of 1949, would be its first graduate.[12]

During Hunt's semester at the University of Arkansas School of Law, twenty-two-year-old Edith Mae Irby applied for admission to the University of Arkansas's College of Medical Sciences in Little Rock. When Dean Henry Chenault received the application, he called the university president for advice. Jones advised him to accept Irby, and she became a student in the fall with some of the same restrictions that Hunt had endured in Fayetteville. She was allowed to attend classes with other students but was required to eat at a separate table and use a separate restroom. Her first days at UAMS were lonely and caused her to question her decision to attend a white medical college, but she overcame her misgivings and remained.

Irby's path to medical college had been long and fraught with some of the same early tragedies that marked Sue Morris's journey to Dunbar High School. Morris suffered the loss of her mother while young, and Irby endured the death of her father in 1930, when she was three years old. Robert Irby appeared on the 1920 census as a farm renter in Danley Township near Conway, Arkansas, and apparently weathered the economic crisis in the farming sector of the 1920s without being driven to the status of sharecropper. Sharecropping was the lowest form of tenancy, one in which the farmer held no tools, implements, or work stock. By 1930, the year he fell from a horse and died, Irby was still tenant farming near Conway, and his property consisted of "a farm wagon, plow, tools, gear, cultivators, and harness." Though modest, this property would have equipped him for tenant rather than sharecropper status. His widow, however, "was forced to assign the estate to the S.C. Smith Company for the sum of $25 and a black horse," leaving her unable to carry on farming operations even had she been capable of doing so. With three young children to support, she was "required to vacate the premises" in January 1931 and moved in with her grandparents. When her older daughter, Juanita, outgrew the rural school in the vicinity, the family moved to Conway. There Juanita continued her education while her mother secured employment as a domestic, occasionally working in the cotton fields for additional income. And there, in Conway, Edith Mae began her formal education in 1933.[13]

The year 1933 was significant for Edith for another reason. Juanita was stricken with typhoid fever, and it was six-year-old Edith who nursed her dying sister. The experience developed her interest in chemistry and biology, and when her family relocated to Hot Springs in 1938, she pursued the subjects in Langston High School. During the war, while Sue Morris was engaged in her struggle with the Little Rock School board, Edith moved to Chicago to live with relatives and work as a clerk-typist. When she had saved enough money, she purchased a train ticket to Knoxville, Tennessee, and enrolled at Knoxville College, a historically black college affiliated with the Presbyterian Church. To pay her way, she worked in the president's office and in the canteen. As graduation drew near, she began applying to medical schools, and because she could qualify for in-state tuition at the University of Arkansas for Medical Sciences, she hoped they would accept her application. She was at home in Hot Springs when a reporter and photographer from *Time Magazine* appeared at the door to announce that UAMS had favored her application.[14]

When Irby arrived in Little Rock in September 1948 to enroll at UAMS, she again found herself short of funds. Family and friends in Hot Springs had collected what they believed was enough money to pay her tuition and registration fees, but upon arriving on campus, she discovered she was $50 short. A friend in Hot Springs had told her to contact Daisy Bates, a civil rights activist and

NAACP member in Little Rock, if she needed help. At two o'clock, just three hours before the registration deadline, she appeared at the *Arkansas State Press*, a black newspaper that Daisy ran with her husband, L. C. When Irby asked for assistance, Bates not only gave her the necessary $50; she also arranged for donations from the Little Rock African American community to help defray Irby's expenses during her first year at UAMS. After that, Montague Cobbs, publisher of the *Journal of the National Medical Association* and an anatomy professor at Howard University College of Medicine, arranged for the Jesse Smith Noyes Foundation to defray some of Irby's expenses. Because of Daisy Bates's efforts, blacks throughout Arkansas continued to contribute to Irby's support.[15]

Even as Irby struggled with the usual difficulties faced by all medical students, she endured additional stress as a result of being the first African American to attend UAMS. Although she was required to eat at a separate table in the dining room, the black cafeteria staff provided fresh flowers daily, and some white students joined her at her table. Two of the three white women students befriended her, and one, Mary Author, even provided transportation to and from campus in her automobile, a gift from her father, a veterinarian who feared for "the safety of his daughter and Edith."[16] But the most important personal relationship Irby formed during this period came when she met James B. Jones, a faculty member at UAPB who had known Ada Sipuel when she was a student there. Jones and Irby married during Edith's second year of medical school. They bought a home in Little Rock but, to enable James to stay on the faculty at UAPB, lived apart much of the time. He traveled with her to New York during the summer of 1950, however, where she interned at Harlem Hospital, and the couple lived in a modest apartment once occupied by Langston Hughes.[17] In the fall they returned to Little Rock, where she continued her internship at the university hospital. When she became pregnant, she faced another hurdle. Although she was able to continue her studies, she was expected to deliver at a hospital that catered only to black patients. However, one of the white doctors, presumably someone she studied with, insisted on taking her to a white hospital, where he had to perform a caesarian section on her. When the administrators at the hospital discharged her earlier than was then customary "because she was Black," the doctor and several staff members at the hospital resigned in protest.[18]

Edith Irby Jones graduated UAMS in 1952 and moved back to Hot Springs, where she opened an office and operated as a general-practice physician until 1958. She had long wanted to study internal medicine and decided to move to Houston to begin a residency in that area at Baylor College of Medicine. The move both fulfilled a long-held dream and removed her family from the racial strife that afflicted Arkansas as a result of the Central High crisis, a crisis to which state legislators responded by passing Act 10, which required that all state employees reveal their membership in certain organizations, including the NAACP. Her husband was still employed at UAPB and would have had to reveal his membership in the NAACP, an organization that Edith had herself become involved with following her first encounter with Daisy Bates. At Baylor Edith still encountered discrimination. She was required to "live separately from other residents" and was assigned only black patients. Nevertheless, she completed her residency without incident and opened a practice in Houston's Third Ward, an area heavily populated by African Americans. She became well known in the black community and in the medical profession and was elected the first woman president of the National Medical Association, the black medical association, in 1985.[19]

By the fall of 1948, when Edith Mae Irby appeared at the office of the *Arkansas State Press* to ask for a loan, Daisy Bates had established a reputation for militancy that discomfited some blacks in Little Rock. As wife of the editor and publisher of a prominent black newspaper, she was eligible for membership in Little Rock's black aristocracy, but her militancy and her background made her unacceptable to many in the elite black community. Like Sue Cowan Morris and Edith Mae Irby, Daisy Gatson Bates hailed from humble circumstances and endured personal tragedies early in life. Born in 1914 and raised by adoptive parents in the small southern Arkansas town of Huttig, Daisy discovered as a teenager that a decade earlier her mother had been raped by three white men and her lifeless body thrown into a pond. Her father purportedly left Huttig shortly afterward never to be seen again—apparently because he could do nothing about the rape and murder of his wife and could not stand to remain in the community under those circumstances. This revelation sparked a sense of injustice in Daisy that smoldered for years. As she told interviewer Elizabeth Jacoway in 1976, "I think I have been angry all my life about what happened to my people" an anger that began when she learned of her mother's murder and realized that "nobody did anything about it."[20]

When Daisy Gatson married L. C. Bates in 1941 and moved to Little Rock to open the *Arkansas State Press,* it is unlikely that she imagined the future in store for her. For the first couple of years she took business-administration classes at Shorter College in Little Rock and worked only part-time at the newspaper. She may have felt some insecurity about her lack of schooling. Although she later claimed to have had a high-school education, it appears that she finished only Huttig's grammar school for African Americans.[21] Nevertheless, she had a forceful personality and strong opinions that ultimately propelled her into the limelight. Her militancy was matched by that of her husband, who had little use for African Americans who tolerated Jim Crow limitations. Upon arriving in Little Rock in 1941, the couple immediately aligned themselves with Harold Flowers, a civil rights activist from Pine Bluff who chafed under the live-and-let-live philosophy of Arkansas's African American leaders. Later Flowers would become one of two civil rights activists who accompanied Silas Hunt to Fayetteville so he could enroll in the law school. Back in 1940, Flowers founded the Committee on Negro Organizations in the hope that he could persuade Arkansas's African American population to adopt a new, more militant stance in support of the right to vote. L. C. Bates quickly let his own opinions be known, praising Flowers openly in the *Arkansas State Press* in 1941 and promoting Sue Cowan Morris's cause beginning in 1942. But another event in 1942 propelled Bates, and his newspaper, into the middle of a racial controversy. A Little Rock policeman murdered a black soldier on Ninth Street—the black business section—on March 22, and the *Arkansas State Press* led the drive for an investigation. When the policeman was acquitted, L. C. Bates called for a federal investigation. The federal grand jury also failed to indict him, but the authorities in Little Rock agreed to assign eight black officers to Ninth Street. This was a meager victory, but it was enough to increase the newspaper's circulation and establish it as a force to be reckoned with.[22]

Daisy's foray into the public arena began as a result of a 1946 strike at the Southern Cotton Oil Mill in Little Rock, just a mile from the newspaper office. The mill workers, members of the Congress of Industrial Organizations, had gone out on strike for higher wages and had begun picketing the mill. As historian Grif Stockley puts it, "In typical Southern fashion, after a [black] picket named Walter Campbell was killed by his replacement, three other [black] pickets were arrested and found guilty of violating Arkansas's right-to-work law and sentenced to a year's imprisonment." The strike-breaker who had killed Campbell was not charged. The arrest, prosecution, and conviction of the three black strikers was "the result of a provision of the right-to-work law. If any violence broke out on a picket line, everybody on the line could be found guilty of it."[23]

Left in charge of the newspaper while her husband was away on a trip, Daisy had just finished writing her story when L. C. returned to the office, and though he had misgivings about her strongly worded article, he approved it and even provided the headline "FTA Strikers Sentenced to Pen by a Hand-Picked Jury." The headline was not what caused them grief, however. It was the implied criticism of Judge Lawrence C. Auten, who had "instructed the jury that the pickets could be found guilty if they aided or assisted, or just stood idly by while violence occurred." Judge Auten, unaccustomed to criticism, especially from members of the black community, ordered the arrest of L. C. and Daisy Bates for contempt of court. They were taken to the police station, photographed and fingerprinted, and then allowed to post bond. Unable to find another attorney to represent them in Little Rock, they secured the services of the union lawyers, but when the case came before Judge Auten on April 29, he sentenced them to ten days in jail and a $100 fine, ruling that the article "implied that the entire court was dishonest and carried an implication that these men [Negro strikers] were railroaded to the penitentiary." He also denied them bail and ruled that they had no right to appeal his decision. The union attorneys immediately took the case to the Arkansas Supreme Court, which ordered their release seven hours later and scheduled the case for hearing later that year. In November the court ruled in favor of the Bateses, citing freedom of the press.[24]

If Judge Auten thought he could intimidate the Bateses, he was badly mistaken. In 1949, white officials in Little Rock, trying to prevent the desegregation of public parks, proposed a bond issue to create a park near a public housing project designated for African Americans. This was an obvious and unsubtle effort to promote segregation in public facilities. Supporters of the bond issue courted black voters with some success, and the measure "passed by a narrow margin." Daisy was contemptuous of those African Americans supporting the measure and, as Grif Stockley has noted, was "making her own voice heard, one that was increasingly critical of her own people's choices."[25]

Daisy and L. C. also became even more active in the NAACP, initially siding with Harold Flowers in an internal struggle for control between the old faction, who treated the organization like a social club, and a more militant faction, led by Flowers, who became "chief organizers of branches" in 1945. Flowers wanted a more aggressive pursuit of African American political and civil rights, and he fought with the president of the Arkansas State Conference of Branches, Rev. Marcus Taylor, for leadership of the organization. By the time Flowers secured the leadership, he had become disenchanted enough with the national office to be exceedingly slow about sending dues to them. In late 1949, similarly disenchanted with the Little Rock chapter, Daisy attempted to organize a new chapter with herself as president. But when the national NAACP rebuffed her efforts, citing the existence of a Little Rock chapter, Daisy remained loyal and accepted the decision. The strife within the Arkansas branch did not please the national organization, which countenanced the older leadership. When Flowers found himself frozen out because of his reluctance to share dues with the national organization, he denounced the NAACP and tried to persuade African Americans in Arkansas to join him in a separate effort. This led to a brief break with L. C. and Daisy Bates, whose loyalty remained with the NAACP.[26]

Daisy's loyalty was rewarded in 1952, when she was elected president of the State Conference, a position she held until 1961. Although the national officers were dubious about her selection, believing her to be too militant, they "permitted" it because she was the state choice and because the Bateses had remained loyal during the affair with Flowers. Daisy's new position gained her greater visibility across the state, and it positioned her to play a prominent role in the integration crisis that arose in 1957. In fact, Daisy was a driving force behind the litigation that sought to force the Little Rock School Board to move more quickly—and beyond tokenism—in integrating the city schools. As a member of the press, she attended meetings called by Little Rock school superintendent Virgil Blossom to promote his plan of integration, a plan Daisy came to understand as an attempt to contravene the intent of the court in the *Brown* decision.[27]

Little Rock had been undergoing a significant increase in its population, brought on first by the availability of jobs during World War II and then by the transformation of the plantation system in the countryside. As mechanization and the use of chemicals on farms and plantations rendered many farm workers redundant, they moved to nearby towns and cities such as Little Rock. The businessmen and promoters of the state's capital city had promoted industry growth with some success, and displaced black and white farm workers found jobs there. Most black women, of course, found their opportunities limited to menial service-related or domestic jobs. Their children, like those of white parents, contributed to the overcrowding of the city school system, so much so that it became necessary to open two new high schools. As originally conceived, Horace Mann would be built in a predominantly black neighborhood and reserved for blacks, and Hall would be built in a predominantly white neighborhood and reserved for whites. But the *Brown* decision presented an unanticipated challenge.

When Blossom met with Daisy Bates and other NAACP officials, he noted that the two new schools would not open on a segregated basis. Although residential zones would continue to exist, integration would be permitted in the two new high schools and in Central, the existing school, which was in a mixed working-class and black neighborhood.[28] But Blossom had been meeting with black groups, promising that his plan would speed integration, and then with white groups, suggesting that his plan would delay integration, and Daisy exposed his duplicity, at least to the black community. As she said in a 1976 interview, "When I found out that he was, you know, saying one thing one place and one another, I didn't quite trust him after that." Responding to criticisms and concerns expressed by the white community, Blossom revised his plan in a way that further limited integration. John Kirk describes the original and revised plans as follows:

> Under the original Blossom Plan, school districts had been gerrymandered to ensure a black majority at Horace Mann High and a white majority at Hall High. The subsequent assignment of black students to Horace Mann, even though they lived closer to Central, confirmed the intention of the school board to limit the impact of desegregation as much as possible. . . . The revised plan, however, allowed white students to "opt out" of attendance at Horace Mann without giving blacks the right to "opt in" to Hall. . . . The school board also declared that it intended to open Horace Mann as a segregated black school in February 1956, a move intended to establish a precedent for all-black attendance the year before the school was to desegregate.[29]

When the US Supreme Court issued its famous *Brown II* decision in 1955, emphasizing the need for "all deliberate speed" in integrating the school systems of the nation, Daisy recognized that it essentially authorized Southern whites to delay integration. This was a sentiment shared by the NAACP nationally, and Daisy played a significant role in laying the groundwork for *Aaron v Cooper,* a case that would play an important role in events leading to the Central High crisis in 1957. She lined up thirty-three African American children in late 1955, and when they were prevented from enrolling, Daisy and other local NAACP activists accompanied nine of them to Virgil Blossom's office, taking an *Arkansas State Press* photographer with her. Blossom could not have been happy to see her. As a member of the press, she had been attending his meetings and press conferences, including those with whites, and exposed his double-talk. The woman who had dogged Blossom at his meetings with black and white audiences the year before—and greatly annoyed him—was ready to take the next step in an effort to speed integration of Little Rock's school system. On February 8, 1956, the case was filed in federal court in Little Rock.[30]

Unfortunately, the federal judge hearing the case, John A. Miller, was the least sympathetic jurist in the state. He had been the prosecuting attorney in the Elaine cases in 1919 and he was an avowed supporter of white supremacy. And the case for the plaintiffs was further handicapped by a breakdown in communication between the local and national NAACP offices. The national office was ready to argue for total and unqualified integration, the position Daisy Bates also advocated. The strategy outlined by the local office, however, was to insist on the implementation of Blossom's original plan of integration, one that would have guaranteed more integration than his revised plan. Daisy had opposed that approach but had been outvoted. When U. Simpson Tate, the attorney dispatched from the national office of the NAACP, made his pitch to Judge Miller for integration of all the city schools, it came as a surprise to Wiley Branton, the Arkansas attorney. His strategy—and that of the state chapter—was in a shambles, and his attempt to recover momentum on appeal was unsuccessful.[31] It is doubtful, however, that Judge Miller would have ruled in favor of either strategy. In a nod to tokenism and a strategy for delaying meaningful integration, he held that the Blossom plan should be allowed to proceed. To no one's surprise, in April 1956 the Eighth Circuit Court of Appeals upheld Judge Miller's decision. Miller had paid lip service to the *Brown II* decision, and no one on the appeals court was willing to mount a challenge to the Supreme Court ruling.[32]

Daisy Bates and other NAACP officials recognized the court's decision as a significant defeat, but the forces of segregation in Arkansas, who viewed even the token integration it permitted as unacceptable, launched a campaign to undermine the Blossom plan. In 1956, Orval Faubus was running for reelection against a rabid racist, Jim Johnson, who made a name for himself by undermining the peaceful integration of schools in Hoxie, Arkansas, an eastern Arkansas town with a progressive administrator. Governor Faubus had earned a reputation as a moderate on the race question, but when Johnson challenged him, Faubus jumped on the segregationist bandwagon. Johnson, a state senator, proposed an "interposition" amendment to the state constitution, an amendment which would have authorized the state to ignore federal court rulings. Governor Faubus, put on the defensive, supported a watered-down version of Johnson's interposition amendment, thus staking out a segregationist position of his own, one that ultimately won him reelection in November 1957. The interposition amendment and a Pupil Assignment Law designed to let the school board maintain segregation also secured enough votes for passage. In 1958 the segregationists continued their campaign to undermine integration. During its session that year, the Arkansas General Assembly passed no fewer than sixteen segregation bills, including Act 10, an affidavit law requiring that state employees reveal their affiliation with certain organizations, particularly the NAACP. Act 10 would come back to haunt Daisy Bates.[33]

Despite the interposition amendment and the Pupil Assignment Law, the Blossom plan was still on track in the spring and summer of 1957. With the sanction of Judge Miller and the Eighth Circuit, Blossom moved ahead with his revised plan, soliciting the names of prospective black students from the principals of Horace Mann High School and Dunbar Junior High without consulting Daisy Bates or any other black activist in Arkansas. Upon learning of his actions, Daisy met with him, but it was clear that he felt empowered by the court's decision in *Aaron v. Cooper* and was determined to make the selection of the students without her advice—or, from his point of view, interference. In the end, nine students, all with excellent academic credentials, were selected. But the forces of segregation had not yet rested. In the summer of 1957, a group of white women organized as the Mothers' League, and began warning of "civil commotion" if the Blossom plan proceeded. Meanwhile, Faubus, having been reelected, seemed to return to a more moderate stand on the issue, but ultimately he called out the National Guard to prevent integration. His biographer and other historians have concluded that his decision was largely a concession to powerful eastern Arkansas legislators, who pressured him relentlessly.[34]

Even as these developments were taking shape, Daisy Bates was working with the nine students, preparing them for Tuesday, September 3, their first day of classes. When Daisy discovered, the evening before, that Faubus had called out the National Guard, she telephoned eight of the nine students, telling them to meet her at the intersection of Twelfth and Park, a few blocks from the school, where they would be joined by some ministers and a police car. She had convinced the city police to provide an escort to Central High School. She was unable to reach Elizabeth Eckford, whose family did not own a telephone, but planned to contact her by some other means the next morning. Unfortunately, Elizabeth set off for school before her family received word of the change of plans, and she met a mob numbering about a thousand and National Guard troops with orders to prevent her from entering the school. With the white mob shouting obscenities and threatening her, she sought to make her way into the "safety" of the school but was blocked by National Guardsmen. She returned to the corner and sat on a bench, waiting for a bus to take her home. One lone white woman sat beside her and admonished her tormentors, and then a bus arrived and whisked her away. The eight remaining students met Daisy as planned and made the trip to Central High. Daisy already knew that they would be turned away, but it was necessary to challenge Faubus's use of the National Guard to prevent integration. Accompanied by two white and two black ministers (and the son of one of the white ministers), Daisy escorted the students to Central High. They endured the same harassment that Elizabeth Eckford had encountered and, like Elizabeth, were turned away.[35]

Over the next three weeks, suits were filed on both sides, segregationist rhetoric heightened, and even President Eisenhower, himself lukewarm to integration, met with Faubus in an effort to convince him to remove the National Guard and let integration proceed. The meeting was cordial, but Faubus refused to back down. Only a September 20 court order reiterating the decision in *Aaron v. Cooper* forced the governor to remove the National Guard. Once again the stage was set for an attempt to integrate Central High, and once again Daisy Bates played the crucial role. On Monday, September 23, the "Little Rock Nine" met at Daisy's home and, with her, climbed into two automobiles for the trip to Central High. Once again they walked through a mob of angry segregationists. But this time they were allowed to enter. The next day saw an even larger crowd of segregationists. At this point, President Eisenhower took action. To maintain order he "nationalized" the Arkansas National Guard and called in a thousand soldiers from the 101st Airborne Division. Throughout the next year the nine students endured harassment, both verbal and physical, but they stood their ground. Only one, Minniejean Brown, was unable to complete the year. Known as someone who would "talk back" to white students who were harassing her, she was provoked into retaliating—dumping a bowl of chili on the heads of two of her male tormentors. In February 1958 she was expelled from Central High, but she was given a scholarship to attend New Lincoln High School in New York City.[36]

Daisy had maintained a running battle to secure protection for the children inside the school, understanding that some white students, encouraged by their parents or other segregationists, were doing things designed to force the nine from Central High. When Minniejean Brown was expelled, they brandished signs that read, "One down, eight to go."

Finally, Daisy managed to secure some protection for the students, but she had problems of her own. From the beginning of the crisis, the Bateses had endured harassment. Crosses were burned on their lawn and shots fired into their home. With the police refusing to protect them, neighbors and friends took turns standing guard. They also endured intimidation from the IRS, which sought to investigate the books of the *Arkansas State Press.* The previous IRS representative in the city had been friendly to them and had routinely reviewed their tax returns as a favor, the new IRS representative was of another persuasion. He levied a fine against them that they were able to pay only with donations from the national office of the NAACP. Finally, Arkansas's attorney general, Bruce Bennett, engaged in his own plan of attack. Using Act 10 as his rationale, he demanded that Daisy, as head of the state chapter of the NAACP, and Rev. J. C. Crenchaw, as president of the Little Rock chapter, hand over the membership rolls. Both refused, and both were arrested in October 1957. Later the charges were dropped against Crenchaw, but Daisy had to pay a $100 fine.

Good news came from another source. The NAACP national board of directors had voted to give the Little Rock Nine the Spingarn Medal, the organization's highest award. Initially they did not include Daisy, but the nine students let it be known that they would not accept the award if it did not include her. At the NAACP's annual convention in Cleveland, Ohio, in July 1958, Bates collected her Spingarn Medal along with the Little Rock Nine. The national office of the NAACP had come to recognize the crucial role Daisy Bates played in the fight against segregation in Little Rock.[37]

Although the Little Rock Nine finished their first year at Central, they were unable to enroll in the fall of 1958 because Governor Faubus had devised another strategy for defeating integration: he closed all city schools in Little Rock. They would remain closed for the entire 1958–59 school year, causing great hardship not only to black students but also to many whites. By this time, Daisy had become a national celebrity, but the ordeal had taken its toll. Segregationist forces had determined to punish Daisy for her efforts, and they managed one major success. White merchants stopped advertising in the *Arkansas State Press,* some counties in eastern Arkansas apparently banned the newspaper, blacks who subscribed or purchased issues were harassed or beaten, and long-term suppliers refused to deal with the Bateses. Although they received donations in an effort to sustain operations, it was all to no avail. The *Arkansas State Press* ceased operations in 1959. At that time, Daisy, the most famous woman civil rights activist in America, began to accept speaking engagements out of state in order to support the Bates household. Her absence from Little Rock blunted the efforts of the NAACP in the state. In 1961, L. C. took over as president of the state chapter, and although he shared Daisy's militant perspective, he was of a retiring disposition and unable to provide her style of leadership. NAACP membership began to decline in the state, but Daisy became a member of the national board and of the SCLC board of directors. She was "appointed by President Kennedy to the Democratic National Committee, and she worked as an advisor on President Lyndon B. Johnson's antipoverty programs. In 1963, Bates was the only woman asked to speak at the March on Washington."[38]

The civil rights struggle was destined to become much more radical, something that a younger version of Daisy Bates would have supported. It is almost certain that, had she been a college student in the early 1960s, she would have welcomed an opportunity to participate in the Freedom Rides or the sit-ins that took place beginning in 1960. As it happens, the arrival of Freedom Riders in Little Rock in March 1960 occurred while Daisy was out of state, but, as historian Ben Johnson reveals, "Daisy and L. C. Bates . . . were nearly alone in praising the students' courage."[39] Nevertheless, as John Kirk puts it, "After the *State Press* closed in 1959, Bates spent most of the following two years either in New York, writing her memoir of the school crisis, or on the road for numerous speaking engagements."[40] A new generation would take the stage in the civil rights struggle, as students at Philander Smith College in Little Rock and UAPB in Pine Bluff began an even more confrontational approach to integrating public facilities and securing the right to vote.

By the time the first sit-ins occurred and the Freedom Riders appeared in Little Rock in the early 1960s, the white businessmen of the city had learned an important lesson from the Central High crisis. As a result of the violence and bad publicity, Little Rock had suffered a shattering loss of business. The cost of defying integration, its civic leaders recognized, was too high. Although they were not integrationists, they were motivated to thwart the segregationists. As a consequence, schools reopened in 1959. When sit-in demonstrations began and Freedom Riders appeared in 1961, Little Rock's civic leaders recognized another potential public-relations fiasco in the making. When Philander Smith students began sit-in demonstrations, in March 1960, they were promptly arrested, but no violence occurred. Four hundred whites were on hand to jeer and taunt the first Freedom Riders, who arrived on July 10, 1961, but, although some black activists were arrested, no one attacked. Little Rock's civic leaders wanted no more negative publicity, and nothing resembling the Central High crisis accompanied the sit-in demonstrations and the appearance of the Freedom Riders. Lunch counters were desegregated quietly and without significant incident.[41]

The real drama in this new phase of the civil rights struggle in Arkansas developed in Pine Bluff, where the Student Nonviolent Coordinating Committee began operations in 1963. In 1960 they had established an office in Little Rock and played a role in the sit-ins there, but it was in Pine Bluff that SNCC found concerted opposition and faced violence and intimidation. As they shifted from merely integrating lunch counters and public facilities to securing voting rights for African Americans, the opposition grew uglier. Among SNCC workers who played a role in Pine Bluff and elsewhere in the Arkansas Delta were several female students at UAPB, including Ruthie Buffington, Joanna Edwards, Shirley Baker, Mildred Neal, Janet Broome, and Hazel Crofton. Along with several male students, in February 1963 they defied the UAPB administration—which feared a backlash against the university—and continued sit-in demonstrations. As a result, they were suspended from UAPB.[42] Black women played a crucial role in SNCC activities during this period, but little has been written about their participation. Activists such as Gould resident Carrie Dilworth, a sixty-five-year-old former secretary of the Southern Tenant Farmers Union, served as role models and provided inspiration for the younger women—and men—of SNCC. Dilworth, a woman of some means, provided a building for organizers to use—until it mysteriously burned.[43] Only a few articles on SNCC's activities in Arkansas have appeared in print to document the efforts of the organization between 1960 and 1967, and women activists such as Carrie Dilworth are not their focus.[44]

Student-activists in the Arkansas Delta were standing on shifting ground, in terms both of the civil rights movement and of plantation agriculture. Between 1950 and 1960, a fundamental rearrangement of plantation operations occurred, a shift dramatically illustrated in the census records. Until 1960, tenancy, particularly sharecropping, represented almost the only "opportunity" for rural African Americans in the Delta. But the emergence of scientific agriculture following World War II transformed the plantation system from a labor-intensive to a capital-intensive enterprise. Sharecroppers, black and white, came so near disappearing that by 1960 the Bureau of the Census dropped that category from its published report. Many former tenants and sharecroppers moved to Little Rock or other Southern cities, where they fueled the civil rights struggle.

By the mid-1960s the transformation of agriculture was almost complete, but the civil rights movement was in the midst of a significant shift, one marked by greater militancy among African Americans and by the willingness of the president and Congress to pass meaningful civil rights and voting-rights legislation. By 1964 even Orval Faubus recognized the potential strength and importance of the black vote and was making overtures to black leaders. But some whites in the Arkansas Delta still resisted SNCC efforts to integrate lunch counters and register African Americans to vote. Violent encounters occurred as the organization spread its activities into Gould, Helena, Forrest City, and other Delta towns. The African American struggle for voting rights was an especially explosive challenge to white control, but courageous African Americans, including such women as Florence Clay of Helena, confronted both racism and male supremacy by running for elected office. In 1964 Clay ran against a popular (white) incumbent, E. C. "Took" Gathings, for a seat in the US Congress.[45] She lost that election, but many other African Americans captured city and town council seats and won mayoral races in towns across the Delta. It was 1980 before an African American woman, Irma Hunter Brown of Little Rock, won election to the state legislature.[46]

As African Americans gained greater access to political power in Arkansas, their economic opportunities expanded as well. An increasing number of African Americans moved into white-collar and professional careers. Significant problems remained, however, particularly in the public school systems in Little Rock and the Arkansas Delta. School districts heavily populated with African Americans suffered from "white flight" and from a retrogressive school-funding structure that tied education funding to local tax collections. And even though a federal court order in 1983 ordered the state to "narrow the gaping disparities in school-district income," the legislature was unable—or unwilling—to allocate funds sufficient to accomplish the task.[47] Despite the efforts of the Black Caucus, which identified the achievement gap between white and black students as among its principal challenges, African American schools continued to be the state's worst facilities.

A significant divide between black and white residents of Arkansas remains in place. Although shaken by the civil rights struggles of the1940s through the 1960s, the state has replaced the Jim Crow system with voluntary segregation that undermines the abilities and thwarts the ambitions of African American children. Yet the sacrifice of those who fought for integration and voting rights was not in vain. It is no coincidence that those counties in Arkansas voting for Barack Obama for president in 2008 were those with the heaviest black populations. Aside from a few white liberal enclaves, such as Fayetteville, the home of the University of Arkansas, the rest of the state went Republican. Political scientists studying the phenomenon have concluded that race continues to be the most significant divide in Arkansas. It is a divide that must be crossed, and black women in Arkansas and elsewhere are likely to play important roles in reshaping race relations in the twenty-first century.

Notes

1. Roy Reed, *Faubus: The Life and Times of an American Prodigal,* (Fayetteville: University of Arkansas Press, 1977); David L. Chappell, *Inside Agitators: White Southerners in the Civil Rights Movement* (Baltimore: Johns Hopkins University Press, 1994); Elizabeth Jacoway, *Turn Away Thy Son: Little Rock, the Crisis That Shocked the Nation* (New York: Free Press, 2007).

2. John A. Kirk, *Redefining the Color Line* (Gainesville: University Press of Florida, 2002).

3. Grif Stockley, *Blood in Their Eyes: The Elaine Massacres of 1919* (Fayetteville, University of Arkansas Press, 2001); Robert Whitaker, *On the Laps of Gods: The Red Summer of 1919 and the Struggle for Justice That Remade a Nation* (New York: Crown Publishers, 2008).

4. John A. Kirk, *Redefining the Color Line: Black Activism in Little Rock, Arkansas, 1940–1970* (Gainesville: University Press of Florida, 2002), 40.

5. Sue Cowan Morris Williams, interview by John A. Kirk, January 1, 1993, Little Rock, Arkansas, Pryor Center for Oral and Visual History, Special Collections Department, University of Arkansas Libraries, Fayetteville, 3; Kirk, *Redefining the Color Line,* 40–41; Grif Stockley, *Race Relations in the Natural State,* (Little Rock: The Butler Center for Arkansas Studies, 2007), 123.

6. Kirk, *Redefining the Color Line,* 40–41; Stockley, *Race Relations in the Natural State,* 123.

7. Kirk, *Redefining the Color Line,* 43. Thomas E. Patterson, *History of the Arkansas Teachers Association* (Washington, DC: National Education Association, 1981), 90–91. The online *Encyclopedia of Arkansas History and Culture* says the District Court of the United States, the Western Division of Eastern Arkansas, heard Morris's appeal in 1943 and decided in her favor. On page 41 of *Daisy Bates: Civil Rights Crusader from Arkansas* (Jackson: University Press of Mississippi, 2005), Grif Stockley says it was the Eighth Circuit in St. Louis that reversed the Little Rock decision. Patterson's *History of the Arkansas Teachers Association* says it was the Eighth Circuit in 1945.

8. Williams, interview by Kirk, 15.

9. Kirk, *Redefining the Color Line,* 43; Stockley, *Race Relations in the Natural State,* 124; John A. Kirk, *An Epitaph for Little Rock* (Fayetteville: University of Arkansas Press, 2008), 92.

10. *Missouri ex rel. Gaines v. Canada,* 305 US 337 (1938).

11. *Sipuel v. Board of Regents of University of Oklahoma,* 332 US 631 (1940).

12. Kirk, *Redefining the Color Line,* 60–62.

13. Manuscript Census of Agriculture, Danley Township, Faulkner County, Sheet 4B, 1920; Lydia E. Brew, *The Story of Edith Irby Jones, M.D.* (n.p., n.p., 1986), 1–5.

14. Brew, *The Story of Edith Irby Jones,* 10–13.

15. Brew, *The Story of Edith Irby Jones,* 15–16.

16. Brew, *The Story of Edith Irby Jones,* 16.

17. Brew, *The Story of Edith Irby Jones,* 20–21.

18. Brew, *The Story of Edith Irby Jones,* 23–24.

19. Brew, *The Story of Edith Irby Jones,* 29, 31, 39.

20. Daisy Bates, *The Long Shadow of Little Rock* (Fayetteville: University of Arkansas Press, 1986; original edition, 1962), 10; Stockley, *Daisy Bates,* 99; Kirk, *Redefining the Color Line,* 47–48; Jacoway, *Turn Away Thy Son,* 164–65. Daisy Bates, interview by Elizabeth Jacoway, October 11, 1976, Interview G-0009, Southern Oral History Program Collection (#4007), University of North Carolina at Chapel Hill (http://docsouth.unc.edu/sohp/G-0009/excerpts/excerpt_946.html).

21. Jacoway, *Turn Away Thy Son,* 164–65; Stockley, *Daisy Bates,* 28, 44.

22. John A. Kirk, "The Little Rock Crisis and Post War Activism in Arkansas," in Kirk, *An Epitaph for Little Rock,* 93.

23. Stockley, *Daisy Bates,* 44–45; Bates, *The Long Shadow of Little Rock,* 39–43.

24. Bates, *The Long Shadow of Little Rock,* 49–43.

25. Stockley, *Daisy Bates,* 51.

26. Stockley, *Daisy Bates,* 53–55; Kirk, *Redefining the Color Line,* 68–73.

27. Stockley, *Daisy Bates,* 53–55.

28. Kirk, "The Little Rock Crisis," 99–100.

29. Bates, interview by Jacoway, October 11, 1976; Kirk, "The Little Rock Crisis," 100.

30. Stockley, *Daisy Bates,* 82; Kirk, "The Little Rock Crisis," 101. (Kirk says thirty-three students, Stockley twenty-seven.)

31. Kirk, "The Little Rock Crisis," 101.

32. Stockley, *Daisy Bates,* 88–89, 96–97.

33. Kirk, *Redefining the Color Line,* 102–3.

34. Kirk, *Redefining the Color Line,* 113–14; Jacoway, *Turn Away Thy Son.* 82–83.

35. Kirk, *Redefining the Color Line,* 116–17; Jacoway, *Turn Away Thy Son,* 168–71; Stockley, *Daisy Bates,* 124–25.

36. Kirk, *Redefining the Color Line,* 122–23; Jacoway, *Turn Away Thy Son,* 238; Stockley, *Daisy Bates,* 174.

37. Kirk, *Redefining the Color Line,* 130–31; Stockley, *Daisy Bates,* 179–80.

38. Kirk, *Redefining the Color Line,* 159, 171.

39. Ben F. Johnson III, *Arkansas in Modern America, 1930–1999* (Fayetteville: University of Arkansas Press, 2000), 149.

40. Kirk, *Redefining the Color Line,* 139.

41. Kirk, *Redefining the Color Line,* 149–50.

42. Holly Y. McGee, "'It Was the Wrong Time, and They Just Weren't Ready': Direct-Action Protest in Pine Bluff, 1963," *Arkansas Historical Quarterly* 66, no. 1 (Spring 2007), 28–29.

43. Stockley, *Race Relations in the Natural State,* 152–53.

44. In addition to McGee's essay, see Jennifer Jensen Wallach, "Replicating History in a Bad Way? White Activists and Black Power in SNCC's Arkansas Project," *Arkansas Historical Quarterly 67,* no. 3 (Autumn 2008), 268–87; Brent Riffel, "In the Storm: William Hansen and the Student Nonviolent Coordinating Committee in Arkansas, 1962–1967," *Arkansas Historical Quarterly* 63, no. 4 (Winter 2004): 405–19; and Randy Finlay, "Crossing the White Line: SNCC in Three Delta Towns, 1963–1967," *Arkansas Historical Quarterly* 65, no. 2 (Summer 2006): 117–37. Jayme Stone, a graduate student at the University of Memphis, has an unpublished paper, "Women of the Arkansas Delta: Grassroots Activism and the Student Nonviolent Coordinating Committee (SNCC), 1963–1966."

45. Finlay, "Crossing the White Line," 127.

46. *Arkansas Democrat-Gazette,* "Education Top Priority for State's Black Caucus," January 9, 2003; American Legacy Foundation, "Irma Hunter Brown," http://blackprwire.com/press-releases/1033-american_legacy_foundation_welcomes_arkansas_state_senator_irma_hunter_brown_to_board_of_directors.

47. Ben F. Johnson III, *Arkansas in Modern America, 1930–1999* (Fayetteville: University of Arkansas Press, 2000), 232–36.

PART II

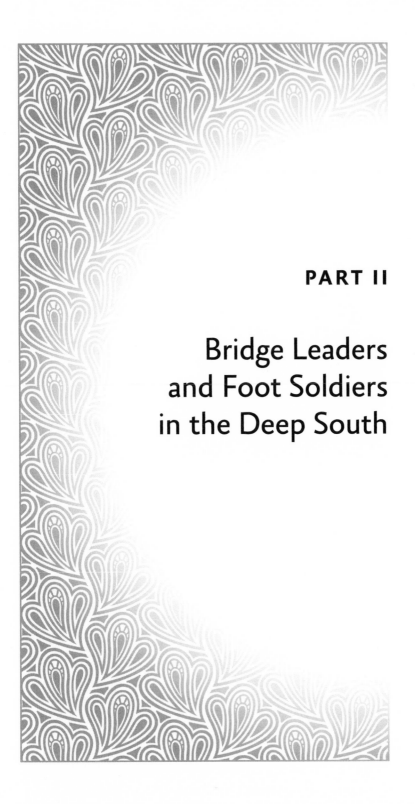

Bridge Leaders and Foot Soldiers in the Deep South

4 Black Women in the Florida Civil Rights Era, 1954–1974

Maxine D. Jones

"Our aim must be to create a world of fellowship and justice where no man's skin color or religion is held against him."
—Mary McLeod Bethune[1]

Florida's Mary McLeod Bethune died on May 18, 1955—one year and one day after the US Supreme Court ruled segregation in public schools unconstitutional. She had devoted her life to insuring that African Americans be treated as full citizens. Bethune asserted her beliefs in speeches and newspaper articles, claiming, "We must challenge, skillfully but resolutely, every sign of restriction or limitation to our full American citizenship. When I say challenge, I mean we must seek every opportunity to place the burden of responsibility upon him who denies it."[2] Though Bethune was pleased with the *Brown* decision, she would have been disappointed with its slow, almost always reluctant implementation. Bethune urged her people to be strong and to understand the "larger meanings of integration." She knew she would not be alive when it happened, but in her "Last Will and Testament" she left a proud legacy and a blueprint for black Americans to follow.[3] December 1, 1955, began a new phase of black activism.

Florida's white sand beaches and sunny skies often masked the racism and discrimination to which its black residents were subjected. Mired in poverty, cordoned off in segregated neighborhoods with limited city and county services, blacks in the Sunshine State depended on individuals such as Bethune, Eartha White, Viola T. Hill, Alice Mickens, Blanche Armwood Beatty and others to voice their concerns and to lobby for equality.[4] Black Floridians were active in pointing out the economic, legal, and social disparities between black and white Floridians. Harry Tyson Moore and his wife, Harriette Simms Moore, were killed for their activism on December 25, 1951. Beginning in 1934, Harry Moore had written hundreds of letters to newspapers and to local, state, and national officials calling attention to grievances in the black community. Those grievances included lynching, injustice in the courts, police brutality, teacher salary inequity, and an inability to vote. Harriette, and their daughters, Annie and Evangeline, helped Moore in his relentless campaign to secure for blacks what the US Constitution guaranteed them. But on Christmas Eve 1951 a bomb exploded under their home in Mims. Harry died that night, and Harriette died on January 3, 1952.[5]

Black women in Florida certainly were concerned about many of the same issues that troubled Harry Moore, but they were equally interested in improving the often-dire conditions that affected the quality of life in the black community. Through individual efforts and through their clubs and organizations, Florida's black women worked to uplift the race and to promote race pride. Many assumed the role of community activists, advocating equal public school education and facilities, decent housing, safe play areas for youth, and affordable childcare for working women. Believing playgrounds reduced crime, Alice Frederick Mickens fought for ten years to get a safe play area for black youth in West Palm Beach. Mickens also helped to establish a day nursery for working mothers and to extend the school year for black students. In 1948, M. Athalie Wilkinson Range complained about the condition of an elementary school in Miami's Liberty City. The school, she observed, had inadequate toilet facilities and "nothing that would be conducive to learning." Range led a campaign that resulted in a school-board decision to build a new school for black students. These women were determined, persistent, yet often subtle and diplomatic in bargaining with the white power structure.[6] But more active protests against discrimination were coming.

On December 1, 1955, black women in Montgomery, Alabama, took a stand against segregation and the mistreatment and disrespect they often received from white drivers on city buses. Five months later a similar movement began in Tallahassee, Florida, the state capital. On Saturday, May 26, 1956, Florida Agricultural and Mechanical University students Wilhelmina Jakes and Carrie Patterson refused to give up their seats at the front of the bus to stand at the back. City police arrested Jakes and Patterson and charged them with "placing themselves in a position to incite a riot."[7] The next day a cross was burned at their off-campus residence. Historian Glenda Rabby wrote, "the young women seemed genuinely stunned that their actions had caused such a turmoil." Very much aware of what was going on in Montgomery, Alabama, FAMU students, in support of their classmates, launched a boycott of city buses on Monday, May 28, 1956. Local black community leaders endorsed the student movement, assumed leadership of the boycott, and organized the Inter-Civic Council. Though the leadership was male, black women played important roles within the ICC and in supporting the boycott. At the grassroots level, Laurie Dixie refused to ride the buses so that her daughter would not have to live in a segregated society. A member of the NAACP, Dixie later became one of the first local women to serve on the board of the Southern Christian Leadership Conference. Hundreds of black women who depended on bus service to get to and from work nevertheless stopped using city buses. Black churchwomen raised the money needed to finance the ICC. Daisy Young and Gladys Harrington, both ICC members, gave freely of their time and talents to the organization. The boycott led to open seating on city buses.[8]

Wilhelmina Jakes and Carrie Patterson refused to be publicly humiliated by the rules of segregation, but they had not intended to initiate a movement challenging those rules. The same cannot be said of Priscilla and Patricia Stephens. These two young sisters, also FAMU students, made a deliberate decision to confront segregation and second-class citizenship head on. During the summer following their freshman year they attended a Congress of Racial Equality workshop in Miami. Their lives were forever changed. Patricia wrote:

> The CORE workshop gave me and Priscilla a very strong conviction that we two could easily motivate other students in Tallahassee to take action against discrimination. Why should we have to attend segregated movie theaters with special balcony sections set aside for Negroes, or separate theaters altogether? Why couldn't we be served at lunch counters like Woolworth and McCrory's, especially since those same stores were more than happy to take our money when we purchased other items? Naively, we also believed that the university itself would support us. In any case, we were excited and ready for action.[9]

In the fall semester of 1959, Patricia and Priscilla Stephens organized the first CORE chapter in Tallahassee, on the FAMU campus. Daisy Young helped them recruit white students from Florida State University. Then, using CORE's nonviolent tactics, they and nine others sought service at the downtown Woolworth on February 20, 1960, nineteen days after the Greensboro, North Carolina, sit-ins. When the waitress refused to serve them, they remained at the counter. Tallahassee police arrested the eleven protesters, which included two high school students and a forty-three-year-old woman, Mary Ola Gaines. Four other women (the Stephens sisters, Angelina Nance, and Barbara Broxton) also were among those arrested. Judge John Rudd found the eleven guilty of disturbing the peace and unlawful assembly. Given the option of paying a $300 fine or serving sixty days in confinement, Patricia and Priscilla Stephens and Barbara Broxton spent forty-nine days in jail along with William Larkins and John Broxton. Gaines lost her job but kept her commitment to the cause.[10]

The actions and bravery of the Stephens sisters and others encouraged more student-led protests. For the next several years, students from both universities united to challenge segregation at Woolworth's, McCrory's, Neisner's, Greyhound and Trailways Bus Depots, city recreational facilities, and the Florida Theater. At great personal sacrifice the Stephens sisters added their voices to the chorus and their names to the list of those who fought for black rights in Florida. Priscilla, scarred by all she had seen and experienced, left the United States in 1964 to live in Africa and remained abroad until 1977. Patricia married fellow freedom fighter John Due and continued to work for the civil rights of people of color in Tallahassee, the state of Florida, and the nation. Patricia Stephens Due shifted her activism "from the street to the places of personal encounter—homes, schools, neighborhoods." She worked as an educator, counselor, and mediator and reenacted for students many moments from the civil rights movement. In 2003, Patricia and her daughter Tananarive Due published *Freedom in the Family,* a poignant autobiographical account of Patricia's work in the movement.[11]

The decade of the 1960s was a tumultuous one in many Florida communities as blacks gathered the strength to confront Jim Crow. In St. Petersburg, C. Bette Wimbish struggled to explain to her children why, when they shopped downtown, they could not have an ice cream cone in a drugstore. She helped her husband, Dr. Ralph Wimbish, president of the local NAACP, organize sit-ins at lunch counters. From March 2 through December 6, 1960, blacks picketed downtown stores, including Webb's City, a conglomerate of stores and a major tourist attraction in St. Petersburg. Speaking of the sit-ins, Wimbish recalled, "It was a very frightening experience. There was always the threat of shooting, beating or spitting. But it had to be done." Their efforts were productive. On January 3, 1961, Webb's City and seventeen other downtown stores opened their lunch counters to blacks.

When Wimbish first ran for the Pinellas County School Board, in 1960, she became the first black to run for office in St. Petersburg and Pinellas County. Whites burned crosses on her lawn, but she was not discouraged. Though she lost, she had garnered more than 10,000 votes and had carried at least one all-white precinct.[12] Continuing in her quest to improve conditions for blacks in St. Petersburg. Wimbish won a seat on the St. Petersburg City Council in 1969. The FAMU law school graduate served as vice mayor from 1971 to 1973.[13]

Both Jacksonville and St. Augustine had their share of upheaval. African Americans in Jacksonville, as in the rest of the country, were impatient with segregation and restless. Male and female youths participated in sit-in demonstrations challenging the city's segregated lunch counters, and mothers challenged the Duval County School Board to let their sons and daughters attend the school of their choice. Sadie Braxton, Iona Godfrey, and Eddie Mae Steward were just a few of the courageous mothers who used legal measures to force the county to listen to them. Hundreds of other brave black mothers reluctantly allowed their sons and daughters to be taunted, spit at, and harassed at predominantly white schools. Their actions benefited thousands.[14]

Blacks in St. Augustine likewise tried to change the status quo. Fannie Fullerwood and Elizabeth Hawthorne led the local NAACP but, according to historian David Colburn, "were rather conservative in their efforts to desegregate St. Augustine. They tried to persuade rather than coerce whites to abandon segregation."[15] All across the South many blacks adopted a conservative stance and a wait-and-see approach because they feared white reaction to their insistence on inclusion. Though circumspect in their approach, Fullerwood and Hawthorne voiced their complaints eloquently. Vice President Lyndon Johnson had accepted an invitation from the St. Augustine Historical Restoration Society to speak at the dedication of the Avero House in March 1963. On February 23, 1963, Fullerwood and Hawthorne wrote to Johnson asking that he reconsider. They revealed that the planning and welcoming committees for the dedication were segregated, and that both St. Augustine and St. Johns County maintained segregated public facilities. The letter described conditions for blacks in the area, including police brutality, and pointed out that blacks were hired, if at all, only as "manual laborers and in non-skilled jobs," on several federally funded projects in the city and the county. They wrote:

> As chairman of the President's Committee on Equal Employment Opportunity and as a leader in the "New Frontier" administration, it is impossible for us to see how you can fulfill an engagement here in St. Augustine because of the conditions which we are now bringing to your attention.

> We are requesting that you reconsider the invitation extended to you for an appearance here at the dedication of the Avero Site, on March 11, unless the nation's oldest city—Saint Augustine—gives concrete evidence of a sincere desire and effort to comply with federal laws relating to the abolition of segregation.[16]

They sent copies of the letter to President John F. Kennedy, Florida Governor Farris Bryant, the mayor of St. Augustine, NAACP officials, and several national magazines and newspapers. When Vice President Johnson indicated that he would not participate in a segregated event, local white officials chose twelve blacks to represent the black community, but none was from the NAACP. Later Fullerwood and Hawthorne penned a letter to President Kennedy asking that he not support St. Augustine's application for a $350,000 federal grant to celebrate its quadricentennial.[17] St. Augustine whites did not agree with Colburn that Fullerwood and Hawthorne's efforts were conservative.

St. Augustine was a powder keg. Although the NAACP followed Fullerwood's leadership and called attention to segregation and other racist policies, many blacks felt the movement had stalled, and whites continued to resist changes in race relations. Because the NAACP was reluctant to use direct-action techniques, the more aggressive male leadership in St. Augustine sought help from the SCLC in 1964. The SCLC chose Easter week to highlight conditions in St. Augustine. A call went out for northern college students to aid in the effort. Among those arrested was Mary Parkman Peabody, the seventy-two-year-old mother of Endicott Peabody, governor of Massachusetts, and the wife of Malcolm Peabody, an Episcopal bishop. Her arrest garnered national attention. St. Augustine whites remained unmoved by the SCLC and Martin Luther King, Jr., until economic pressure was applied. The city was dependent on tourism, and the SCLC pleaded with tourists to avoid the segregated city. The economic consequences were so severe that business owners abandoned their racist practices. (This did not, however, signal a change in attitude.) The events in St. Augustine in 1964, including those involving black women, played an important part in the passage of the Civil Rights Act of 1964.[18]

The movements to eradicate segregation and racism in Tallahassee, Jacksonville, and St. Augustine were replicated in some form all across Florida. Blacks worked diligently to change their lives and the way that whites treated them. Their strategies were varied. Many willingly faced the possibility of being beaten, jailed, and even killed to secure their rights. Some, such as Fannie Fullerwood in St. Augustine, took a moderate approach; others, such as Patricia Stephens Due, took a more direct, confrontational stance. Many welcomed white support; some supported Black Power or black-only protests. But what changes transpired in the day-to-day lives of average black people? What effect did federal legislation have—the Civil Rights Act of 1964, the Voting Rights Act of 1965, and the 1968 Civil Rights Act? Did life change significantly for black Floridians between 1954 and 1974? How did the lives of black women change? Expectations were high, but across the board, change was slow.

In 1965, Daniel Patrick Moynihan, assistant secretary of labor, issued a report entitled *The Negro Family: The Case for National Action.* Dubbed "the Moynihan Report," it addressed the state of black America ten years after *Brown v. Board of Education.* Moynihan assessed conditions in the nation's black community by looking at poverty, housing, unemployment, school-dropout and illegitimacy rates, and the fabric of the black family. According to the report: "Individually, Negro Americans reach the highest peaks of achievement. But collectively, in the spectrum of American ethnic and religious and regional groups . . . Negroes are among the weakest." [19] The report concluded that, despite the perceived victories won with the *Brown* decision, the numerous protests to eliminate racism and discrimination, and the passage of the Civil Rights Act of 1964, "The circumstances of the Negro American community in recent years has [*sic*] probably been getting worse, not better. Indices of dollars of income, standards of living, and years of education deceive. The gap between the Negro and most other groups in American society is widening."[20]

How could this be? Certainly, the drive for first-class citizenship continued. The battle for voting rights was ongoing, as was the goal of open housing. Many had believed that the Civil Rights Act of 1964 would bring immediate change. Nevertheless, as the Moynihan Report shows, there was a huge difference between Equality of Opportunity and equality of results:

> The demand for Equality of Opportunity has been generally perceived by white Americans as a demand for liberty, a demand not to be excluded from the competitions of life—at the polling place, in the scholarship examinations, at the personnel office, on the housing market. Liberty does, of course, demand that everyone be free to try his luck, or test his skill in such matters. But these opportunities do not necessarily produce equality: on the contrary, to the extent that winners imply losers, equality of opportunity almost insures inequality of results.
>
> The point of semantics is that equality of opportunity now has a different meaning for Negroes than it has for whites. It is not (or at least no longer) a demand for liberty alone, but also for equality—in terms of group results.[21]

Obviously achieving equality of results takes time. But had the goals/benefits of the civil rights movement been deceptive? Or had only the black middle class reaped the real and tangible gains? According to the report: "A middle-class group has managed to save itself, but for vast numbers of the unskilled, poorly educated city working class the . . . cycle of poverty and disadvantage will continue to repeat itself."[22] An examination of education, transportation, politics, and economic opportunity reveals that although the *Brown* decision ultimately increased opportunities for all African Americans, early gains were limited primarily to the upper and middle classes.

Florida's black population grew from 603,101 in 1950 to 808,186 in 1960.[23] But blacks remained at the bottom of the economic ladder, still striving for acceptance and first-class citizenship. The church and the school continued to be strong institutions in the black community. For generations school boards had funded African American schools at different levels than white schools, but black schools were the pride of black communities across the state. And they employed hundreds of African American women as teachers and administrators. In Duval County, Lucille G. Coleman, Helen G. Roux, Adrienna N. Wesson, Eva L. Guyton, Olivia Baldwin, Aldonia C. Joyner, and Sadie Tillis served as principals during the 1957–58 school year. Desegregation had an enormous impact on their positions as teachers and administrators. When Florida finally implemented the *Brown* decision, many principals and teachers in black schools lost their jobs.[24]

Because whites were resistant to change, the federal court order to desegregate public schools initially had little effect. In Florida, school districts stalled, and white parents fought desegregation. But black parents fought back. When the Pinellas County School Board continued to build separate schools, C. Bette Wimbish, the mother of two children and a concerned citizen, took action, as she stated in a 1973 interview with Douglas Fleming:

> I was very outraged in the 50s about the attempt on the part of the local board of public instruction to condone and continue what I called involuted segregation. This is where they arbitrarily drew lines and said that this is the black community, and all schools serving the black community must be constructed within the confines of these lines. And to that end and in collusion with the then city council they proceeded to convey the park, Campbell Park on which they were going to build a five million dollar high school on less than two acres of land. And we all know that the state guidelines at that time called for forty acres for a

> high school. And of course I was outraged at that too. So actually I investigated and found out that the park was dedicated in perpetuity for park purposes. Yet still the city council at that time was going to convey it to the school (board) to build a high school to keep down the possibility of integration. And of course the community rallied behind me and as you see it was never built at that particular spot.[25]

Wimbish was unafraid to challenge the white power structure. Nor was she an advocate for her children only, but also for the children of all black mothers in the county who felt they lacked the skills or the voice to challenge the power structure that sought to maintain separate and unequal schools.

NAACP legal action and court rulings finally forced many districts to desegregate their schools. In 1964, Iona Godfrey's Jacksonville home was bombed because her six year-old son was one among thirteen who integrated an all-white elementary school. When school opened in 1965, only 137 of approximately thirty thousand African American students attended previously all-white schools. No white students enrolled in black schools. Compelled by a federal court order, Duval County schools finally integrated in 1971. Students did not attend desegregated schools until 1970 in St. Augustine and St. Johns County. Integration promised so much more than separate but equal, but rarely were those promises fulfilled.[26]

When Florida schools were desegregated, increasing numbers of black women completed high school and attended college. Even so, they were at a disadvantage by comparison with white women. Between 1960 and 1974 the percentage of black females finishing high school increased from 45 to 75. But the percentage of white female graduates in 1974 was 83. Similarly, in 1970, 41 percent of black females between ages sixteen and twenty-four who were not enrolled in school had completed high school; 49 percent of white females in the same category were graduates. Of black women between the ages of twenty and twenty-four not enrolled in school, fewer than 3 percent had completed four years of college; 8 percent of white females in that category had done so. In 1970, more than 8,300 black females between the ages of sixteen and thirty-four were enrolled in college in Florida; 67,381 white females in the same category were enrolled.

National statistics for 1965 indicate that the rate of college attendance was the same both for black men and for black women: approximately 10 percent. In 1973, however, black men outnumbered black women in college. Of black males ages eighteen to twenty-four, 19 percent attended college; 14 percent of black females in the same category had done so. In 1974, 20 percent of black men between the ages of eighteen and twenty-four attended college; 16 percent of black women did so.[27]

It was in the political arena, not the educational, that effective changes occurred in Florida. The Voting Rights Act of 1965 along with the Twenty-Fourth Amendment produced the most immediate and visible gains for blacks Americans, including those in Florida. These measures prohibited literacy tests and the poll tax as a requirement for voting. Signed into law by President Lyndon B. Johnson on August 6, 1965, the Voting Rights Act added approximately 250,000 blacks to the voting rolls in Southern states by the end of that year. On April 4, 1964, 240,616 blacks were registered to vote in Florida. Though not as dramatic an increase as in other Southern states, two years later the number of registered black voters was 283,269. In 1972 more than 311,000 blacks were on the voting rolls in Florida. Most blacks elected to office may have been privileged, but for the first time African Americans of all classes were voting.[28]

More important, black women were voting and running for office. In 1965, M. Athalie Wilkinson Range ran for the Miami City Commission. She lost the election, but later that year Mayor Robert High King appointed her to the City Commission. Voters elected her twice more. In 1971, when Governor Reubin Askew named Range Secretary of the Department of Community Affairs, she became the first African American to head a state agency in Florida.[29]

In 1967, voters elected Jacksonville natives Sallye Brooks Mathis and Mary Littlejohn Singleton to the Jacksonville City Council. From the black middle class, Mathis and Singleton were the first African Americans to earn a seat on the council in more than sixty years. A 1930 graduate of Stanton Institute in Jacksonville, Mathis attended several schools, including South Carolina's Benedict College and Bethune Cookman College before graduating from Tuskegee Institute in 1945 with a degree in education. During her more than twenty-five years teaching in public schools, Mathis worked diligently for the equalization of teacher salaries, and in 1962 she helped integrate the Jacksonville League of Women Voters. As a member of the Jacksonville City Council, Mathis became an advocate for the voiceless of all races—children and the elderly. She held her seat until her death in 1982.[30]

Born in Jacksonville in 1926, Mary Littlejohn Singleton attended a private school, Boylan Haven Industrial Training School. From there she matriculated at Hampton Institute, where she majored in horticulture before leaving at the end of her second year. She graduated from FAMU in 1949 and in 1955 married

Jacksonville businessman Isadore Singleton. In 1965, Governor Farris Bryant appointed her to the Local Government Study Commission of Duval County.

Singleton's election to the Jacksonville City Council in 1967 was only the beginning of her political career. In 1972 she was voted into the Florida House of Representatives, and in 1974 she was reelected. In that chamber, Singleton strongly supported education and served as vice chair of the House Committee on Education. Governor Reubin Askew named her to the Host Committee for the 1972 Democratic National Convention held in Miami. Bruce Smathers, Florida Secretary of State, appointed the talented Singleton to head the State Supervisor of Elections Office in 1976. In 1978, Former Governor Claude Kirk named Singleton as his running mate in his unsuccessful bid to return to the state's highest office. Then, in 1980, the highly regarded Singleton succumbed to cancer.[31]

By the time of her death she had earned the respect of an entire city. In 1991, Jacksonville established an annual Mary L. Singleton Memorial Day for Peace, Justice, and Social Harmony. Jim Saunders, of the *Jacksonville (Florida) Times-Union,* called her a builder "because she worked to bring members of the community together, regardless of race," and a trailblazer because she "helped lead the way for blacks into the previously all-white political system."[32] At the first Mary L. Singleton Day for Peace, Justice and Social Harmony, Jake Godbold, a white former mayor of Jacksonville, paid her tribute: "Where have all the Marys gone? Mary Singleton was a politician in the most honorable sense of the word. She saw politics and public service as a way to improve the lives of the people she served. Mary knew that strong people build coalitions and work together, while the weak and afraid work to divide us. Mary was strong. Mary knew she lived in a city torn by racial strife, and she worked to make us one community of neighbors who cared about each other."[33]

Like Mary Singleton, other black women acquired public support. In 1970, when Gwendolyn Sawyer Cherry was elected Representative of Florida's 96th District, she became the first African American woman elected to the Florida legislature. Cherry was born in Miami in 1923 and raised in an upper-class family. Her father, William B. Sawyer, was a physician trained at Meharry Medical School in Nashville, Tennessee, and her mother, Alberta Preston, operated the family-owned, exclusive Mary Elizabeth Hotel. A child of privilege, Cherry attended private and public primary and secondary schools and attended Fisk University and Howard University before graduating from FAMU in 1946 with a major in biology and a minor in chemistry. In 1950 she earned a master's degree from New York University in Human Relations and attended law school at FAMU from 1962 to 1965, graduating cum laude. For eighteen years Cherry taught science in the Dade County School System, and she was one of the first black women to teach in an integrated school.[34]

Before seeking a seat in the Florida Legislature, Cherry held a number of jobs, including special assistant and inspector for the Office of Economic Opportunity, professor of law at FAMU, attorney at a private law firm, and civilian attorney with the US Coast Guard. With support from the Hispanic community, Cherry received more votes than her three competitors in the 1970 Democratic primary election but was forced into a runoff against Harvey Ruvin, whom she defeated by a margin of 4,464 votes. She had no Republican opposition in the general election. On November 17, 1970, Gwendolyn Sawyer Cherry became the first black woman to serve in the Florida Legislature. Cherry's primary concern was equal rights for women and minorities. She was also a strong advocate for children's rights and became a "legislative pioneer in the quest for statewide affordable child-care centers." Cherry tackled controversial issues. She supported abortion rights, asserting that it was "a matter between a woman and her doctor." Prison reform, the establishment of rape centers for victims of sexual assault, and an end to capital punishment were also top priorities. Cherry's legacy was important: she laid the groundwork for black Floridians to follow in her footsteps, and she believed that a black woman could become president of the United States. Cherry supported Shirley Chisholm's bid to do so in 1972. Gwendolyn Sawyer Cherry served Florida residents until her death in an automobile accident in 1979. Carrie Meek, another strong African American woman, completed Cherry's term and later became the first African American woman to serve in the state senate.[35]

By 1970 more than one million blacks called the Sunshine State home. Florida's black middle class had taken advantage of opportunities made available through the efforts of the modern civil rights movement. They had the resources and the wherewithal to move forward. More blacks of all classes were voting, and a few were attending desegregated schools. Unfortunately the mass of black Floridians stagnated in a world all too familiar. In 1970 the median income for females fifteen years old and over in Florida was $1,637 for blacks and $2,240 for whites. Nationally, the median income for females fourteen years and over was $2,063 for blacks and $2, 226 for whites. During the period 1970–74, black females received the least compensation of all workers. Work experience apparently made no difference. A professional class of black women in Florida earned their living as architects, lawyers, engineers, pharmacists, registered nurses and teachers, but black women remained underrepresented in higher-paying jobs.

In 1973 and 1974, black women posted the highest unemployment figures in the nation.[36]

African American women and the black community made significant advances in the twenty years following the *Brown* decision, but statistical gains can be misleading. In reality blacks had so much catching up to do that even "significant gains" left them far behind the majority population. In his 1981 study, Walter Allen noted that "black women, because of their membership in two discriminated groups, are more disadvantaged in total than either blacks or women alone." Having studied four race and sex subgroups, Allen noted, "black women were consistently under-educated, underpaid, underemployed, victims of marital dissolution and in poorer health." And he concluded: "The ethos of black women in the United States is one characterized largely by disadvantage. They represent a minority hidden within two minorities (black, women), subject not only to racial and sexual discriminations' independent effects, but their conjoint effects as well. Along the entire bio-psycho-social continuum, black women find themselves at the eye of the storm."[37] It is safe to conclude that the national trend reflected the status of black women in Florida.

By 1974, black women in Florida and across the country had moved closer to full citizenship. Federal legislation had removed the restrictions and limitations that prevented blacks and women from participating fully in American society. The high-school graduation rate increased for black women, and those who continued their education had more choices. Black women could attend Florida State University and the University of Florida, historically white institutions. Doby Flowers chose to attend Florida State University in 1967, and in 1970 she became the school's first black homecoming princess. Flowers earned a B.A. in 1971 and an M.A. two years later. In 1972, Florida State University President Stanley Marshall invited Freddie Lang Groomes, a recent PhD, to serve as his executive assistant. Groomes became the first woman and African American in the University's central administration, and during the next thirty years he used her position to serve not only the university but the state and nation as well. From 1973 to 1978 she served on the Florida Governor's Commission on the Status of Women. In 1979, President Jimmy Carter appointed Groomes to the President's Advisory Committee for Women.[38]

Tangible gains were achieved for black women in Florida between 1954 and 1974. At the end of that period they were actively involved in politics and served in decision- and policy-making positions in state institutions. Fewer worked in service positions, and more found employment as professionals and clerical workers. Yet all was not well for black women in Florida or nationally. Despite all the apparent gains, parity with white women and men eluded them. Black women experienced the highest unemployment rate in the country. In 1974 for black women twenty years and older, the unemployment rate was 8.7 percent. In addition, black women held few high-paying, high-status jobs. In 1970 and 1974, black women still made less than white women and black men.[39]

Despite civil rights legislation and the opportunities it created, economic security eluded black Americans and particularly black women. With the desegregation of schools and residential areas, middle-class blacks were able to move to safer neighborhoods and provide better educational opportunities for their children. Those who left and those who remained in segregated African American communities lamented the loss of community and black-owned businesses. Some blacks deliberately chose not to leave the familiarity of their environs, but economic circumstances trapped thousands in neighborhoods with poor schools and high crime. Poverty, the major concern of the 1968 Poor Peoples Campaign, plagued black America. The 1,822,000 black families with female heads in 1973 only confirmed what the Moynihan Report had predicted in 1965.[40]

In July 1974, more than thirty thousand people gathered in the nation's capital for the dedication of a monument to honor Florida's Mary McLeod Bethune. Bethune left her people a legacy of love, hope, and faith. In her will, she bestowed upon black Americans a thirst for education, a respect for the uses of power, the challenge of developing confidence in one another, racial dignity, and a desire to live harmoniously with others. Bethune would have been sorely disappointed by the economic status of black America in 1974. Twenty years after the *Brown* decision not all shared in the promise of America. Black women in Florida and in the United States remained on the periphery of a great society.[41]

Notes

1. "My Last Will and Testament; As Life Drew to a Close, America's First Negro Lady Prepares for Her People's Legacy of Love." *Ebony* 10 (August 1955): 105–110.

2. Mary McLeod Bethune Papers. The Bethune Foundation Collection, Part 1, Reel 2, Frame 612, University Publications of Bethesda, Maryland.

3. Joyce A. Hanson, *Mary McLeod Bethune and Black Women's Political Activism* (Columbia: University of Missouri Press, 2003), 203.

4. See Maxine D. Jones's "Without Compromise or Fear: Florida's African American Female Activists," in Jack E. Davis and Kari Frederickson, eds., *Making Waves: Female Activists in Twentieth-Century Florida* (Gainesville: University Press of Florida, 2003), 269–92.

5. Although many consider Harry T. Moore to be "America's first civil rights martyr," his

name is not on the monument in Montgomery, Alabama. The monument honors only those who died between 1954 and 1968 in the struggle for black equality. See Ben Green, *Before His Time: The Untold Story of Harry T. Moore, America's First Civil Rights Martyr* (New York: The Free Press, 1999), 166–88; see also Caroline Emmons Poore, "Striking the First Blow: Harry T. Moore and the Fight for Black Equality" (Master's thesis, Florida State University, 1992); http://www.splcenter.org/crm/memorial.jsp.

6. Lottie Montgomery Clark, "Negro Women Leaders of Florida," (Master's thesis, Florida State University, 1942), 57–61 Athalie Range with Bea L. Hines, "Breaking Racial Barriers," in Abraham D. Lavender and Adele L. Hines, eds., *Black Communities in Transition: Voices from South Florida* (Lanham, Md.: University Press of America, 1996), 50.

7. Glenda Alice Rabby, *The Pain and the Promise: The Struggle for Civil Rights in Tallahassee, Florida* (Athens: University of Georgia Press, 1999), 9–10.

8. Rabby, *The Pain and the Promise,* 12–15, 29; http://www.floridamemory.com/items/show/34726.

9. Tananarive Due and Patricia Stephens Due, *Freedom in the Family* (New York: One World Books, 2003), 40–43.

10. Due and Due, *Freedom in the Family,* 48–50; Rabby, *The Pain and the Promise,* 88–89; http://www.floridamemory.com/items/show/26927.

11. Due and Due, *Freedom in the Family,* 228–29; *Tallahassee Democrat,* February 2, 1993.

12. *St. Petersburg Times,* June 28, 1970, March 18, 1979, and March 9, 1998; Pamela D. Robbins, "Stack 'em High and Sell 'em Cheap: James 'Doc' Webb and Webb's City, St. Petersburg, Florida" (PhD diss., Florida State University, 2003), 110; Doug Fleming, "Toward Integration: The Course of Race Relations in St. Petersburg, 1868–1963" (Master's thesis, University of South Florida, 1973), 56.

13. *St. Petersburg Times,* June 28, 1970, March 18, 1979, March 9, 1998; Fleming, *Toward Integration,* 56, 57.

14. Abel Bartley, *Keeping the Faith: Race, Politics and Community Development in Jacksonville, Florida, 1940–1970* (Westport, Conn.: Greenwood Press, 2000), 81–83, 92, 105, 111. See chapter 6 for a discussion of the 1960 and 1964 riots.

15. David Colburn, *Racial Change and Community Crisis: St Augustine, Florida, 1877–1980* (Gainesville: University Press of Florida, 1991), 30–31.

16. Mrs. Fannie Fullerwood and Mrs. Eliza Hawthorne to Vice President Lyndon B. Johnson, 23 February 1963, Papers of the Governor's Office, Florida State Archives, Department of State, Tallahassee, Florida.

17. Colburn, *Racial Change and Community Crisis,* 32–34.

18. Colburn, *Racial Change and Community Crisis,* 64–67, 44–151, 212; http://oasis.lib.harvard.edu/oasis/deliver/~sch011 16 .

19. Daniel Patrick Moynihan, *The Negro Family: The Case for National Action.* Office of Policy Planning and Research, United States Department of Labor, March 1965. http://www.dol.gov/oasam/programs/history/webid-meynihan.htm; Deborah Gray White, *Too Heavy a Load: Black Women in Defense of Themselves, 1894–1994* (New York: W. W. Norton and Co., 1999), 198.

20. Moynihan, *The Negro Family: The Case for National Action.*

21. Moynihan, *The Negro Family: The Case for National Action.*

22. Moynihan, *The Negro Family: The Case for National Action.*

23. Allen Morris, *The Florida Handbook, 1969–1970* (Tallahassee: Peninsular Publishing Co., 1969), 430.

24. Eartha M. M. White, comp., "Who is Who in Jacksonville Business and Professions," unpublished document, Eartha White Collection, University of North Florida, Jacksonville, Florida.

25. Fleming, *Toward Integration,* 53.

26. Bartley, *Keeping the Faith,* 107, 125, 126, 130–33; Abel Bartley, "Reading, Writing and Racism: The Fight to Desegregate the Duval County Public Schools System," *The Journal of Negro History* 86 (Summer 2001): 336–47; Colburn, *Racial Change and Community Crisis,* 200–201.

27. US Census Bureau, *The Social and Economic Status of the Black Population in the United States, 1973* (Washington, DC: US Government Printing Office, 1974), 3, 65, 67; table 147 in *1970 Census of the Population* (Washington, DC, US Government Printing Office, 1973), 651–52; table 65 in *The Social and Economic Status of the Black Population in the United States, 1974* (Washington, DC: US Government Printing Office, 1975), 94.

28. http://www.usnews.com/usnews/documents/docpages/document_page100.htm; Tabulation of Official Vote, Florida Primary Elections: Democratic and Republican, May 5, 1964, and May 26, 1964, compiled from Official Canvass by Tom Adams, Secretary of State and Chairman of the State Canvassing Board, 1; Tabulation of Official Vote, Florida Primary Elections: Democratic and Republican, May 3, 1966 and May 24, 1966, compiled from Official Canvass by Tom Adams, Secretary of State and Chairman of the State Canvassing Board, 1; Tabulation of Official Votes Cast Presidential Preference Primary Election, March 14, 1972, and Special Election, November 2, 1971, compiled by Richard (Dick) Stone, Secretary of State.

29. Range with Hines, "Breaking Racial Barriers," 51–52; Florida Commission on the Status of Women; "Athalie Range: The Pioneer," *South Florida, CEO,* October 2004, http://www.highbeam.com/doc/1G1-125413855.html.

30. Barbara Walch, "Sallye B. Mathis and Mary L. Singleton: Black Pioneers on the Jacksonville, Florida, City Council" (Master's thesis, University of Florida, 1988), 57, 74, 77, 110.

31. Jones, "Without Compromise or Fear," 285; Maxine D. Jones and Kevin McCarthy, *African Americans in Florida* (Sarasota: Pineapple Press, 1993), 122; *Jacksonville Times Union,* February 1, 1991, February 9, 1992; *Tallahassee Democrat,* November 28, 1976.

32. Walch, "Sallye B. Mathis and Mary L. Singleton," 62–71; http://www.fldoe.org/gr/Bill_Summary/2007/SB1160.pdf; Jacksonville, Florida *Times-Union,* February 1, February 9, 1992.

33. Jacksonville, Florida *Times-Union,* February 1, 1992.

34. Roderick Dion Waters, "Sister Sawyer: The Life and Times of Gwendolyn Sawyer Cherry" (PhD diss., Florida State University, 1994), 27–28, 35–36, 40, 41–44, 54–58, 54–65.

35. Waters, "Sister Sawyer," 73–75, 77–80, 108, 112–14, 220; Jones, "Without Compromise or Fear," 284–85.

36. US Census Bureau, *1980 Census of Population* (Washington, DC, US Government Printing Office, 1983), 86; tables 13 and 35 in US Census Bureau, *The Social and Economic Status of the Black Population in the United States, 1974,* 28, 61; table 67 in US Census Bu-

reau, *The Social and Economic Status of the Black Population in the United States, 1973,* 95; Walter R. Allen, "The Social and Economic Statuses of Black Women in the United States," *Phylon* 42, no. 1 (March 1981): 33; table 171 in US Census Bureau, *1970 Census of Population,* 826.

37. Allen, "The Social and Economic Statuses of Black Women in the United States," 40.

38. *Florida State Times,* April/May 2004, 1–2; http://www.presidency.ucsb.edu/ws/index.php?pid=31738#axzz1L1mVb8No.

39. US Census Bureau, *The Social and Economic Status of the Black Population in the United States, 1974,* 1–6, 65, 80; US Census Bureau, *A Statistical Portrait of Women in the United States: 1978* (Washington, DC: US Government Printing Office, 1980), 93–95, 110, 114.

40. US Census Bureau, *Female Family Heads* (Washington, DC, US Government Printing Office, 1974), 4, 6.

41. *Amsterdam (New York) News,* February 21, 1976; "My Last Will and Testament; As Life Drew to a Close, America's First Negro Lady Prepares For Her Peoples' Legacy of Love." *Ebony* 10 (August 1955): 105–110.

5 Black Women in Alabama, 1954–1974

Stefanie Decker

In his 1963 inauguration speech as governor of Alabama, George Wallace proclaimed his platform for his coming term by promising, "Segregation now! Segregation tomorrow! Segregation forever!"[1] Wallace made good on that pledge when, a few months following his speech, he defiantly stood in a doorway at the University of Alabama to bar the first African-American students from enrolling. One of those students was Viviane Malone, a young woman who had watched other strong women in Alabama fight for freedom and justice through the 1950s and into the 1960s. The civil rights movement, often termed the "Second Reconstruction," brought a transformation in Southern society as it sought to break the century-old institutions of segregation and discrimination. Black men and women alike were instrumental in the success of the movement. Male leaders generally gained the national spotlight, and women worked diligently and patiently behind the scenes organizing and sustaining the movement. But some women, matriarchs of freedom, came to the forefront with brave, often defiant, actions.

By 1974 the civil rights movement had made massive inroads in the state of Alabama. Slowly, deliberately, in the face of white resistance and violence, African Americans dismantled the Jim Crow system. Following the *Brown* decision, in 1954 the modern civil rights movement began a new phase of black protest: direct action. The NAACP had led slow but often successful court challenges, but the emerging civil rights organizations demanded a more immediate change in the Southern landscape. The Montgomery Bus Boycott produced the first major direct-action protest by African Americans and assured that their voices would be heard and their actions seen. Often in the forefront, and always in the background, black women in Alabama did more than their share to ensure future generations equality and liberty in the United States.

African American women in Alabama faced more than their share of obstacles before 1954. Most faced economic inequality and substandard pay. Those who worked were employed as service workers, janitors and cooks, and farm laborers.[2] Almost 50 percent worked as domestics in private households.[3] Because most of their employers were white women, historian Barbara Ellen Smith and others term black domestic labor "occupational segregation."[4] The median income of black women was $380 annually; that of white women, $925. Furthermore, most black women completed fewer than six years of formal education, and fewer than 7 percent received a high school education.[5] Professional opportunities were limited. The law, the social structure, and the economic system, placed black women at the bottom of the scale. Race, therefore, was "not just a matter of difference, but a social relationship of power, privilege, and contestation."[6] Given the harsh realities of life as an African American woman in Alabama, it is no surprise that the direct-action phase of the civil rights movement started from the insubordinate action of one black woman.

On December 1, 1955, Rosa Parks decided not to give her bus seat to a white man. The bus system in Montgomery established whites-only seating in the front of the bus with the black section in the back. Separating the two sections was an invisible floating line, which got moved farther back as more whites boarded the bus. If no more seats were available in the white section, blacks were forced to give up their seats and stand. Many African Americans had criticized the segregated busing system, but only a handful, mostly women, had refused to obey the laws. Bus drivers treated women particularly poorly, often calling them names or assaulting them.[7] On that historic day in December, however, Rosa Parks did refuse to obey.

Parks's arrest sparked a wave of massive protest in Montgomery and demonstrated to African Americans that direct action protest could be successful and peaceful. Although her detention took the black community of Montgomery by surprise, the resulting boycott was years in the making. The Women's Political Council, led by Jo Ann Robinson, a professor of English at Alabama State College, had debated similar action numerous times, waiting only for the right time. The WPC, which numbered two hundred fifty women at the time of the boycott, existed to fighting discrimination, and much of its activity focused on voter registration, but because Robinson had experienced her own humiliation on a Montgomery bus in 1949, she vowed that ending segregation on city buses would be the primary goal of the WPC.[8]

Parks was not the first black woman arrested in Montgomery for having violated the city-bus segregation order. A few months earlier, Claudette Colvin, then only fifteen, had refused to move to the black section of a city bus. After Colvin's arrest, Robinson felt that the time had come to stage the planned bus boycott. Others in the community, however, were more cautious. Colvin was young, they argued, had resisted arrest, and, as it turned out, was unmarried and pregnant. The black community had similar misgivings about another woman who had been arrested for violating the city bus ordinance that October. Mary Louise Smith, who was older than Colvin, came from a poor family, and her father was rumored to be an alcoholic.[9] But when Parks defied the order and was arrested, the black community of Montgomery had a very different reaction.

If black Montgomery was prepared for the ensuing bus boycott, so too was Rosa Parks prepared for her defiance. Although employed as a seamstress at a local department store, Parks was a long-time active member of the NAACP and had attended workshops at Highlander Folk School, a labor and civil rights training school in Tennessee.[10] Parks was a respected member of Montgomery's black community and was described by Martin Luther King, Jr., as "soft spoken and calm in all situations. Her character was impeccable and her dedication deep rooted."[11] Park's respectability and demeanor provided the black community a star witness to challenge the segregation law. After Park's arrest, Jo Ann Robinson and the Women's Political Council printed more than thirty-five thousand leaflets encouraging Montgomery's African American community to boycott the buses the following Monday. With the help of her students, Robinson spent the night distributing the handbills. E. D. Nixon, a sleeping-car porter who had been active in civil rights in the city for more than twenty years, scheduled a mass meeting at Holt Street Baptist Church. At that historic meeting, a twenty-six year old minister, Martin Luther King, Jr., was elected head of the Montgomery Improvement Association, which spearheaded the boycott. Jo Ann Robinson, an MIA leader, worked tirelessly for the duration of the protest. With thousands of people in attendance, the participants decided that the boycott should continue until the bus companies provided better service for their black customers. Ultimately, the boycott lasted more than a year.[12]

Black women were instrumental in the success of the boycott. Because many worked as domestics in white neighborhoods, their dedication to the protest was essential. According to Lynne Olson, "The true heroines [of the boycott] were the [women] doing the walking."[13] Johnnie Carr, one of the women who helped lead the boycott, worked closely with the Montgomery Improvement Association (MIA), the organization that led the protest. Carr's primary job was to organize car pools to get blacks to work. During the boycott, many women in the Women's Political Council volunteered their cars for use, and these carpools worked through the entire year. One white woman who supported the boycott, Virginia Foster Durr, recalled that many white women would pick up their domestics and drive them home each day. Most black women refused to support the boycott openly when confronted by whites. Instead they made excuses to cover their participation.[14] It was an elderly black woman, "Mother" Pollard, who gave voice to the boycott when she said, "My feets is tired, but my soul is rested."[15]

During the boycott, Fred Gray, a black Montgomery lawyer, filed a civil-action suit against the city with four women, Aurelia Browder, Susie McDonald, Claudette Colvin, and Mary Louise Smith, as plaintiffs. Browder, a thirty-four-year-old widow and mother of four, bravely took the stand and told the judge she simply wanted "better treatment."[16] In June 1956 a district court ruled, in *Browder v. Gayle,* that segregation on city buses violated the Fourteenth Amendment. The bus boycott not only galvanized and unified the black community of Montgomery, it also excited African Americans in many parts of the South. More and more activists took to the streets in protest of segregation and discrimination, and similar boycotts broke out in Birmingham and Mobile and even in Florida.[17] A black janitor expressed the sentiment of many African Americans after the boycott when he said, "We got our heads up now, and we won't bow down again—no, sir—except before God!"[18]

Two years after the monumental *Brown* case, many schools in the South remained segregated. Among those most reluctant to integrate were the universities. State money spent on black colleges lagged far behind that spent on white institutions. In the 1939–40 academic year, black universities received a little over $131,000 compared to almost two million for white colleges. Tuskegee was allotted only $10,000. The one land-grant college for blacks, Alabama Agricultural and Mechanical Institute, offered only a two-year degree. Few PhDs sat on black university faculties, and most libraries had substandard holdings.[19] For many African Americans in the state, separate was far from equal, and the only opportunity to receive an equal education was to attend a white university. The white university of choice for many blacks was the hallmark of white elitism—the University of Alabama in Tuscaloosa. According to E. Culpepper Clark, "Tuscaloosa became the Appomattox of segregation."[20]

In 1955, Autherine Lucy and Pollie Ann Meyers sought admission to the University of Alabama as students in library science, and after a four-year court battle, the NAACP obtained a court order prohibiting the university from rejecting Lucy's application based on race. Meyers was not accepted, but the university did admit Lucy. In February 1956, Lucy registered as a student at the University of Alabama, becoming the first African American admitted to an all-white university in the state. After her first day of class, however, mobs gathered on campus yelling "Keep Bama White" and "Hey, hey, ho, ho, Autherine's got to go." And eventually the mob began rioting. Cars full of blacks were attacked, and rocks and firecrackers were hurled at any African American in sight. When many in the crowd began yelling that they intended to kill Lucy, she was rushed into Graves Hall for safety. After three hours, highway patrolmen managed to sneak her out and to safety. Within the week, arguing that her presence created an unsafe environment, the university expelled her. And despite efforts to overturn the expulsion, the state upheld the school's justifications for her dismissal.[21] Lucy did not return to the university until the 1990s, but her bravery paved the way for other black students to attend.

In 1963, Viviane Malone and James Hood took over the fight that Lucy had begun in 1955. By then, however, whites in the state had elected George Wallace, a virulent segregationist, to the governorship. Malone, one of eight children, was born to parents who were determined to be in the fight against segregation. Malone wanted to major in accounting, but neither Alabama State nor Alabama A&M offered degrees in the subject. She also wanted to fight segregation. With the full backing of the NAACP, she and Hood arrived at the university in June 1963 to pay for their fall tuition, but Wallace barred their entry by standing in the doorway. Then National Guardsmen, dispatched by President John Kennedy, arrived at the university, and Wallace reluctantly stood aside.[22] Nevertheless, Wallace's infamous "Stand in the Schoolhouse Door" demonstrated how far African Americans in Alabama had yet to go almost ten years after the *Brown* decision.

When white racists attacked their men and children, many women in the civil rights movement sacrificed their physical well-being in defense of their families. Ruby Shuttlesworth, wife of Birmingham activist and preacher Fred Shuttlesworth, tried to desegregate Phillips High School by enrolling her daughter Ricky. Fred had initiated the challenge, but Ruby rode with him and their two daughters to the school, where a mob dragged Fred from the car and attacked him with clubs and chains. As they yelled, "Kill him!" Ruby tried to get out of the back seat, all the while hitting men with her purse, but was stabbed in the hip. Before losing consciousness, Fred managed to return to the car and drive to a hospital. Similarly, Mattie Jones tried to defend her son, Robert, when a white mob broke into her house to attack him for having attended a prayer vigil. Mattie told the men they would get her son "over her dead body," but they left her with a broken leg and head wounds. Fortunately neither Mattie's nor Robert's injuries were life-threatening. [23]

By the early 1960s, Alabama again became central in the fight for black civil rights. In 1960 the Supreme Court had ruled, in *Boynton v. Virginia,* that racial segregation in busing violated the Interstate Commerce Act.[24] The plaintiff, Bruce Boynton, was the son of Amelia, who, with her husband, Samuel, had been active in the civil rights movement in Tuskegee since the 1930s and 1940s. (In 1932 she had bravely registered to vote in the town in order to cast her ballot for Franklin Roosevelt.[25])

The *Boynton* ruling prompted the 1961 Freedom Rides, which were intended to test the validity of the ruling. The first group of Freedom Riders, most of them members of the Congress of Racial Equality, left Washington, DC, on May 4, 1961, with the intent of traveling to New Orleans. Black and white riders participated. Some were women. Despite a few minor incidents, the Freedom Riders faced little violent opposition until they reached Anniston, Alabama. A few miles outside the town a white mob firebombed the bus and attempted to burn the riders alive by barring the bus door shut. Amid shouts of "roast 'em," the riders managed to escape through broken windows. Arriving late, state troopers laughed as they approached the scene. The violence continued when a second bus reached Birmingham: as the riders disembarked at the station, members of the Ku Klux Klan assaulted them. One rider was beaten so severely that he was paralyzed for life; a black woman's assailant stopped beating her only when he realized that the police were on their way.[26] There was talk of suspending the rides, but Diane Nash, a Nashville activist and a cofounder of the Student Nonviolent Coordinating Committee, argued that to stop the rides would be to risk losing the meaning of the protest. Gathering a group of riders, she attempted to finish the rides, only to be jailed in Birmingham. Nash was not an Alabama native (she was born in Illinois), but she worked tirelessly in the state to register voters and to organize protests.[27]

Despite the promised protection by state troopers, more violence followed in Montgomery, where white mobs again attacked and beat the riders. More than a thousand people joined together outside Ralph Abernathy's church to hear King, James Foreman, and others speak in support of the riders. Thousands more threatened violence, but, under pressure from President Kennedy, Governor Patterson ordered the Alabama National Guard to disperse the mob. The rides continued throughout the summer with similar arrests and protests in Mississippi and Louisiana. Ultimately the rides forced President Kennedy to issue an act enforcing the *Boynton* decision.[28] Hundreds of riders, black and white, men and women, participated. The Freedom Rides gave life to the civil rights movement, particularly among younger activists. According to historian Clayborne Carson, the rides "contributed to the development of a self-consciously radical southern student movement prepared to direct its militancy toward other concerns."[29]

Notes

1. George Wallace, as quoted in Diane McWhorter, *Carry Me Home: Birmingham, Alabama: The Climactic Battle of the Civil Rights Revolution* (New York: Simon and Schuster, 2001), 311.

2. *Census of the Population, 1950,* vol. 2, part 2, "Characteristics of the Population: Alabama," 2–42, 2–220.

3. http://www.census.gov/prod/www/abs/decennial/1950cenpopv2.html, *Census of the Population, 1950,* vol. 2, part 2, "Characteristics of the Population: Alabama," 2–42, 2–220.

4. Barbara Ellen Smith, "The Social Relations of Southern Women," in Barbara Ellen Smith, ed., *Neither Separate Nor Equal: Women, Race, and Class in the South* (Philadelphia: Temple University Press, 1999), 22.

5. *Census of the Population, 1950,* vol. 2, part 2, "Characteristics of the Population: Alabama," 2–248, 2–155.

6. Smith, "Social Relations," 15.

7. Juan Williams, *Eyes on the Prize: America's Civil Rights Years, 1954–1965* (New York: Penguin Books, 1988), 61; Lynne Olson, *Freedom's Daughters: The Unsung Heroines of the Civil Rights Movement from 1830 to 1970* (New York: Simon and Schuster, 2001), 88.

8. Olson, *Freedom's Daughters,* 91; See David Garrow, ed., *The Montgomery Bus Boycott and the Women Who Started It: The Memoir of Jo Ann Robinson* (Knoxville: University of Tennessee Press, 1987); Williams, *Eyes,* 61; Olson, *Freedom's Daughters,* 89.

9. Williams, *Eyes,* 63; Taylor Branch, *Parting the Waters: America during the King Years, 1954–1963* (New York: Simon and Schuster, 1988), 123, 127; Olson, *Freedom's Daughters,* 94. In 1942, Mildred McAdory moved a "segregator," a wooden bar separating the black and white sections, on a Birmingham streetcar. She was beaten and jailed. Although a protest against the streetcars was discussed, it never materialized. McWhorter, *Carry Me Home,* 90–91.

10. J. Mills Thorton III, "Challenge and Response in the Montgomery Bus Boycott of 1955–1956," *Alabama Review* 33 (1980): 195; John M. Glen, *Highlander: No Ordinary School,* 2nd ed. (Knoxville: University of Tennessee Press, 1996), 136; Branch, *Parting,* 125.

11. Martin Luther King, Jr., *Stride toward Freedom: The Montgomery Story* (New York: Harper and Brothers, 1958), 44.

12. Garrow, *The Montgomery Bus Boycott,* 16–17; Williams, *Eyes,* 69; John White, "E. D. Nixon and the White Supremacists," in Glenn Feldman, ed., *Before Brown: Civil Rights and White Backlash in the Modern South* (Tuscaloosa: University of Alabama Press, 2004), 199–

206; Rev. Thomas R. Thrasher, "Alabama's Bus Boycott," in David J. Garrow, ed., *The Walking City: The Montgomery Bus Boycott, 1955–1956* (New York: Carlson Publishing, 1989), 61; *Montgomery Advertiser,* 6 December 1955.

13. Olson, *Freedom's Daughters,* 117.

14. Olson, *Freedom's Daughters,* 389; Williams, *Eyes,* 78; Hollinger Bernard, ed., *Outside the Magic Circle: The Autobiography of Virginia Foster Durr* (New York: Simon and Schuster, 1985), 282–83; Olson, *Freedom's Daughters,* 117, 119.

15. Mother Pollard, as quoted in Frye Gaillard, *Cradle of Freedom: Alabama and the Movement That Changed America* (Tuscaloosa: University of Alabama Press, 2004), 27.

16. Gaillard, *Cradle,* 34.

17. Williams, *Eyes,* 87–88, 89.

18. Abel Penn, "Report on Montgomery a Year After," *New York Times Magazine,* December 29, 1957, 36.

19. E. Culpepper Clark, *The Schoolhouse Door: Segregation's Last Stand at the University of Alabama* (New York: Oxford University Press, 1993), xv–xvi.

20. Clark, *The Schoolhouse Door,* xix.

21. Clark, *The Schoolhouse Door,* xviii, 71–80, 96–98; McWhorter, *Carry Me,* 97–99; Branch, *Parting,* 167–68.

22. Branch, *Parting,* 175, 177, 209, 225–234; see also, Dan T. Carter, *The Politics of Rage: George Wallace, the Origins of the New Conservatism, and the Transformation of American Politics* (New York: Simon and Schuster, 1995).

23. McWhorter, *Carry Me Home,* 127–28, 153. Surprisingly, neither Shuttlesworth was seriously injured in the attack at Phillips High School.

24. Branch, *Parting,* 390; the *Boynton* decision also made segregation illegal in waiting rooms, restrooms, and restaurants in interstate travel. McWhorter, *Carry Me Home,* 195.

25. Gaillard, *Cradle,* 62.

26. Williams, *Eyes,* 147–48; McWhorter, *Carry Me Home,* 203–207.

27. Olson, *Freedom's Daughters,* 151–60, 182–85. See also Lisa Mullins, *Diane Nash: The Fire of the Civil Rights Movement* (Miami, Fla.: Barnhardt and Ashe Publishing, 2007).

28. Powledge, *Free,* 254–65.

29. Clayborne Carson, *In Struggle: SNCC and the Black Awakening of the 1960s* (Cambridge, Mass.: Harvard University Press, 1981), 36.

6 "Call the Women"

The Tradition of African American Female Activism in Georgia during the Civil Rights Movement

Clarissa Myrick-Harris

> "Somewhere I read a story, that in one of those western cities built in a day, the half-dozen men of the town labored to pull a heavy piece of timber to the top of a building. They pushed and pulled hard to no purpose, when one of the men on the top shouted to those below: "Call the women." They called the women; the women came; they pushed; soon the timber was seen to move, and ere long it was in the desired place. Today not only the men on top call, but a needy race,— the whole world calls loudly to the cultured Negro women to come to the rescue. Do they hear? Are they coming? Will they push?"[1]
>
> —Lucy Craft Laney, Founder, Haines Normal and Industrial Institute, Augusta, Georgia

Hundreds of black women in Georgia heeded "the call" to lead when it was issued back in 1899 by educator and activist Lucy Craft Laney. During the mid-twentieth century, the women who responded hailed from a variety of socioeconomic and educational backgrounds, and they brought a range of skills and experiences that informed their contributions. Some were part of the black "cultured" elite class; many came from the rural and urban working class and the underclass. These committed activists ranged from domestic workers, cotton pickers, and hairdressers to social workers, teachers, schoolgirls, and ministers' wives. Some joined the movement after experiencing personal epiphanies; others became involved as a natural outgrowth of their religious convictions and church work; many carried on family traditions of activism; and a significant number married into the movement when they wedded men of like mind, sharing leadership responsibilities with them but rarely the public recognition.

Whatever their backgrounds and reasons for joining the movement, African American women activists in Georgia generally made their contributions without fanfare. Most downplayed the importance of their personal leadership, focusing instead on ensuring the success of collective efforts that they organized and directed. They devoted themselves to claiming voting rights, improving quality of life, and obtaining equal access to education, jobs, and public facilities.

Examining the tradition of black women's leadership in Georgia from 1954 to 1974—the most intense period in the modern-day struggle for social change—reveals that the movement was not a monolithic wave directed by only a small cadre of charismatic black male leaders. It is better characterized as a network of interdependent local movements led and sustained by the complementary efforts of African American women and men of diverse backgrounds. These activists made their contributions through a host of community-based organizations and institutions as well as through key national civil rights organizations.[2]

The local movements in Georgia can be understood as unfolding and converging during four periods beginning more than a decade before *Brown v. Board of Education* The first period (1940–49) was a time for "Laying the Foundation" for the decades of activism to come. During the second period, "Retrenchment and Redirection" (1950–59), black activists sought to reinforce and reinvigorate initiatives to strengthen black organizations and voting power. The third period (1960–65), an intense and concentrated timeframe, emphasized "Direct Action and Integration." The fourth period (1966–74), which emerged as the integrationist thrust waned, mirrored the militant national quest for Black Power.[3] This essay discusses the tradition of black female activism in key cities and towns in Georgia during these four phases. Citing specific little-known and well-known black women in Georgia as exemplars, it focuses on three critical aspects of their civil rights activities: how they came to take on pivotal roles in the movement; their leadership styles and major accomplishments; and challenges they encountered while making essential contributions to local, state, and even national civil rights efforts.[4]

Laying a Foundation (1940–49)

In Georgia three factors provided an opportunity for community organizers to strengthen existing civil rights initiatives and establish new ones during the 1940s: the lowering of the voting age from twenty-one to eighteen in 1943; the abolition of the "whites only" primary in 1944; and the temporary end to the poll tax in 1945. From the beginning, women were among the leaders headquartered in Atlanta and Savannah who ignited activism among black Georgians. They carried out mass voter-education and -registration drives in their cities, swelled the rolls of their political organizations, and established NAACP chapters in towns and hamlets throughout the state. They encouraged African Americans to support moderate white candidates for local and state offices.[5] When moderate candidates won, black leaders negotiated with them for such concessions as the hiring of black police officers in Atlanta and Savannah (the first in the South since Reconstruction), the selection of black jurors on court cases, the extension of hospital privileges to black doctors, and increases in funding for black public schools.[6]

During this foundational period, Georgia's black women carried on their tradition of agency and advocacy through leadership roles in the NAACP and the Urban League and behind the scenes in school, church, and social organizations and in civic clubs.[7] By the spring of 1946 the number of registered black voters across Georgia had risen from fewer than 30,000 to 125,000. Although that was only 18 percent of black citizens eligible to vote, it was the largest black electorate in any southern state at the time. In Atlanta alone that year, the number of blacks registered to vote rose from approximately 3,000 to more than 21, 000, in large measure because of women activists within a coalition called the All Citizens Registration Committee. Historian Kathryn Nasstrom writes: "The conduct of the drive at the level of community organizations also suggested women's equal, and at times superior, contribution. Women's organizations were among the groups to which ACRC made special appeals, and when asked, women responded, at times outdistancing the men. They became models held up for emulation."[8]

Black women educators, who made up the majority of African American public-school teachers in Georgia, played a pivotal role in voter registration and education. Among the many educator/activists, three stand out. Narvie Harris, an Atlanta teacher/activist who began her career in a one-room schoolhouse in rural Georgia and taught in DeKalb County schools for almost forty years, affirmed that "if you can reach the child, you can reach the parent." Florence "Frankie" Victoria Adams, an Atlanta University social-work professor and activist, taught and trained African American social workers and budding activists during this period. She developed courses and trained students in the newly emerging disciplines of community organization and group work. Clark College education professor Pearlie Dove raised the political awareness of the young women and men she trained to teach. Dove also supported the efforts of black leaders and educators to equalize the pay of black and white teachers during the 1940s. All three of these women continued their activism in subsequent phases of the movement in Georgia.[9]

Black women who established models for leadership in Georgia civic and political organizations during the 1940s include Grace Towns Hamilton, executive director of the Atlanta Urban League, Atlanta community organizer Ruby Blackburn, and NAACP leader Eloria Gilbert of Savannah. Born into Atlanta's black elite, Grace Towns Hamilton did not consider herself a civil rights activist. However, her work was essential to building a strong black electorate in that city and establishing a state infrastructure for the movement during the 1940s. Hamilton earned a bachelor's degree from Atlanta University and, in 1929, a master's from Ohio State University. In 1943 she was named the first female director of the Atlanta Urban League, and she initiated demographic surveys of the black community to assist canvassing efforts during the 1946 voter-registration blitz. Hamilton became an adept strategist and negotiator, emphasizing coalition-building among black leaders and organizations, conducting extensive research on problems faced by the black community, and working with the white power structure to effect change.[10]

As early as 1946 the Atlanta Urban League, under Grace Towns Hamilton, spearheaded the establishment of the Temporary Coordinating Committee on Housing. This committee, the embodiment of efforts to spur social change in the city, set the agenda and tone for all subsequent efforts to solve the housing shortage for blacks within the framework of segregation. The committee, which consisted of representatives from Atlanta's black and white businesses, social agencies, and government, outlined a plan for identifying and purchasing land for new African American communities, arranging construction of housing on the land, and implementing the program.[11] All these skills served Hamilton well in the later phases of the civil rights movement in Georgia.

Ruby Blackburn, a hairdresser and former domestic worker, used her grassroots community-organizing style to persuade hundreds of working-class and middle-class black women and men to register to vote and push for social change during the 1946 mass campaign. Beyond that, she focused on improving the quality of life for African Americans, especially women. Through her organization's To Improve Conditions club and the Atlanta Cultural League and Training Center she operated nationally respected training programs for domestic workers and the unemployed. Ultimately TIC involved more people than any other black organization in Atlanta.[12]

Eloria Gilbert of Savannah was at the forefront of the initiative to increase and strengthen the Georgia NAACP in the 1940s. Generally her husband, Ralph Mark Gilbert, a dynamic Savannah minister, is given the credit not only for heading and revitalizing the Savannah branch of the NAACP during the period 1942–50, but also for organizing and overseeing at least forty branches in rural Georgia. However, as Reverend Gilbert acknowledged, he was able to build a pervasive NAACP presence in the state because he "divided the territory between the wife and myself."[13] At a time when membership in the NAACP in the South carried with it the threat of violent reprisal by white supremacists, Eloria Gilbert traveled across the state to monitor activities of existing branches and delivered speeches on behalf of the organization in locations up and down the East Coast. In addition, she established an NAACP branch in Luthersville, Georgia. In nearly every Georgia town where Gilbert spoke, white sheriffs stood in the back to hear what she had to say. As soon as she finished speaking, she would leave before the local authorities had time to harass or arrest her.[14] Because of the work of both Eloria Gilbert and Reverend Gilbert, by the end of 1946 there were fifty-one NAACP branches in the state and membership had risen from fewer than 1,000 to 13,595.[15]

As African American women and men worked to lay the foundation for social change in Georgia in the 1940s, the fear of black empowerment sparked a virulent white backlash—and black women suffered along with the men. The state reaffirmed its long tradition of violence against black women in 1945 when it convicted and executed a domestic worker named Lena Baker who killed the white man who had sexually abused her, imprisoned her, and threatened to shoot her in rural Cuthbert, Georgia. She became the only woman ever executed in the state. In 2001, Lela Bond Phillips published *The Lena Baker Story* about this heinous episode.[16]

A year later the Moore's Ford Bridge in Monroe, Georgia, became the site of what is called the last known mass lynching in American history. In a gruesome, racially motivated lynching, Mae Murray Dorsey and her husband, George, George's sister Dorothy Dorsey Malcolm, and her husband, Roger, were viciously murdered in July 1946. Dorothy Malcolm was seven months pregnant. An unmasked mob beat them, shot them multiple times, and then cut out the unborn baby with a knife. No one was ever arrested or even indicted for the murders.[17] And during the gubernatorial campaign of 1948 a reinvigorated Ku Klux Klan terrorized black Georgians.[18] The sadistic behavior, which reflected the anti-black state of Georgia society, led black women leaders to continue their struggle. During the next decade, even as they celebrated and worked to realize the promises of *Brown v. Board of Education,* black women activists in Georgia worked with black men against new roadblocks to civil rights.

Retrenchment and Redirection (1950–59)

During this phase, leaders of civil rights initiatives throughout the state fought to maintain cohesion and black voter strength in spite of renewed legal and extralegal measures put in place to further disfranchise African Americans, discredit the NAACP, block public-school desegregation, and deny adequate housing and services for African Americans. Throughout the decade, black women played major roles in reinforcing and maintaining movement initiatives. And at the end of the decade they worked to create the infrastructure for and to launch a new national organization, the Southern Christian Leadership Conference, whose purpose was to use direct action in confronting barriers to black empowerment.

In the 1950s, Grace Towns Hamilton continued her method of black coalition building and negotiation with the white power structure to address the housing shortage for African Americans. Under her leadership, the Temporary Coordinating Committee on Housing was responsible for nearly half of the 10,550 housing units constructed for blacks in Atlanta between 1945 and 1956.[19]

In the *Brown* era, Ruby Blackburn remained a stalwart member of the NAACP in the face of the state government's declaration of war on the organization. Her own civic organizations successfully prodded Atlanta's city government to construct two elementary schools for black students and to improve public bus service in her neighborhood, Dixie Hills. In 1951, after being rejected for membership in the all-white League of Women Voters, Blackburn founded and led the Georgia League of Negro Women Voters. The driving goal of the Georgia League was to register "every woman and girl who becomes of age." A key to Blackburn's success was her hands-on approach to community organizing and her adeptness at not only registering people to vote but also educating them about the political process, demonstrating to them how to use a voting machine, and encouraging them to use their votes to support candidates and initiatives that would benefit the black community. Blackburn personally swore in poll workers and even led a group of women to the 1957 session of the Georgia legislature to "check up" on elected state officials. By 1958, Blackburn had earned a spot on the Fulton County Democratic Party Executive Committee because of her political acumen and participatory approach to activism.[20]

New leaders arrived in Georgia, especially because Atlanta had become the headquarters of a number of civil rights organizations. One prominent black woman leader and activist was Ella Jo Baker. Born in Norfolk, Virginia, Baker graduated from Shaw University in Raleigh, North Carolina, and then lived almost half her life in New York City. She spent fewer than five years in Atlanta, beginning in 1958 when she was fifty-five years old. Yet for that brief period she was at the center of an intense, tumultuous shift in focus from litigation and negotiation to aggressive direct action. During her years in Georgia, Ella Baker became an icon of the civil rights movement for two primary reasons: her crucial roles in establishing the Southern Christian Leadership Conference and later the Student Nonviolent Coordinating Committee and her unwavering advocacy of principles of participatory democracy—grassroots leadership—and direct action to effect social change.[21]

Martin Luther King, Jr., asked Ella Baker to come to Atlanta soon after he and a cadre of Southern black ministers had established SCLC there in the fall of 1957. The ministers conceived the organization to continue the momentum achieved as a result of the Montgomery Bus Boycott in 1955–56 and the passage of the 1957 Civil Rights Act. Although the men in this network were respected and skilled church leaders, they needed a seasoned administrator to develop the infrastructure of their fledgling organization as well as to plan and implement their first project, the Crusade for Citizenship, a voting-rights campaign that would be conducted throughout the South. Ella Baker fit the bill.[22]

In Atlanta, Baker was a staff of one as she set up the SCLC office on "Sweet Auburn" Avenue, the center of black institutions and businesses in the city. She launched the SCLC Crusade for Citizenship in a matter of weeks, and over the following months she attempted to insulate herself against the friction between her, Dr. King, and other ministers in the organization. The campaign was successful, but her relationship with Dr. King and others in the organization had deteriorated. Baker knew that the ministers' notions about the place of a woman—especially an outspoken, middle-aged black woman like herself—were behind the tensions. Nor did the SCLC ministers appreciate Baker's belief that the grassroots masses rather than a charismatic handful should lead civil rights organizations. In later years, Baker explained: "After all, who was I? I was female. I was old. I didn't have any PhD . . . I did not just subscribe to a theory because it came out of the mouth of the leader."[23]

Baker left SCLC in the summer of 1960, but not before she brought female and male student leaders together at Shaw University, her alma mater, where she advised them to establish their own organization—which eventually was named the Student Nonviolent Coordinating Committee. The students embraced Ella Baker's collective-leadership approach to social change.[24]

Direct Action and Integration (1960–65)

In the early 1960s, as in the previous decade, the movement in Georgia focused on the development of organizations and initiatives devoted to claiming black voting rights, improving African Americans' quality of life, and obtaining equal access to education, jobs, and public facilities. The emergence of the student movement and its use of nonviolent direct action as a tactic to gain various citizenship rights helped define this phase. In addition to direct action, the students' collective leadership style and their focus on encouraging group-centered leadership among the grassroots were distinctive. Though friction sometimes erupted between the veterans of the civil rights movement and the new activists of the student movement, a synergistic relationship emerged. The students were inspired by the contributions of their elders, and the elders benefited from and participated in many robust initiatives of the younger generation.

A number of women came of age and emerged as leaders during the student movement in Georgia. As early as 1957, students at Atlanta's Spelman College, the premiere historically black liberal-arts college for women, had defied the institution's conservative administration as well as state and local laws by attempting to sit in the "whites only" section of the galleries in the state capitol. When the speaker of the house ordered them to leave, they did so unwillingly but their return on subsequent days contributed to the later desegregation of the galleries. In the early 1960s, many of these young women became dedicated leaders of the Atlanta Student Movement and the national movement.[25] In 1963, white historian Howard Zinn was fired from his position as chair of Spelman's History Department because of his role in raising the awareness of his students. Decades later he said: "I was lucky to be at Spelman at a time when I could watch a marvelous transformation in my students, who were so polite, so quiet, and then suddenly they were leaving the campus and going into town, and sitting in, and being arrested, and then coming out of jail full of fire and rebellion."[26]

The brave young Spelman women who continued their lives of activism include children's advocate Marian Wright Edelman, novelist Alice Walker, and educator Hershelle Sullivan Challenor. Another Spelman student, Ruby Doris Smith-Robinson, had a profound impact on the local, state, and national movement in the 1960s. In fact she devoted the last years of her short life to answering the call to lead.

The sit-ins by college students in Greensboro, North Carolina, early in 1960, inspired Atlanta native Ruby Doris Smith, her fellow Spelmanites, and students at Morris Brown, Morehouse, and Clark colleges and at Atlanta University. These activists founded the Atlanta Student Movement and organized the Committee on Appeal for Human Rights. Through the committee they conducted sit-ins at lunch counters in local stores, boycotted businesses and restaurants, published an "Appeal for Human Rights," and won a lawsuit against the city that eventually resulted in the desegregation of the city's public facilities.[27]

After heeding the call to serve, Smith quickly became executive secretary of the Atlanta Student Movement. By February 1961 she had become involved in the national student movement through the newly established Student Nonviolent Coordinating Committee. (The first SNCC conference had been held at the Atlanta University Center in October 1960.) Under the guidance of the SCLC executive director, Ella Baker, SNCC provided a way to harness the energy and idealism of black and white youth. Smith immersed herself in the movement and became its first full-time Southern campus coordinator. Known for her fearlessness and resolve, in 1961 she joined the Freedom Riders to push for the desegregation of interstate buses throughout the South. She also established SNCC's "jail, no bail" policy. In 1963 she was appointed SNCC's administrative secretary and a full-time member of the central office staff.[28]

Smith married in 1964 and had a child, but she continued her intense level of work with the movement. As Ruby Doris Smith-Robinson she was elected to the national post of executive secretary of SNCC in 1966, planning and overseeing grassroots organizing initiatives in the South and North early in the organization's Black Power phase. Male chauvinism and sexism most certainly existed within SNCC, but that was balanced, indeed countered, both by the presence of such women as Ruby Doris Smith-Robinson and by the young SNCC workers' acknowledgement of the tradition of black women's leadership. Although Smith often clashed with her male colleagues, she most often prevailed. Tragically, her leadership ended abruptly when, in January 1967, she died of cancer.[29]

The infrastructure and systems that Ruby Doris Smith-Robinson established during her tenure as a central administrator in SNCC helped facilitate the work of its field staff during mass voter-registration drives and demonstrations against segregation in the cities and towns of southwest Georgia, the rich black belt and former slave stronghold of the state. Beginning in the fall of 1961 and continuing through the summer of 1962 the Albany Movement emerged as a coalition of African American local and national organizations coordinating their efforts to desegregate movie theaters, bus stations, and other public facilities. Women, as always, were part of the struggle. Marion King, beaten severely by local jail guards, suffered a miscarriage. Ola Mae Quarterman, a teen-aged girl who sat toward the front of a bus and was told to move, was arrested for using obscene language. More than a thousand African American demonstrators, including Ruby Doris Smith-Robinson and civil rights icon Martin Luther King, were jailed in Albany and surrounding rural counties at the height of this local movement. Soon Albany would witness the first mass movement in the modern civil rights period attempting to desegregate a large rural community.[30]

The Albany Movement called forth scores of rank-and-file activists from across the country, including such women as Prathia Hall, a SNCC worker from Philadelphia, Pennsylvania, and New Yorker Doris Derby, who came to the city to "check on a friend" who was involved in the movement and ended up in marches and demonstrations herself. The majority of the protesters, however, were women, men, and youths of Albany and surrounding southwest Georgia communities. Bernice Johnson Reagon, an Albany native, joined SNCC at this time and became a definitive voice of the both the local movement and the national civil rights struggle.[31]

Bernice Johnson, the daughter of a minister, entered Albany State College (now University) in 1959. There she became secretary of the junior chapter of the NAACP. Later, as a student leader in the Albany Movement, she helped rally hundreds of Albany State students to march after local police had arrested her fellow students for attempting to buy tickets at the white ticket counter of the Trailways bus station. When the NAACP chastised her for her direct action, she joined SNCC. There she marched, sat-in, and went to jail, at which point, Albany State expelled her. It was then that she found her calling as a freedom singer. She had always sung—in church and public gatherings—but after she joined the movement, her voice was transformed in a way that reflected her spiritual and political transformation. Conveying the life-and-death struggle of the movement, her singing became a powerful experience for all who heard her.

As a member of the SNCC Freedom Singers, Johnson used her powerful voice as an instrument of the movement throughout the nation. While in that quartet, she wrote new lyrics for spirituals and hymns of the Black Church, freedom songs that energized the movement. Her commitment to the movement permeated her personal life as well. She married Cordell Reagon, one of the three original SNCC field workers who helped spark the Albany Movement through the voter-registration drive in southwest Georgia. Bernice Johnson Reagon continued her life of activism and inspiration on a national and international level.[32]

Many historians argued that the Albany Movement failed to win civil rights for African Americans in that city primarily because Martin Luther King's involvement failed to spur change. Many of Albany's black citizens, however, refute that assertion. The Albany Movement, they say, became a catalyst for activism that generated political power for black people in Albany during the sixties and seventies. Even though de facto racism and discrimination remained for decades, in the spring of 1963 the city commission removed all segregation statutes from its books, thus paving the way for efforts to desegregate public facilities and schools and to elect black public officials.[33]

During this segment of the movement, male and female students in Savannah worked with veteran activists in the NAACP to conduct sit-ins at eight downtown lunch counters. They also demanded the desegregation of facilities, the use of courtesy titles (Mr., Mrs., Miss, instead of the usual "boy" or "girl") for African American adults, and the hiring of black clerks and managers. To win these demands, they called for a boycott of white-owned downtown stores. The protests and boycott forced some of the large stores into bankruptcy and eventually led to the desegregation of parks, swimming pools, and busses in the city.[34]

The Savannah Movement ignited the activism of numerous young black women, such as Mercedes Arnold and Carolyn Q. Coleman, and reinvigorated the defiant spirit of older women, such as Addie Byers, an English teacher who fought to desegregate the public libraries of Savannah in the 1950s and 1960s. Well aware of the influence of teacher-activists in the movement, the state ruled that any teacher affiliated with the NAACP would be permanently banned from teaching in Georgia. Undeterred, Byers provided funds to allow other teachers to join the NAACP. Her activism became an inspiration to hundreds of women and men in Savannah and throughout the state. Eventually she became the first African American woman to serve on the board of the Chatham-Effingham-Liberty Regional Library, and in 1985 she received the NAACP Freedom Award.[35]

By the summer of 1963 the focus in southwest Georgia was on Americus. There an atrocious incident, referred to by Lynne Olson as "an horror story to end all horror stories," transpired in late July when more than thirty young girls, arrested for demonstrating against segregation, were beaten, burned with cattle prods, and secretly sent to a stockade in neighboring Lee County. The girls' plight came to light when SNCC photographer Danny Lyon took pictures while several of the imprisoned girls distracted a guard. The girls, ranging in age from ten to sixteen, had been kept for six weeks in the filthy stockade. The toilets overflowed, the windows were barred, and flies, gnats, and mosquitoes harassed the young women. In the overpowering heat of summer, they had no bed or bedding; they could only lie down on wet, slippery concrete floors. Gun-toting guards served them inedible food, threw a rattlesnake into the stockade, and even threatened to take them out and shoot them.[36]

The girls' time in the stockade was the continuation of a nightmare that began on July 19, 1963, when they became foot soldiers in the movement. Emmarene Kaigler Streete was fourteen years old when she participated in peaceful SNCC marches and demonstrations to protest the segregated bus station and theater in Americus. "We were marching at least once a week and every weekend," she said. "A lot of us were sneaking out of the house and doing it against our parents' wishes." A stinging blast of water from a fire hose knocked thirteen-year-old LuLu Westbrooks to the ground during the assault on the protesters. When she stood up, a policeman hit her in the head with a baseball bat. Her bleeding wound went untreated for a month while she was under lock and key in the stockade. Memories of their capture and the acts of terrorism they suffered continue to haunt the women called "the lost girls of Americus, Georgia."[37]

The desegregation of public schools in Georgia was a protracted process that continued decades after the height of the civil rights movement. In response to the Supreme Court ruling in *Brown,* the state vowed to close public schools rather than integrate. However, a crack in the barriers to integration appeared in January 1961 when native Atlantans Charlayne Hunter and Hamilton Holmes integrated the University of Georgia.[38] That victory was followed by the admittance of Mary Frances Early to the master's degree program in music education in August. In 1962, Early became the first African American graduate of the University of Georgia. In the wake of those victories, the state legislature struck down its school segregation law and laid the foundation for the long battle to desegregate Georgia's elementary and secondary schools. Charlayne Hunter went on to become an award-winning journalist, and Mary Frances Early became a respected music professor in the Atlanta University Center.[39]

In the early 1960s, both the SCLC and student leaders continued the fundamental civil rights imperative of voter education and registration. The SCLC

Citizenship Education Program became the vehicle for systematizing this work. In 1961, Dorothy Forman Cotton joined SCLC to help establish the CEP. She worked for the organization for twelve years, serving as the SCLC education director, the only woman on the organization's executive staff. The daughter of a widowed tobacco farmer, Cotton attended Shaw University, where she worked as housekeeper for the president of the institution to support herself while she earned her bachelor's and master's degrees. Later, as a young wife living in Petersburg, Virginia, Cotton became involved in the movement when her minister, Rev. Wyatt Walker, started a campaign to protest the segregated Woolworth's lunch counter and the city's whites-only public library.[40]

In 1961, when Martin Luther King, Jr., invited Walker to join SCLC in Atlanta, Cotton went with him. She, Andrew Young, and Septima Clark were the team charged with establishing the CEP by exporting the Highlander Folk School's citizenship program to SCLC. At the SCLC Dorchester Center in South Georgia, Cotton taught basic literacy, together with the workings of the government, in preparation for literacy tests. She also trained grassroots African Americans to establish citizenship schools and organize protests in their own communities. Cotton looked for potential leaders—male and female—among preachers, beauticians, undertakers, and others.[41]

Like Ella Baker, Cotton encountered sexism within the leadership of SCLC. "We [women] were programmed to serve men. . . . I was not mad about it." Also like Baker, however, Cotton never wavered on or deferred matters related to her work as the organization's director of education. Cotton remained with SCLC after the assassination of Martin Luther King, Jr. and later served as vice president of field operation for the Martin Luther King, Jr. Center for Nonviolent Social Change, established by the slain civil rights leader's wife, Coretta Scott King.[42]

Cotton's work was reinforced by that of many other women, such as native Atlantan and community organizer Ella Mae Brayboy. Brayboy was an effective activist who, beginning in 1962, worked in voter registration with Atlanta's All Citizen Registration Committee and the SCLC Voter Education Project. The work of these women as organizers and teachers helped to increase the number of registered black voters in the state and helped lay the groundwork for the passage of the 1965 Voting Rights Act. By the end of 1965, eleven African Americans successfully ran for seats in the Georgia legislature. One of those new lawmakers, Grace Towns Hamilton, a veteran in the fight for black rights, became the first African American woman elected to serve as a state representative in Georgia.[43]

The Quest for Black Power (1966–74)

In the fourth phase of the civil rights struggle in Georgia, the SCLC and the SNCC increased their efforts to stir activism in inner-city neighborhoods. Both organizations also continued to mobilize foot soldiers for the movement in Georgia's rural communities. The voter education, literacy, and black-history programs initiated by the CEP were deemed major components in that process. The Voter Education Project of the Southern Regional Council supported some of these activities. In addition, community organizer Ella Mae Brayboy implemented innovative programs in the city to empower women to deal with the challenges of motherhood as well as overcome spousal abuse and unemployment in the late 1960s and early 1970s.[44]

The radicalization of SNCC occurred principally through its Atlanta Project, beginning in 1966. The Project shifted the focus of SNCC from organizing African Americans in the rural South to creating a grassroots model for social change in inner-city communities, beginning with neighborhoods in Atlanta. The Atlanta Project encouraged black women, men, and youths in Atlanta to take control of their communities through aggressive participation in electoral politics and engagement in activities meant to improve their quality of life. Along with this shift in venue came a shift in philosophy as SNCC departed from its earlier focus on passive resistance and integration and issued a passionate, militant call for "Black Power" and separatism.

This was a time when the ardent affirmation of African American manhood was viewed as prerequisite to the empowerment of all black people. Consequently conflicts erupted within the organization about what Black Power meant and how it should be expressed in the organization and in the world. The debates exacerbated the undercurrent of chauvinism that always had run through the movement. Black women in SNCC acknowledged and abhorred sexism in the organization, but many also agreed that the reclaiming of black manhood was central to the liberation of all black people. On the other hand, a position paper authored primarily by white women staffers in SNCC lambasted the organization as hypocritical in its treatment of women as second-class citizens while it fought to elevate the status of all African Americans.[45]

Subsequently, in keeping with the new emphasis on black control of the freedom struggle, Atlanta Project activists spearheaded the push to expel white women and men from SNCC, and other movement organizations followed suit. Ultimately, the debates around sexism within the movement became a catalyst that ignited the modern feminist movement in America, and the emergence of SNCC as an exclusively black organization heralded a period of increased black pride and focus on self-determination and self-definition in African America.[46]

The assassination of Martin Luther King in April 1968 sent the movement reeling in Georgia and the nation. However, a number of black women, including the wives of some of the most prominent civil rights leaders, worked quietly and relentlessly to restore balance and continue the fight for equality. Those black women included Coretta Scott King, Juanita Jones Abernathy, Jean Childs Young, and Evelyn Gibson Lowery. All these women had worked side by side with their husbands in the movement and established and maintain a balanced home life for their families. In addition to publishing *My Life with Martin Luther King, Jr.,* Coretta Scott King continued working for civil rights on behalf of black Americans. She established the Martin Luther King, Jr., Center for Nonviolent Social Change and advocated a holiday memorializing her husband. Juanita Jones Abernathy was inducted into the International Women's Hall of Fame in 2006. Jean Childs Young's career, which spanned almost four decades, included her work as an educator and advocate for children's rights as well as her civil rights activism. President Jimmy Carter appointed her chair of the 1979 International Year of the Child, a program in which more than one hundred countries commemorated the twentieth anniversary of the United Nations Declaration of the Rights of the Child. Young left some of her ideas in "What to remember about Me," written shortly before her 1994 death from liver cancer. A middle school in southwest Atlanta is named in her honor. Evelyn Gibson Lowery courageously continued her efforts even after being shot at twice by Ku Klux Klansmen. Lowery, wife of SCLC leader Rev. Joseph Lowery, is responsible for the Civil Rights Heritage Educational Tour, for the Civil Rights Freedom Wall, and for the SCLC's sister organization, the Women's Organizational Movement for Equality Now, set up in 1979.[47]

But the struggle was not complete. Three women who brought new energy, new goals, and new ideas to the Georgia civil rights movement were Dorothy Bolden, Jondelle Johnson, and Xemona Clayton Brady. In 1968, the year of King's death, Dorothy Bolden, herself a domestic worker, began organizing Atlanta's domestic workers into a union that became the National Domestic Workers Union with Bolden as president. That she was successful was owed in no small measure to her organizing abilities as well as to support from the Urban League and the Georgia Council of Human Relations. What had become obvious, despite the myriad successes of the Georgia civil rights movement, was that the poorest African American Georgians remained impoverished. Bolden's efforts helped change the picture for some, but in the twenty-first century much more remains to be accomplished.[48]

During the early seventies, Atlanta journalist, public school educator, and civil rights worker Jondelle Johnson led editorial crusades against police brutality and segregation at the city prison farm and discrimination in the postal system. In 1972, after being elected executive director of the Atlanta branch of the NAACP, Johnson revitalized the organization when she convened the nation's first community coalition on broadcasting and launched a pivotal lawsuit against Cox Enterprises, which resulted in hundreds of jobs for African Americans in the cable industry in Atlanta. Johnson was also instrumental in negotiating several Fair Share Agreements with businesses in Atlanta and throughout the country.[49]

Oklahoma-born Xemona Clayton Brady, nee Brewster, also figured prominently in keeping alive the African American quest for justice and equality. Following work as an undercover agent for Chicago's Urban League and as a teacher for a school-dropout program in Los Angeles, Clayton joined the SCLC to help with fund-raising. However, she is best known for her organizing skill and her power of persuasion, as demonstrated in 1966 and 1967 when she helped Atlanta's black physicians force the integration of segregated hospitals in the city and when she became the catalyst for the decision of Georgia's Ku Klux Klan Grand Dragon Calvin Craig to leave that organization and denounce racism and white supremacy. In 1968 Clayton hosted a successful show in Atlanta that featured well-known blacks such as Lena Horne and Harry Belafonte. Later she joined Turner Broadcasting and became assistant corporate vice president of urban affairs. A recipient of numerous awards, Clayton published her autobiography, *I've Been Marching All the Time.* Thanks to the continued efforts of black women such as Brady, even the death of Martin Luther King did not disrupt the civil rights effort in Georgia.[50]

Black women also sought voting and political rights. Currently black Georgia women constitute the largest voter bloc in the state. As a result, they can influence elections and become candidates. In 1966, Grace Towns Hamilton became the first black woman elected to the Georgia legislature. In 1970, Juanita Terry Williams unsuccessfully sought the state comptroller's position. State representative Mildred Glover raised the stakes in 1982 when she ran in the Democratic primary for the office of governor. Glover had entered the political arena earlier and in 1974 was elected to the Georgia House of Representatives, replacing Julian Bond. However, in her gubernatorial race she picked up little backing from leading Georgia blacks, lacked money, relied on a small staff, and received limited media coverage. Even though she was a skilled politician with support from black districts, she still managed only 1 percent of the vote. Former Georgia state representative and congresswoman Cynthia McKinney attempted the largest step when she received the Green Party nomination for president of the United States in 2008. That she was one of many black candidates for president and vice president that year reflects the importance of the civil and voting rights movements. Georgia-born McKinney lost, but an African American, Barack Obama, did win the presidency.[51]

Black Georgia women have played prominent and welcome roles in the civil rights movement as organizers, bridge builders, activists, educators, and leaders. Their influence has been felt throughout the state, the region, and the nation. They accepted Lucy Craft Laney's challenge, heeded her call, and contributed mightily to the Georgia civil rights movements.

Notes

1. Lucy Craft Laney, "The Burden of the Educated Colored Woman," 1899, in Patricia Liggins, *Call and Response: The Riverside Anthology of the African American Literary Tradition* (New York: Houghton Mifflin Company, 1998), 635.

2. Stephen G. N. Tuck, *Beyond Atlanta: The Struggle for Racial Equality in Georgia, 1940–1980* (Athens: University of Georgia Press, 2001) discusses the network of local movements that contributed to the battle for civil rights in Georgia. For a brief overview of Georgia's civil rights movement, see Stephen Tuck, "Civil Rights Movement," *The New Georgia Encyclopedia* (http://www.georgiaencyclopedia.org).

3. These phases were adapted from an essay by Clarissa Myrick-Harris and Norman Harris, "Atlanta's Story" in Atlanta in the Civil Rights Movement, 1949–1970, http://www.atlantahighered.org/civilrights/atlantasstory.asp.

4. Tuck, *Beyond Atlanta*, 248; Harry G. Lefever, *Undaunted By the Fight: Spelman College and the Civil Rights Movement, 1957–1967* (Macon, Ga.: Mercer University Press, 2005); William G. Anderson, "Reflections on the Origins of the Albany Movement," *Journal of Southwest Georgia History* 9 (Fall 1994): 1–14; Michael Chalfen, "The Way out May Lead In: The Albany Movement Beyond Martin Luther King, Jr.," *Georgia Historical Quarterly* 79 (1995): 560–98; Charlayne Hunter Gault, "'Heirs to a Legacy of Struggle': Charlayne Hunter Integrates the University of Georgia," in Bettye Collier-Thomas and V. P. Franklin, eds., *Sisters in the Struggle: African American Women in the Civil Rights-Black Power Movement* (New York: New York University Press, 2001), 75–82 ; Cynthia Griggs Fleming, "Black Women and Black Power: The Case of Ruby Doris Smith Robinson and the Student Nonviolent Coordinating Committee," in Collier-Thomas and Franklin, eds., *Sisters in the Struggle*, 197–213; Cynthia Griggs Fleming, *Soon We Will Not Cry: The Liberation of Ruby*

Doris Smith Robinson (Lanham, Md.: Rowman & Littlefield, 1998). On Georgia civil rights efforts, see also Paul Bolster, "Civil Rights Movement in Twentieth Century Georgia" (PhD diss., University of Georgia, 1972).

5. Kathryn L. Nasstrom, "Francis Freeborn Pauley: Using Autobiography and Biography to Interpret a White Woman's Activist Identity," in Gail S. Murray, ed., *Throwing Off the Cloak of Privilege: White Southern Women Activists in the Civil Rights Era* (Gainesville: University Press of Florida, 2004), 77–100; Kathryn L. Nasstrom, *Everybody's Grandmother and Nobody's Fool: Francis Freeborn Pauley and the Struggle for Social Justice* (Ithaca: Cornell University Press, 2000); Constance Curry, *Deep in Our Hearts: Nine White Women in the Freedom Movement* (Athens: University of Georgia Press, 2000); Alisa Y. Harrison, "Women and Girls' Activism in Southwest Georgia: Rethinking History and Historiography," in Angela Boswell and Judith N. McArthur, eds., *Women Shaping the South: Creating and Confronting Change* (Columbia: University of Missouri Press, 2006), 229–58; Alisa Y. Harrison, "'Ain't Gonna Let Nobody Turn Me Round': The Southwest Georgia Freedom Movement and the Politics of Empowerment" (Master's thesis, University of British Columbia, 2001); Kay Pedrotti, "Relationships," *Atlanta Journal-Constitution* (April 22, 1997); Lynne Olson, *Freedom's Daughters: The Unsung Heroines of the Civil Rights Movement from 1830 to 1970* (New York: Simon and Schuster, 2001), chaps, 13, 14; Kathryn L. Nasstrom, "Down to Now: Memory, Narrative, and Women's Leadership in the Civil Rights Movement in Atlanta, Georgia," *Gender and History* 11 (1999): 113–44. For a popular account, see Grace Walker, "How Women Won the Quiet Battle of Atlanta," *Good Housekeeping* (May 1961): 76–77, 194–207.

6. Tuck, *Beyond Atlanta,* 40–66. In 1947, Savannah became one of the first Southern communities to hire black policemen since Reconstruction; Atlanta followed in 1948. See W. Marvin Dulaney, *Black Police in America* (Bloomington: Indiana University Press, 1996), 42–46.

7. Tuck, *Beyond Atlanta,* chap. 2; Clarence Bacote, "The Negro in Georgia Politics Today," *Journal of Negro Education* 26 (1957): 307–18; Hugh Carl Owen, "The Rise of Negro Voting in Georgia, 1944–50" (Master's thesis, Emory University, 1951).

8. Tuck, *Beyond Atlanta,* 66; Nasstrom, "Down to Now: Memory, Narrative, and Women's Leadership in the Civil Rights Movement in Atlanta, Georgia," 113–44, quote on 122.

9. Nasstrom, "Down to Now," 113–44, quote cited on 123; "Adams, Florence V. 'Frankie,'" *Notable Kentucky African Americans Database* (http://www.uky.edu/libraries/NKAA); "Dove, Pearlie" (http://dc.lib.unc.edu/cdm/singleitem/collection/sohp/id/1063/rec/2).

10. The Atlanta Urban League was established in 1920 as an affiliate of the National Urban League, which was established in 1911 when two northern social-service organizations merged to address the education, employment, housing, health, and social-service needs of African Americans flooding into cities in the North and South.

11. Lorraine Spritzer and Jean B. Bergmark, *Grace Towns Hamilton and the Politics of Southern Change* (Athens: University of Georgia Press, 1997); Sharon Mitchell Mullis, "The Public Career of Grace Towns Hamilton: A Citizen Too Busy to Hate" (PhD diss., Emory University, 1976); Delores P. Aldridge, "Hamilton, Grace Towns," in Darlene Clark Hine, Elsa Barkley Brown, and Rosalyn Terborg-Penn, eds., *Black Women in America: An Historical*

Encyclopedia (Bloomington: Indiana University Press, 1993), 1: 520–21; Sowande' Mustakeem, "Hamilton, Grace Towns," in Darlene Clark Hine, ed., *Black Women in America,* 2nd ed. (New York: Oxford University Press, 2005), 2: 8–10

12. Tuck, *Beyond Atlanta,* 58–61; *New York Times,* December 26, 1945; Myrick-Harris and Harris, "Atlanta's Story." Blackburn, a leading and energetic organizer, was overlooked and ignored.

13. Tuck, *Beyond Atlanta,* 51; Eloria Sherman Gilbert, telephone interview by Clarissa Myrick-Harris, August 6, 2008.

14. On page 51 in *Beyond Atlanta,* Stephen Tuck wrote that Eloria Gilbert organized the NAACP chapter in Hazlehurst, Georgia. Gilbert says that is an error; she organized the NAACP chapter in Luthersville, Georgia, in 1946. Eloria Sherman Gilbert, telephone interview by Clarissa Myrick-Harris, August 6, 2008.

15. Tuck, *Beyond Atlanta,* 51, 248; Eloria Sherman Gilbert, telephone interview by Clarissa Myrick-Harris, August 6, 2008.

16. Lela Phillips, "Lena Baker Case," *The New Georgia Encyclopedia* (http://www.georgiaencyclopedia.org); Lela Bond Phillips, *The Lena Baker Story* (Atlanta: Wings Publishing, 2001).

17. Tuck, *Beyond Atlanta,* 68; E. M. Beck and Stewart E. Tolnay, "Lynching," *The New Georgia Encyclopedia* (http://www.georgiaencyclopedia.org); Wallace H. Warren, "'The Best People in Town Won't Talk': The Moore's Ford Lynching of 1946 and Its Cover-Up," in John C. Inscoe, ed., *Georgia in Black and White: Explorations in the Race Relations of a Southern State, 1865–1950,* (Athens: University of Georgia Press, 1994), 266–88.

18. Tuck, *Beyond Atlanta,* 74–79.

19. See note 11.

20. See note 12.

21. Barbara Ransby, *Ella Baker and the Black Freedom Movement: A Radical Democratic Vision* (Chapel Hill: University of North Carolina Press, 2003); Joanne Grant, *Ella Baker: Freedom Bound* (New York: Wiley, 1998); Ellen Cantarow and Susan Gushee O'Malley, "Ella Baker: Organizing for Civil Rights," in Ellen Cantarow, Susan Gushee O'Malley, and Sharon Hartman Strom, eds., *Moving the Mountain: Women Working for Social Change* (New York: Feminist Press, 1980), 53–93; Carol Mueller, "Ella Baker and the Origins of 'Participatory Democracy,'" in Vicki L. Crawford, Jacqueline Anne Rouse, and Barbara Woods, eds., *Women in the Civil Rights Movement: Trailblazers and Torchbearers, 1941–1965* (Bloomington: Indiana University Press, 1993), 51–70.

22. Ransby, *Ella Baker and the Black Freedom Movement,* chap. 6; Barbara Ransby, "Behind-the-Scenes View of a Behind-the-Scenes Organizer: The Roots of Ella Baker's Political Passions," in Collier-Thomas and Franklin, eds., *Sisters in the Struggle,* 42–57.

23. Ransby, *Ella Baker and the Black Freedom Movement,* chap. 6, quote on 174.

24. Pamela Petty, "Non-positional Leadership: The Case of Ella Baker and the Student Nonviolent Coordinating Committee" (PhD diss., University of Michigan, 1997); Barbara Ransby, "Baker, Ella Josephine," in Darlene Clark Hine, Elsa Barkley Brown, and Rosalyn Terborg-Penn, eds., *Black, Women in America: An Historical Encyclopedia* (Bloomington: Indiana University Press, 1993), 1: 70–74.

25. Tuck, *Beyond Atlanta,* 118–19; Harry G. Lefever, *Undaunted By the Fight;* Karen Vanlandingham, "In Pursuit of a Changing Dream: Spelman College Students and the Civil Rights Movement, 1955–62" (Master's thesis, Emory University, 1983).

26. Excerpt from Howard Zinn's commencement speech at Spelman College in 2005, forty-two years after the institution had fired him: http://www.newtondialog.org/Speeches/ZinnAtSpelmanCollege.htm.

27. Tuck, *Beyond Atlanta,* 112–19.

28. Clayborne Carson, *In Struggle: SNCC and the Black Awakening of the 1960s* (Cambridge, Mass.: Harvard University Press, 1981); Mueller, "Ella Baker and the Origins of 'Participatory Democracy,'" 51–70; Fleming, "Black Women and Black Power."

29. Fleming, "Black Women and Black Power"; Cynthia Griggs Fleming, *Soon We Will Not Cry;* Cynthia Griggs Fleming, "Smith-Robinson, Ruby Doris," in Darlene Clark Hine, Elsa Barkley Brown, and Rosalyn Terborg-Penn, eds., *Black Women in America: An Historical Encyclopedia* (Bloomington: Indiana University Press, 1993), 2: 1085–86.

30. "Albany," *The New Georgia Encyclopedia;* Clayborne Carson, "SNCC and the Albany Movement," *Journal of Southwest Georgia History* 2 (Fall 1984): 16–25; Slater King, "The Bloody Battleground of Albany," *Freedomways* 4 (Winter 1964): 93–101; Howard Zinn, *SNCC: The New Abolitionists* (Boston: Beacon Press, 1964), chap. 7.

31. Clarissa Myrick-Harris, "Behind the Scenes: Two Women of the Free Southern Theater," in Crawford, Rouse, and Woods, eds., *Women of the Civil Rights Movement.*

32. Olson, *Freedom's Daughters,* 225–27, 231–34, 337–38; Veterans of Hope, interview by Bernice Johnson-Reagon (http://veteransofhope.org/show.php?vid=38&tid=9&sid=21).

33. Clayborne Carson, "SNCC and the Albany Movement," *Journal of Southwest Georgia History* 2 (Fall 1984): 16–25; Slater King, "The Bloody Battleground of Albany," *Freedomways* 4 (Winter 1964): 93–101; Howard Zinn, *SNCC: The New Abolitionists* (Boston: Beacon Press, 1964), chap. 7; Tuck, *Beyond Atlanta,* 147–53; Veterans of Hope, interview with Bernice Johnson-Reagon.

34. Stephen Tuck, "A City Too Dignified to Hate: Civic Pride, Civil Rights, and Savannah in Comparative Perspective," *Georgia Historical Quarterly* 79 (Fall 1995): 539–59; Tuck, *Beyond Atlanta,* 127–37.

35. Buddy Sullivan, "Savannah," *The New Georgia Encyclopedia* (http://www.georgiaencyclopedia.org); Arlinda Smith Broady, "Addie Bird Byers, Educator, Activist, dies, 97," *Athens Banner-Herald* (December 7, 2003); "Addie Bird Byers" (http://www.lifeinlegacy.com); Tuck, *Beyond Atlanta,* 99.

36. Glenn M. Robins, "Americus Movement," *The New Georgia Encyclopedia* (http://www.georgiaencyclopedia.org); Donna M. Owens, "Stolen Girls," *Essence Magazine* (June 2006): 162; Olson, *Freedom's Daughters,* 246–47, quote on 246; Zinn, *SNCC: The New Abolitionists,* 182–83; Tuck, *Beyond Atlanta,* 173–86.

37. Glenn M. Robins, "Americus Movement," *The New Georgia Encyclopedia* (http://www.georgiaencyclopedia.org); Olson, *Freedom's Daughters,* 246–47, quote on 246; Zinn, *SNCC: The New Abolitionists,* 182–83; Tuck, *Beyond Atlanta,* 173–86. For a personal account, see Lulu Westbrooks-Griffin, *Freedom Is Not Free: Forty-five Days in Leesburg Stockade, A Civil Rights Story* (Hamlin, N.Y.: Heirloom, 1998).

38. Charlayne Hunter Gault, "'Heirs to a Legacy of Struggle': Charlayne Hunter Inte-

grates the University of Georgia," in Collier-Thomas and Franklin, eds., *Sisters in the Struggle,* 75–82; Calvin Trillin, *An Education in Georgia: Charlayne Hunter, Hamilton Holmes, and the Integration of the University of Georgia* (Athens: University of Georgia Press, 1991; reprint of 1964 edition); Charlayne Hunter-Gault, *In My Place* (New York: Knopf, 1993).

39. R. O. Johnson, "Desegregation of Public Education in Georgia," *Journal of Negro Education* 24 (Summer 1955): 228–47; Maurice C. Daniels, "Mary Francis Early," *Unsung Foot Soldiers* (http://www.footsoldier.uga.edu); Maurice C. Daniels, *Horace T. Ward: Desegregation of the University of Georgia, Civil Rights Advocacy, and Jurisprudence* (Atlanta: Clark Atlanta University Press, 2001).

40. Tavis Smiley, "Dorothy Cotton Interview," *Tavis Smiley Show,* April 3, 2008 (http://www.pbs.org/kcet/tavissmiley); Clayborne Carson and Stephanie Brookins, "Dorothy Foreman Cotton," in Hine, Brown, and Terborg-Penn, eds., *Black Women in America,* 1: 286–87; Olson, *Freedom's Daughters,* 222, 262.

41. Smiley, "Dorothy Cotton Interview"; Clayborne Carson and Stephanie Brookins, "Dorothy Foreman Cotton," 1: 286–87; Olson, *Freedom's Daughters,* 222, 262.

42. Carson and Brookins, "Dorothy Foreman Cotton," 286–87; Olson, *Freedom's Daughters,* 222, 262.

43. "Inventory of the Ella Mae Wade Brayboy Papers," *Digital Library of Georgia* (http://dlg.galileo.usg.edu/aafa/html/aafa_aar194-012.html): Clarissa Myrick-Harris and Norman Harris, "Atlanta in the Civil Rights Movement," *Atlanta Regional Council for Higher Education* (http://www.atlantahighered.org/civilrights); Alton Hornsby, Jr., "The Negro in Atlanta Politics, 1961–73," *Atlanta Historical Bulletin* 21 (1973): 7–33.

44. See note 51; Tuck, *Beyond Atlanta,* chap. 6.

45. Emily Stoper, *The Student Nonviolent Coordinating Committee: The Growth of Radicalism in a Civil Rights Organization* (Brooklyn: Carlson Publishing Co., 1989); Tuck, *Beyond Atlanta,* chap. 6.

46. Stoper, *The Student Nonviolent Coordinating Committee;* Myrick-Harris and Harris, "Atlanta in the Civil Rights Movement"; Kristen Anderson Bricker, "'Triple Jeopardy': Black Women and the Growth of Feminist Consciousness in SNCC, 1964–1975," in Kimberly Springer ed., *Still Lifting, Still Climbing: Contemporary African-American Women's Activism* (New York: New York University Press, 1991), 49–69. On male-dominated Atlanta, see also Alton Hornsby, Jr., "A City That Was Too Busy to Hate: Atlanta Businessmen and Desegregation," in Elizabeth Jacoway and David R. Colburn, eds., *Southern Businessmen and Desegregation* (Baton Rouge: Louisiana State University Press, 1982), 120–36.

47. Clayborne Carson and Angela D. Brown, "King, Coretta Scott," in Hine, Brown, and Terborg-Penn, eds., *Black Women in America,* 1: 678–80; Coretta Scott King, *My Life with Martin Luther King, Jr.* (New York: Holt, Rinehart and Winston, 1969); Juanita Jones Abernathy, interview by Clarissa Myrick-Harris, February 10, 2005; Carla Morrison, "On the Move with Atlanta's Women of Vision," *Chit Chat Communications* (http://www.chitchat communications.com); Jean Childs Young, "What To Remember About Me," *Atlanta Journal and Constitution* (September 20, 1994).

48. Dorothy Cowser Yancy, "Bolden, Dorothy Lee," in Hine, Brown, and Terborg-Penn, eds., *Black Women in America,* 1: 144–45; Barbara Laker, "The Fighter," *Atlanta Constitution* (January 6, 1983); "Dorothy Lee Bolden Thompson," (http://pba.org/programming/

programs/voicesofchange); "Inventory of the Dorothy Lee Bolden Thompson Collection," Auburn Avenue Research Library (http://dlg.galileo.usg.edu/aafa/print/aafa_aar196-005.html); Dorothy Cowser Yancy, "Dorothy Bolden, Organizer of Domestic Workers: She Was Born Poor but She Would Not Bow Down," *Sage* 3 (Spring 1986): 53–55.

49. "Jondelle Johnson Drive" (http://legis.state.ga.us/legis/1999_00); Myrick-Harris and Harris, "Atlanta in the Civil Rights Movement."

50. Xemona Clayton Brady, *The History Makers* (http://www.thehistorymakers.com/biography/xernona-clayton-40); Xemona Clayton and Hal Gulliver, *I've Been Marching All the Time: An Autobiography* (Atlanta: Longstreet Press, 1991).

51. Tuck, *Beyond Atlanta,* 193; Hanes Walton, Jr., and Johnny Campbell, Jr., "The First Black Female Gubernatorial Candidate in Georgia: State Representative Mildred Glover," in Hanes Walton, Jr., ed., *Black Politics and Black Political Behavior: A Linkage Analysis* (Westport, Conn.: Praeger, 1994), 235–49, 332–33.

7 Women in the South Carolina Civil Rights Movement

W. Marvin Dulaney

Just as in other parts of the South, black women were important participants in the civil rights movement in South Carolina. In the struggle for social justice, voting rights, and equal opportunity in all facets of American life, these women were prominent contributors. Indeed, they influenced the movement throughout the South, and several received national attention for their efforts on behalf of social justice and equal rights.

Despite the prominent role of African American women in the movement in South Carolina, historians focus—as they do in other states—on the male leaders. In South Carolina, for example, historians have written much about Edwin A. Harleston, I. S. Leevy Johnson, I. DeQuincey Newman, J. Arthur Brown, Joseph A. DeLaine, and Matthew Perry. By contrast, only two women, Septima Clark and Modjeska Simkins, have received much attention.[1]

Of these two women who have come to epitomize the role of black women in the civil rights movement in South Carolina, Modjeska Monteith Simkins had the longer, more consistent civil rights career. In 1899 she was born in Columbia to Henry Clarence Monteith and Rachel Evelyn Hull. She and her seven siblings traced their ancestry directly to enslavement. In 1921 she earned her bachelor's degree from Benedict College, and she taught school until 1929, when she married Andrew W. Simkins, a prosperous businessman. Because married women were not permitted to teach in public schools in Columbia, she was asked to resign. Simkins did not work again until 1931, when she was hired as Director of Negro Work for the South Carolina Tuberculosis Association. Her work with the SCTBA brought her in contact with African Americans from all levels of life and made her keenly aware that their impoverishment was the result of racism, segregation, and overall powerlessness. She joined the Columbia NAACP in 1929 and became its secretary. Her work with the SCTBA enabled her to extend her social-service and social-justice efforts throughout the state. In 1931, for example, she wrote to Governor Ibra C. Blackwood asking that he pardon two African Americans convicted of murdering a white man and sentenced to death in Lexington County. She argued that they had not received a fair trial. The governor did not act on her request, but she was not discouraged. She continued her activism on behalf of African Americans in the state. In fact she was so bold that when Franklin D. Roosevelt visited Columbia in 1938, she requested an audience with him to discuss more jobs for African Americans in his New Deal programs. Roosevelt's secretary turned down her request by stating that time constraints did not permit him to meet with her.[2]

Simkins' statewide connections served her well when the NAACP organized its state conference in Cheraw in 1939. Simkins became a charter member and was appointed state secretary. For three years, as she traveled throughout the state working on behalf of the SCTBA, she also recruited members for the NAACP, increasing the number of chapters from 10 to 110. In 1942, however, she lost her SCTBA job. The state agency reflected the white supremacy of the era, and her supervisor viewed her NAACP work as subversive.[3]

Undaunted by this turn of events, Simkins continued her NAACP work in behalf of equal rights for African Americans in South Carolina. If anything, her firing from the SCTBA seemed to radicalize her. She took on even more challenges in the struggle for equal rights and social justice. And then, in 1944, when *Smith v. Allwright* made white primaries illegal and Governor Olin B. Johnston said the state would pass new measures to prevent "inferior negroes" from voting in Democratic Party primaries, Simkins challenged him to a debate: "Resolved: the Concept of 'White Supremacy' Is Sound—Biblically, Historically, and Scientifically." She stated further: "In your presentation, I am challenging you to prove, unequivocally and conclusively, that you are superior to me, to say nothing of the hundreds of Negroes and other nationally and internationally renowned persons of color." She requested that the debate be held in the South Carolina General Assembly. Johnston did not respond.[4]

Most of Simkins's work for the NAACP was less confrontational, but it was important and often groundbreaking. As state secretary from 1939 to 1957, she worked with the national office and its leadership to pursue some of the state's most important civil rights cases, including the Teacher Salary Equalization case, the *Elmore v. Rice* white-primary case, and the *Briggs v. Elliott* school-desegregation case. She raised money, organized and supported the plaintiffs, and coordinated the statewide effort to publicize and develop support for them in the African American community.

Her first challenge as state secretary was to organize black teachers to fight for salaries equal to those of white teachers. Salary equalization emerged as part of the three-pronged NAACP attack on segregated and inferior education for African American school children in the South.[5] To achieve salary equalization in South Carolina, Simkins had to fight the state *and* overcome the resistance of black teachers who feared losing their jobs for being involved with an NAACP campaign. To reach individual teachers, she coordinated her efforts through the Palmetto State Teachers' Association, an African American teachers association organized early in the century. Partnering with that organization, she helped teachers raise money to support their case, wrote letters, published articles in black newspapers, and arranged meetings to discuss the inequities in teacher salaries. She not only set up a Teachers' Defense Fund to support teachers who lost their jobs because of their support for the case; she also formed an organization to accept donations from teachers who did not want to be identified as contributors to the NAACP campaign. African American teachers won salary equalization in Charleston in 1944 and in Columbia in 1945.[6]

In 1957 Simkins was forced out of office as state secretary of the NAACP. Several factors contributed to her removal. As early as 1954 her friend and fellow civil rights activist John H. McCray charged that she was too dominant in chapter activities and was trying to take over the organization. McCray's charge had little merit. He was reacting to her decision to shut down his newspaper, *The Lighthouse and Informer,* after she had been forced to manage it while he served a sixty-day jail term for libel. McCray's charge had more to do with their business arrangement than with her work in the NAACP. More serious, however, was the charge that she was a communist. Her activities and relationships with "communist front" organizations and "known communists" led to her name being mentioned during US House Un-American Activities Committee hearings. Committed to social justice, in the late 1940s and early 1950s she had attended meetings and conferences with the Southern Negro Youth Congress and the Southern Conference for Human Welfare. HUAC later cited and listed these organizations as "communist front" organizations simply because they had "known communists" as members. She also associated and had attended meetings with "known communists" such as Paul Robeson and W. E. B. DuBois. Retrenching after an attack by the state legislature following the *Brown* decision, the NAACP did not want to be linked to communism, and its national and state leadership thought it best to purge from its leadership people such as Simkins, who had associated with alleged communists and communist organizations.[7]

In 1958, after the snub, Simkins resigned from the NAACP, but she continued her activism in other areas. In her hometown of Columbia, she became more active in a local community organization that she had helped organize in 1956, the Richland County Citizens' Committee. Under the auspices of the RCCC she continued her advocacy for health care among African Americans by agitating to improve conditions at the Negro Hospital in Columbia. She challenged the county to improve services and conditions at the hospital and to make its staff more accountable. Simkins also became more active in politics. Before leaving the NAACP, she had been active in both the Democratic and the Republican Parties and in the Progressive Democratic Party, organized by African Americans in 1944 to challenge the seating of South Carolina's all-white delegation at the 1948 Democratic National Convention. As a leader of the RCCC she supported the organization's endorsement of candidates in each election and its twenty-year battle to change the electoral system in Columbia from at-large, citywide city council seats to single-member districts. In addition she ran for office three times, twice for the city council and once for the state legislature.[8]

By the time of her death, in 1992, Modjeska Montieth Simkins had received numerous accolades for her civil rights activism. In South Carolina she was known as the "Grand Old Lady of Civil Rights" and as the "matriarch of civil rights activists." These were fitting tributes for a woman who had spent six decades of her life fighting for social and political justice and equality for African Americans.[9]

Like Simkins, Septima Poinsette Clark had a long legacy of civil rights activism. The two women also had a similar history. Clark was born in 1898 in Charleston, the daughter of Peter Poinsette and Victoria Warren Anderson. Her father had been enslaved. She attended Avery Normal Institute, the city's premier private school for African American children, graduated in 1916, and then obtained a certificate to teach in the state public schools. She began her teaching career in the rural community of Johns Island, where she first encountered the stark poverty that restricted the lives of African Americans in the Sea Islands communities of South Carolina. On Johns Island she also learned of the gross inequities in teachers' salaries based on race. She and another teacher taught 132 children and made $60 a month combined while the white teacher at the white school across the road made $85 for teaching only 3 students. Returning to teach at her alma mater, Avery Institute, in 1919, she joined the NAACP and participated in a petition campaign to hire black teachers on the Charleston peninsula, where they had been prohibited from teaching. In 1920 she married Nerie Clark, and she followed him in his career as a merchant marine until his death in 1925. Her travels with him took her to Dayton, Ohio, and to his hometown in Hickory, North Carolina.[10]

In 1929 she returned to Columbia, where she taught elementary school until 1942, when she decided to complete her bachelor's degree at Benedict College. Then, taking classes over the course of three summers, she earned her master's degree in education at Hampton Institute in 1946. Her thesis was entitled "An Experiment in Individualizing Instruction in Reading in a Sixth Grade Class." Using the students in her sixth-grade class at Saxon Elementary School in Columbia as her subjects, she described how she developed a methodology that enabled them to improve their reading skills by letting them use their own language expressions and to develop their reading skills at their own pace.[11] This methodology became the basis for her instruction of adults in the citizenship schools she organized twelve years later in the Sea Islands of South Carolina.

During her eighteen years in Columbia, Clark engaged in a limited amount of civil rights activism. While she was teaching in Columbia, she participated only in the teacher-salary equalization suit. Although she remained a member of the NAACP, having joined the organization during the petition campaign in Charleston in 1919, she did not remain active throughout her life.[12]

In 1947, Clark returned to Charleston, where she immediately became active in several organizations to improve the lives of African Americans in the city. She worked with the YWCA and the Shaw Boys Club. She also became active in the Charleston branch of the NAACP, becoming chair of the Auditing Committee in 1951 and vice president in 1954. Unlike the residents of Columbia, whom she found open and less rigid racially, Charlestonians drew the color line two ways: whites did not respect or associate with blacks, and upper middle-class blacks did not associate with lower-class blacks. In 1947, for example, when Clark and two white women met with Mayor William M. Morrison to solicit his support for the Boys Club, he did not acknowledge Clark's presence, turned his back on her, and spoke with the white women, who were not directly involved in the project. In 1951 she wrote to her friend Elizabeth Waring, wife of federal judge J. Waties Waring, that the *Charleston News and Courier* refused to print a story about African American workers for the Community Chest because the story used "Mr. and "Mrs." before the workers' names. She also observed that her social standing among middle-class African Americans in Charleston was lower because her father had been enslaved.[13]

Clark taught in the Charleston public schools until 1956, when the school board refused to renew her contract because of her membership in the NAACP. That year, when the state legislature passed a law prohibiting municipal, state, and county employees from having NAACP memberships, teachers throughout South Carolina lost their jobs. Clark tried to persuade other teachers who were victims of the law to stand together and challenge it. She wrote 726 letters to black teachers across the state, arguing that "if whites could belong to the Ku Klux Klan, then surely blacks could belong to the NAACP." Only 26 teachers responded. Clark succeeded in convincing eleven of the forty-two teachers who were dismissed in Charleston County to meet with the school superintendent and file a formal protest. Only six teachers showed up, and the superintendent dismissed them by stating that they were "living far ahead of their time."[14]

Clark's dismissal was fortuitous. Having met Myles Horton, a founder of Highlander Folk School, in Monteagle, Tennessee, in 1954 while attending a workshop on desegregation, she accepted a position with Highlander as director of education.[15] After working with Horton and others at Highlander to refine its education program, in 1957 she returned to South Carolina to start one of the civil rights movement's most important innovations—Citizenship Schools. These schools taught basic literacy, reading, and writing as well as practical skills such as balancing a checkbook. But the most revolutionary component of the schools was how they helped prepare African Americans to take and pass the state literacy test, register to vote, and participate in the democratic process.[16]

The Citizenship Schools began when Horton and Clark responded to a request from Esau Jenkins, a community organizer and businessman on Johns Island, for an adult-education program. Jenkins recognized that because many people in his community could not read or write, they would never be able to challenge their oppressors. Initially he asked the school district and local churches to help improve literacy among adults on Johns Island, but both rejected his request. Then he turned to Horton and Clark (she having taught him to read and write in the school on Johns Island), and they responded. Clark, recognizing that the community needed a teacher whom the people would trust and who would work with them as she had, brought in her cousin, Bernice Robinson, to teach the first Citizenship School.[17]

Bernice Robinson, a beautician, became one of South Carolina's unsung heroines in the civil rights movement. Like her cousin Septima Clark, she was born in Charleston in 1914 and attended Charleston's public high school for Negroes—which provided students instruction only for grades one through nine. In 1936 she moved to New York City intending to become a musician. Instead she went to beauty school and remained in New York City until her mother became ill in 1947. At that time she returned to Charleston, joined the NAACP, and became its secretary and membership chairperson. In 1954, when she accompanied Septima Clark to Highlander, she began her association with Esau Jenkins and his community organization, the Progressive Club. She was the right person at the right time to teach the first Citizenship School.[18]

When Robinson began teaching the Citizenship School, in January 1957, she took an unconventional approach by asking the first fourteen students—all adults—what they wanted to learn. They said that they wanted to learn how to write their names, how to read the voter election laws to qualify and register to vote, and how to fill out money orders at the post office. For three months the class met two nights per week for two hours. At the end of the course the fourteen students took South Carolina's literacy test; eight passed and were registered to vote.[19]

Under Robinson's leadership and with Clark's support, the schools continued. By February 1958, Robinson had taught two more classes. Then in 1958–59, four Citizenship Schools opened, one each on Edisto Island, Johns Island, and Wadmalaw Island and one in North Charleston. Robinson and Clark developed a curriculum that, with eighty hours of instruction, prepared adults who had not been able to read or write to pass South Carolina's literacy test. The schools were so successful that in 1961 Martin Luther King and the Southern Christian Leadership Conference adopted them and hired Clark to implement them throughout the South. By 1963, Citizenship Schools were responsible for registering fifty thousand new voters in the South. In addition the Freedom Schools organized by SNCC in Georgia and Mississippi, especially during the 1964 Freedom Summer Project, borrowed extensively from the models developed by Clark and Robinson.[20]

In 1970, Clark and Robinson left SCLC and their work with the Citizenship Schools. Clark retired, but in 1976 she was elected to the Charleston County School Board. Robinson took a position with the South Carolina Commission for Farm Workers, ran unsuccessfully for Congress in 1972, and then continued her work with the SCCFW until 1977. Before Clark's death in 1987 and Robinson's in 1994, both women were heralded for helping grassroots and rural African Americans participate in the electoral process and thereby in the civil rights movement. As one scholar observed, after lauding Clark and Robinson, and Dorothy Cotton of SCLC, for having taught and trained older people in the South, "Had it not been for Clark and her mastery at teaching illiterate adults how to read and write, the 1965 Voting Rights Act would have been meaningless."[21]

Few women had careers in the movement to equal those of Simkins, Clark, or Robinson, but many participated at the grassroots level and as foot soldiers in the various campaigns for equality in education and employment, for equal access to public facilities, and for voting rights. Among them were Lottie Polk Gaffney of Gaffney, South Carolina, Sarah Z. Daniels of Columbia, and Annie Belle Weston of Manning. Contemporaries of Septima Clark and Modjeska Simkins, these three women pioneered in the voting-rights campaign by challenging the Democratic white primary and by participating in the Progressive Democratic Party when it was organized in 1944.

Lottie Polk Gaffney served as a teacher and principal at Petty Town School in Cherokee County. She was also very active in politics and, like any other American citizen, felt that she should be able to vote and elect politicians who best represented her interests and those of African Americans. In 1940, Gaffney and two other women tried to register in the Democratic Primary in Cherokee County, but they were turned away. In 1942, with the assistance of the NAACP, Gaffney filed a lawsuit against the Cherokee County Registration Board for denying her and her companions a ballot in violation of the Fifteenth Amendment. The federal district court in Spartanburg acquitted the election officials for refusing to register African Americans, citing insufficient evidence to convict them.[22]

For her efforts Gaffney became the target of reprisals from her employers and other whites in the Cherokee County area. The post office refused to deliver her mail. Despite her excellent record as a teacher, she lost her job. After she obtained a signed petition of endorsement from the parents whose children she taught attesting to her competence, the school board then charged that she had faked her credentials from the Colored Normal, Industrial, Agricultural and Mechanical College in Orangeburg. She went to the college and obtained an official transcript to verify that she had more than enough credits to certify her as a teacher. Finally, the school officials admitted that she had lost her job because she had participated in the voting-rights case. But they did not rehire her.[23]

Gaffney's predicament did not deter her from continuing her political activism. When African Americans formed the Progressive Democratic Party in 1944, Gaffney attended the founding convention and became one of the delegates who challenged the white Democrats at the party's national convention in Chicago. In 1948 she attended the Democratic National Convention as a delegate. There she was joined by three other women who were members of the PDP. Among them were Sarah Z. Daniels and Annie Belle Weston.[24]

In 1945, the PDP had formed a women's auxiliary, and Sara Z. Daniels had become its chair. Daniels was also president of the Manning chapter of the NAACP, a home-demonstration agent, and president of the Clarendon County Teachers' Association. She organized two women's PDP auxiliaries. Like Modjeska Simkins, she used the contacts she had made as a home-demonstration agent to support her political activism. In her roles as the president of the NAACP and chair of the women's auxiliary of the PDP she promoted voter registration in Clarendon County and linked together her job and activism as a way to encourage women to become more politically active and to make sure that they were represented in local and national political meetings. Eventually she suffered the same fate as Simkins, Clark, and Gaffney: during the 1950 Clarendon County school-desegregation suit she lost her job as a demonstration agent because of her participation in and support of the suit.[25]

Annie Belle Weston of Columbia, a professor at Benedict College, helped to link the PDP to the colored women's clubs in South Carolina. She served as state secretary of the PDP, but she was also active in the South Carolina Federation of Colored Women's Clubs. At a time when women did not participate openly in politics and deferred to men, Weston not only served as state secretary but also, along with Gaffney and Daniels, served as a delegate to two Democratic National Conventions. She worked with the women's organizations in the state to involve them in politics and to use their organizational skills to improve the lives of their families and their communities. She urged women to join the PDP, to fight for the right to vote, and to fight for first-class citizenship.[26]

According to Cherisse Jones-Branch and Peter Lau, Annie Belle Weston and other women like her, who were active in the PDP as well as in the South Carolina Federation of Colored Women's Clubs, typified women throughout the state who connected their work for women's clubs and associations with the civil rights movement. The club movement developed among African American women in South Carolina as a result of their commitment to racial uplift. As the women formed clubs and associations to address social and economic problems that adversely affected African Americans, they also developed a commitment to political activism and social justice that eventually drew them into the civil rights movement. When club members understood that the effectiveness of programs they sponsored was limited by the racial proscriptions demanded by a segregated society, they shifted their focus from racial uplift to politics and the struggle for equal rights and social justice.[27]

Two of the largest women's organizations in the state, the South Carolina Federation of Colored Women's Cubs and the Woman's Baptist Educational and Missionary Convention of South Carolina, exemplified the transition from racial uplift to political rights and social justice. Middle-class and professional African American women led these two organizations, and by the 1940s and 1950s the women in them supported a variety of educational programs and political campaigns, the interracial cooperation movement, and court cases that involved them in the civil rights movement.[28]

From its founding in 1909 and throughout its long history, the South Carolina Federation of Colored Women's Clubs and its local affiliates sponsored and supported a wide variety of uplift activities: Negro Health Week, schools for African-American orphans, libraries in communities where segregation denied African Americans access to public libraries, and branches of the YWCA. And they worked with white women's organizations on issues that crossed racial lines. The Federation of Colored Women's Clubs was most noted for its school for delinquent young women, Fairwold Industrial School for Girls, in Cayce, founded in 1917 by its long-serving president, Marion Birnie Wilkinson. But its member organizations also supported the NAACP anti-lynching campaign, sponsored forums to discuss voting and civil rights issues, worked with the interracial-cooperation movement in Greenville and Charleston, and worked with local chapters of the NAACP to increase membership. In fact, thanks to the women of the Woman's Baptist Convention and the membership drives of the Federation of Colored Women's Clubs, the majority of NAACP members in the state were women.[29]

As with the Federation of Colored Women's Clubs, the mission of the Woman's Baptist Convention—the largest organization of black Christian women in South Carolina—did not at first involve its members in the civil rights movement. In 1888 it was established to support Baptist colleges in South Carolina and to promote missionary work among its members. Eventually, however, the organization expanded its mission to address the social and political issues that confronted its members. In the 1940s, for example, the Woman's Baptist Convention held an "Inter-Racial Hour" at its annual conventions and invited white Baptists to discuss how Christians could improve race relations in the state. The organization also began to address politics by inviting I. S. Leevy and Modjeska Monteith Simkins to its meetings to discuss voting rights and what women needed to do to gain full citizenship rights. The organization bought an annual membership in the NAACP and encouraged its members to buy individual memberships. After the 1954 *Brown* decision, the Woman's Baptist Convention issued a statement publicly endorsing the desegregation of public schools and encouraging its members to support the decision. The organization also stated that its members should not be intimidated by the state campaign against the NAACP or bought off by the state legislature's offer to build new, segregated schools for black children. When sit-ins and other demonstrations began in the 1960s at colleges supported by the Woman's Baptist Convention, specifically at Friendship Junior College in Rock Hill and Benedict College in Columbia, the members of the organization supported the students by raising bail money for them and providing food and support for those who remained in jail to support the principle of "jail, no bail."[30]

Although the Federation of Colored Women's Clubs and the Woman's Baptist Convention were the largest and most active women's organizations in the state working with black men and white women for political participation and social justice, other women's organizations also participated in the struggle and laid the basis for the civil rights activism among women in the 1960s. In her 1997 master's thesis, Cherisse Jones-Branch shows that several interracial women's organizations, such as the YWCA, the Women's Christian Council, and the South Carolina Council on Human Relations, attempted to address the disadvantages, unequal conditions, and violence facing African Americans. But few black and white women were able to build interracial relationships based on equality. Jones-Branch argues that many white women who acted on their Christian values and sense of fair play to better race relations still assumed that once they had helped African Americans develop "separate but equal" educational, recreational, and health facilities and their own YWCAs and YMCAs, these separate facilities would take care of the needs of African Americans and segregation could continue unfettered. According to Jones-Branch, white women interracial activists in the 1940s and 1950s were unwilling to challenge or change the racial status quo.[31]

Thus, it was African-American women, collectively and individually, who had to challenge the racial status quo in South Carolina. As we have seen with Modjeska Monteith Simkins, Septima P. Clark, and Lottie P. Gaffney, African American women risked their livelihoods as well as their physical well-being to challenge racism and segregation in South Carolina. They were often unheralded and received little recognition for their efforts. This was especially true for Sarah Mae Flemming Brown.

In June 1954, eighteen months before Rosa Parks refused to surrender her seat and move to the back of the bus in Montgomery, Alabama, Sarah Mae Flemming defied a similar order from a white bus driver in Columbia, South Carolina. In addition to refusing to move to the back of the bus, Flemming tried to exit through the front door, which was reserved for white passengers. At that, the bus driver hit her in the stomach with his forearm and forced her to exit through the back door. The blow from the white bus driver, Warren H. Christmus, was so severe that it bent Flemming over in pain. Upon arriving home, she had to place ice on her stomach to reduce the pain, and eventually she went to the hospital.[32]

Sarah Mae Flemming was only twenty-one years old when she refused to move from her seat in the front section of the bus in Columbia. She was not unlike many other women who challenged racism and segregation in South Carolina and in other parts of the South. She worked as a domestic for a white family in Columbia, and like many another African-American woman who became the focal point of the civil rights movement, she took a serious risk by challenging the bus company. She had never intended to become a civil rights activist or the plaintiff in a significant civil rights case.[33]

After Flemming's encounter on the bus, Modjeska Simkins convinced her to file a lawsuit against the bus company. Thus, even before Rosa Parks's arrest in Montgomery, Flemming filed a lawsuit against South Carolina Electric and Gas, the corporation that owned the bus company. Simkins also recommended that Flemming retain a white attorney, Philip Wittenberg, who had represented other African-American plaintiffs in Columbia and won cases on their behalf. After retaining Wittenberg, Flemming charged the bus driver and SCE&G with violating her civil rights. She also sought $25,000 in damages for the injury to her stomach. Federal District Court Judge George B. Timmerman, one of two judges whose rulings against the plaintiffs had led to the *Brown* school-desegregation decision by the US Supreme Court, dismissed Flemming's case and forced her to appeal it. With the assistance of NAACP attorneys Thurgood Marshall and Matthew Perry, Flemming did appeal, to the Fourth Circuit Court of Appeals in Richmond. In July 1955 the Fourth Circuit, reversing Judge Timmerman's ruling, declared that segregated seating on buses was unconstitutional. The judges of the Fourth Circuit extended the *Brown* decision to public transportation, thereby reversing the *Plessy* decision of 1896. Eventually the case went back to Judge Timmerman's court, and in June 1957 a jury in Columbia heard the case. After hearing Christmus testify that he had not struck Flemming during the 1954 altercation on the bus and receiving biased instructions on the case from Judge Timmerman, the all-white, all-male jury refused to reward Flemming the $25,00 she had requested in damages.[34]

Nevertheless, *Flemming v. SCE&G* established the precedent that overturned segregated seating on buses in the South.[35] Although the District and

Appeals courts took three years to declare segregated buses unconstitutional and to deny Flemming compensation for her injury, her case helped Rosa Parks and the Montgomery Improvement Association win the 381-day bus boycott in 1955–56. Indeed, in *Browder v. Gayle* the US District Court for the middle district of Alabama essentially adopted the ruling of the Fourth Circuit in *Flemming v. SCE&G* to end segregated seating on buses in Montgomery, Alabama. Few people, however, know that Sarah Mae Flemming Brown's case established the precedent that made victory possible in Montgomery.[36]

As we have seen, Sarah Mae Flemming Brown, Modjeska Simkins, and Septima P. Clark were part of the generation of people who helped launch the modern civil rights movement in South Carolina. As the movement emerged in the late 1940s and the early 1950s, women who were not members of the middle-class social clubs also participated. In 1950, twenty African American citizens in Clarendon County signed a petition demanding better schools for their children. African American women who, along with their husbands, signed the petition suffered economic reprisals and harassment. One signatory, Annie Gibson, later recalled that she and her husband were evicted from the land they were sharecropping and were unable to find work to support themselves. Like Clark and Simkins, many African American teachers lost their jobs for refusing to renounce their NAACP membership. In 1955, Mamie H. McCollum, wife of the Orangeburg's NAACP president, was fired from her job as a teacher at Bowman Elementary School. In 1956, when the South Carolina legislature passed its law barring membership in the NAACP for state, county and municipal employees, twenty-one teachers—eighteen of them women—in Elloree, South Carolina, resigned from their jobs rather than disown the NAACP. Six years later the Orangeburg School Board fired Gloria Rackley from her teaching job for refusing to renounce the NAACP and for her "civil rights activities." Rackley had sued to desegregate the city's hospital and led demonstrations protesting discrimination in city public facilities. She was arrested for using the "whites only" restroom in the county courthouse.[37]

Other young women also were drawn into the movement—not always by choice. After the *Brown* decision, J. Arthur Brown, president of the State Conference of the NAACP, decided to use his two daughters as plaintiffs in a case he would file to desegregate Charleston's public schools. In 1960 he filed the first in the name of his elder daughter, Minerva,[38] but when she graduated before the resolution of the case, he continued the case in the name of Millicent. When Millicent won *Brown v. Charleston* in 1965, she became the first African American student to integrate public schools in Charleston. Inadvertently, Millicent became a civil rights pioneer in South Carolina and suffered three years of harassment and abuse during her effort to desegregate Charleston's Rivers High School. In 1963, while the Browns were awaiting the outcome of their school-desegregation case in Charleston, Rebecca Monteith and her sister, Modjeska Monteith Simkins, had NAACP attorney Matthew Perry file a lawsuit to force the University of South Carolina in Columbia to admit Rebecca's daughter, Henrie Dobbins Monteith. Henrie won the suit in the spring of 1963, enrolled in the fall, survived harassment and ill treatment from some of her fellow white students, and became the first African American graduate of the University of South Carolina.[39]

Desegregation of public schools in Charleston and at the state's flagship university attracted the most media attention, but those students who served as desegregation pioneers in some of the state's smaller cities encountered some of the same problems and resistance. In 1964, June Manning desegregated Orangeburg High School. Unlike Millicent Brown in Charleston, Manning attended a "freedom school" during the summer to prepare her for the ordeal she would face once she enrolled in the all-white high school. But, as she later recalled, nothing could have prepared her for the three years of name-calling, harassment, and petty, gratuitous nastiness she faced at Orangeburg High School. She survived the three years and eventually attended and helped integrate Furman University in Greenville, South Carolina. After state troopers killed three students and wounded twenty-nine during a student demonstration at South Carolina State in her hometown in 1968, she decided to finish her education at Michigan State University.[40]

In 1969, four years after Millicent Brown had integrated Charleston's Rivers High School, there occurred in Charleston what historians have called "the last major campaign of the civil rights movement." Quite appropriately, it involved the status of African American women who worked as nurse aides and assistants at the Medical College of South Carolina hospital. More than three hundred African American women worked as nurse aides at the hospital, where they did some of the most basic work required to run a teaching hospital: bathing patients, cleaning rooms, emptying bedpans, and other tasks that white LPNs, RNs, and doctors did not want to do. For their efforts, these women were paid $1.30 per hour (below the national minimum wage of $1.60), abused, and mistreated by the white professional staff, who called them "monkey grunts" and "niggers." In the spring of 1969 they formed a union, Local 1199B, and affiliated with the AFL-CIO. They elected one of their fellow workers, Mary Moultrie, as their president and sought recognition from the medical college and redress of their grievances over pay and working conditions. The president of the medical college refused to meet with twelve of their representatives. In his absence the twelve women staged a sit-in in his office and were fired.

To protest the arbitrary firing of their representatives, the women in Local 1199B went out on a 115-day strike. The strike was joined by 450 women from the city's two hospitals, and the women raised the community's awareness of their cause with demonstrations, picketing, marches, and a boycott of downtown stores. To support their cause, the women argued that they were fighting for the basic rights given to most American workers: the right to receive livable wages, decent working conditions, and collective bargaining. The strike received national attention, and the women's cause received support from SCLC. Coretta Scott King, Ralph Abernathy, and Andrew Young journeyed to Charleston to join the women in marches and demonstrations. After a series of confrontations with the police, the imposition of a curfew, and the mobilization of the National Guard to quell the violence that accompanied the strike, the women won most of the concessions they had sought. Their wages were raised to the national minimum, $1.60; the 12 women who had been fired were rehired; and the medical college instituted a six-point grievance procedure and created a credit union for its workers. The medical college did not recognize Local 1199B or agree to collective bargaining, but the women felt that they had won something even more important—respect and dignity. No longer would they allow the administration and staff at the Medical College of South Carolina hospital to treat them as less than first-class citizens.[41]

As the "last major campaign in the civil rights movement," the strike by the women at the Medical College of South Carolina symbolized what African American women had sought from the beginning of their participation in the movements for racial uplift and civil rights: defense of their honor and human dignity. African American women in South Carolina had participated in movements for racial uplift and civil rights primarily to improve the lives of their families and to support the African American community in general, but the 1969 hospital strike brought their efforts full circle—back to a demand for honor and dignity for themselves. Moreover, whereas earlier organizational activity in the state had been led primarily by middle-class African American women such as Septima Clark, Modjeska Simkins, and the women in the churches and social clubs, the hospital strike symbolized the emergence of grassroots leaders such as Mary Moultrie who were ready to act in their own behalf by demanding treatment equal to that of any other citizen in South Carolina. The "last major campaign of the civil rights movement," led by women, symbolized both the success of the movement and the need to continue it.

Notes

1. For sources that document the tendency to emphasize the leadership role of men in the civil rights movement in South Carolina, see Edward Ball and Edwina Whitlock Harleston, *Sweet Hell Inside: The Rise of An Elite Black Family in the Segregated South* (New York: Harper Perennial, 2002); William Lewis Burke, Belinda F. Gergel, and Randall F. Kennedy, *Matthew Perry: The Man and His Times, and His Legacy* (Columbia: University of South Carolina Press, 2004); Sonny DuBose, *The Road to Brown: The Leadership of a Soldier of the Cross, Rev. J. A. DeLaine: Recollections of Courage* (Orangeburg, S.C.: Williams Publishing, 2002); R. Scott Baker, *Paradoxes of Desegregation: African American Struggles for Educational Equity in Charleston, South Carolina, 1926–1972* (Columbia: University of South Carolina Press, 2006); and Peter F. Lau, *Democracy Rising: South Carolina and the Fight for Black Equality since 1865* (Lexington: University of Kentucky Press, 2006). In fairness, Baker and Lau provide considerable coverage of the role of women in South Carolina's civil rights movement, especially the roles of Septima P. Clark and Modjeska M. Simkins. It would be hard for them to ignore the considerable scholarship on the seminal role of Septima P. Clark in the movement in South Carolina, including her two first-person narratives: Septima P. Clark with Leggette Blythe, *Echo in My Soul* (New York: E. P. Dutton and Co., 1962), and Septima Clark with Cynthia Stokes Brown, *Ready from Within: Septima Clark and the Civil Rights Movement* (Navarro, Calif.: Wild Trees Press, 1986), and the numerous secondary accounts documenting her life. Here are several of those sources: Grace Jordan McFadden, "Septima P. Clark and the Struggle for Human Rights," in Vicki L. Crawford, Barbara Woods and Jacqueline A. Rouse, eds., *Women in the Civil Rights Movement: Trailblazers and Torchbearers, 1941–1965* (Bloomington: Indiana University Press, 1990), 85–98; Charles M. Payne, *I've Got the Light of Freedom: The Organizing Tradition and the Mississippi Freedom Struggle* (Berkeley: University of California Press, 1995), 68–77; and Jacqueline A. Rouse, "'We Seek to Know . . . in Order to Speak the Truth': Nurturing the Seeds of Discontent—Septima P. Clark and Participatory Leadership," in Bettye Collier-Thomas and V. P. Franklin, eds., *Sisters in the Struggle: African American Women in the Civil Rights–Black Power Movement,* (New York: New York University Press, 2001), 95–120.

Less has been written about Modjeska Simkins, but her role in the movement has been documented fairly well. See Barbara Woods Aba-Mecha, "Black Woman Activist in Twentieth Century South Carolina: Modjeska Monteith Simkins," (PhD diss., Emory University, 1978); Barbara Woods, "Modjeska Simkins and the South Carolina Conference of the NAACP, 1939–1959" in Crawford, Rouse, and Woods, eds., *Women in the Civil Rights Movement,* 99–120; and William A. Elwood, "An interview with Modjeska Simkins," *Callaloo* 14 (Winter 1991): 191–210. Even one of the most recent studies, based on a 2003 civil rights conference at The Citadel in Charleston, includes only one essay specifically about the role of women in the movement: Stephen Preskill, "The Developmental Leadership of Septima Clark, 1954–1967," in Winfred B. Moore, Jr., and Orville Vernon Burton, eds., *Toward the Meeting of the Waters: Currents in the Civil Rights Movement of South Carolina during the Twentieth Century* (Columbia: University of South Carolina Press, 2008), 222–38.

2. Woods, "Modjeska Simkins and the South Carolina Conference of the NAACP," 99–110; *Charleston Post and Courier,* February 13, 1998; Elwood, "Interview with Modjeska Simkins," 197; Modjeska Monteith Simkins to Governor Ibra C. Blackwood, February 25, 1931; Mrs. Andrew Simkins to President Franklin D. Roosevelt, October 28, 1938; Maloria C. Thomsen to Modjeska M. Simkins, October 31, 1938; Modjeska Monteith Simkins Collection, Correspondence, Reel 4678, South Caroliniana Library, University of South Carolina, Columbia, S.C.

3. Woods, "Modjeska Simkins and the South Carolina Conference of the NAACP," 107.

4. Lau, *Democracy Rising,* 135; Modjeska Monteith Simkins to the Honorable Olin D. Johnston, Governor of South Carolina, April 17, 1944, Simkins Collection.

5. Richard Kluger, *Simple Justice: The History of* Brown v. Board of Education *and Black America's Struggle for Equality* (New York: Vintage Books, 1977), 133–38.

6. *Columbia Lighthouse and Informer*, June 3, 1945, clipping, Simkins Collection, Reel 4702; Ada F. Coleman, "The Salary Equalization Movement," *Journal of Negro Education* 16 (Spring 1947): 240; Woods, "Modjeska Simkins and the NAACP," 108–9; Lau, *Democracy Rising,* 132–33; "Come, See and Hear Mrs. A. W. Simkins," May 20, 1945, flyer, Simkins Collection, Reel 4678.

7. Lau, *Democracy Rising,* 210–11; Woods, "Modjeska Simkins and the South Carolina Conference of the NAACP," 115. On October 23, 1955, *Charleston News and Courier* first published the fact that Simkins's name had been cited four times in HUAC exhibits on "communist front" organizations, Simkins Collection, Reel 4702. For Simkins's connections to "communist front" organizations and "known communists," see Mrs. A. W. Simkins to "Dear Fellow Citizens," a circular announcing a leadership training school for Negro Youth in Irmo by the Southern Negro Youth Congress, July 17, 1946; a letter, from S. Tanner to Modjeska Monteith Simkins, November 12, 1946, congratulating her on her election to the Southern Conference of Human Welfare; and a letter, from Paul Robeson to Mrs. Andrew W. Simkins, October 28, 1947, inviting her to a meeting with himself, W. E. B. DuBois, John Johnson of *Ebony,* Benjamin E. Mays, and others. All the correspondence is in the Simkins Collection, Reel 4678.

8. Woods, "Modjeska Simkins and the South Carolina Conference of the NAACP," 116; Modjeska Monteith Simkins, interview by Jacquelyn Hall, July 28–31, 1976, Southern Oral History Program, University of North Carolina, Simkins Collection, Reel 4678; Cherisse Jones-Branch, "'To Speak When and Where I Can': African American Women's Political Activism in South Carolina in the 1940s and 1950s," *South Carolina Historical Magazine* 17 (July 2006): 217–20. Articles in the following newspapers document Simkins's work with the Richland County Citizens' Committee and her three campaigns for elective office: *The Columbia State,* January 12 and February 23, 1966, May 3, 1973, June 28, 1981, and January 28, 1984; *Columbia Palmetto Leader,* March 26, 1966; *Columbia Record,* February 18, 1966, October 7, 1976, April 3, 1981, March 2, 1983, and July 31, 1983. All are in the Simkins Collection, Reel 4704.

9. *The Columbia State,* June 28, 1981, Simkins Collection, Reel 4678; *The Columbia State,* April 10, 1992, Simkins Collection, Reel 4704.

10. McFadden, "Septima P. Clark and the Struggle for Human Rights," 85–87; Clark, *Ready from Within,* 104.

11. Clark, *Ready from Within,* 114–17; Septima Clark, "An Experiment in Individualized Instruction in Reading in a Sixth Grade Class" (Master's thesis, Hampton Institute, 1946), Box 15, Folder 4, Septima Poinsette Clark Papers, Avery Research Center for African American History and Culture, College of Charleston, Charleston, S.C.

12. Clark, *Ready from Within,* 35–36, 117.

13. "Septima Poinsette Clark: Educator Humanitarian," Box 1, Folder 6, Septima Poinsette Clark Papers; Septima P. Clark to Elizabeth Waring, September 3 and 23, 1951, Box 1, Folder 1, Judge J. Waties and Elizabeth Waring Papers, Avery Research Center; Clark, *Ready from Within,* 117.

14. Clark, *Ready from Within,* 36–38.

15. Highlander Folk School was founded in 1932 as an adult-education center. It soon branched out to train labor and community organizers and, eventually, civil rights organizers such as Dr. Martin Luther King, Jr., Rosa Parks, and Septima Clark. Because of its success and its interracial clientele, it was branded a "communist training school." See Donna Langston, "The Women of Highlander"; Crawford, Rouse, and Woods, eds., *Women in the Civil Rights Movement,* 145–67.

16. Sandra B. Oldendorf, "The South Carolina Sea Island Citizenship Schools, 1957–1961," in Crawford, Rouse, and Woods, eds., *Women in the Civil Rights Movement,* 171–72.

17. Langston, "The Women of Highlander," 153–56; Oldendorf, "The South Carolina Sea Island Citizenship Schools," 172; Clark, *Ready from Within,* 48–51.

18. Bernice Robinson, interview by Sue Thrasher and Elliott Wigginton, November 9, 1980, Box 1, Folder 5, Bernice Robinson Papers, Avery Research Center.

19. Langston, "The Women of Highlander," 155–56.

20. McFadden, "Septima Clark and the Struggle for Human Rights," 90–95; Rouse, "Septima Clark and Participatory Leadership," 106–117; Oldendorf, "The South Carolina Sea Island Citizenship Schools, 172–74; and Peter Ling, "Local Leadership in the Early Civil Rights Movement: The South Carolina Citizenship Education Program of Highlander Folk School," *Journal of American Studies* 29 (December 1995): 399–422. For an example of the Citizenship School curriculum, see "Curriculum for Citizenship Education," Box 5, Folder 4, Bernice Robinson Collection.

21. Septima Clark's awards and tributes fill a whole box in the Clark Papers. Remarkable among them is a letter from Senator Strom Thurmond (who opposed black voting rights and civil rights through most of his life) congratulating her for the honorary degree she received from the College of Charleston in 1978. See Strom Thurmond to Mrs. Septima Clark, February 28, 1978, Box 1, Folder 6, Clark Papers. Oldendorf, "The South Carolina Sea Island Citizenship Schools," 179–80; Robinson interview by Thrasher and Wigginton; Langston, "The Women of Highlander," 163. The quotation is from Bernice McNair Barnett, "Invisible Southern Black Women Leaders in the Civil Rights Movement: The Triple Constraints of Gender, Race and Class," *Gender and Society* 7 (June 1993): 169.

22. "South Carolinians Are Refused Registration," *The Crisis* (October 1940), 324, and the *Chicago Defender*, June 7, 1941, February 28 and March 7, 1942, and April 29, 1944.

23. Jones-Branch, "To Speak When and Where I Can," 204–6.

24. *Chicago Defender*, July 29, 1944; Miles S. Richards, "The Progressive Democrats in Chicago, July 1944," *South Carolina Historical Magazine* 102 (July 2001): 219–37.

25. Lau, *Democracy Rising*, 199; Jones-Branch, "To Speak When and Where I Can," 209–11.

26. Jones-Branch, "To Speak When and Where I Can," 212–15; Lau, "Democracy Rising," 162.

27. Lau, *Democracy Rising*, 36–37; Jones-Branch, "To Speak When and Where I Can," 216–24.

28. Theodore Hemmingway, "Prelude to Change: Black Carolinians in the War Years, 1914–1920," *Journal of Negro History* 65 (Summer 1980): 221; Asa S. Gordon, *Sketches of Negro Life and History in South Carolina*, (Columbia: University of South Carolina Press, 1971; reprint of 1929 edition), 180–85; W. Marvin Dulaney and Damon Fordham, "Doing the Best They Could with What They Had: The WBEMC, 1920–1960," in W. Marvin Dulaney, ed., *Born to Serve: A History of the Woman's Baptist Educational and Missionary Convention of South Carolina* (Atlanta: Publishing Associates, 2006), 36–38; Cherisse Jones, "'Loyal Women of Palmetto': Black Women's Clubs in Charleston, South Carolina, 1916–1965" (Master's thesis, University of Charleston, 1997), 40–41; Edwin D. Hoffman, "The Genesis of the Modern Movement for Equal Rights in South Carolina, 1930–1939," *Journal of Negro History* 44 (October 1959): 361–68.

29. Lau, *Democracy Rising*, 37–38; Jones, "Loyal Women of Palmetto," 40–56.

30. W. Marvin Dulaney and Damon Fordham, "Doing the Best They Could With What They Had," and Alada Shinault-Small, "WBEMC: 1960–2005," in *Born to Serve*, 56, 62–64, and 75–77.

31. Cherisse Renee Jones, "'Repairers of the Breach': Black and White Women and Racial Activism in South Carolina, 1940s–1960s," (PhD diss., Ohio State University, 2003), "Introduction" and 112–30.

32. *The Columbia State*, March 30, 2003; Judge Cameron McGowan Currie, "Before Rosa Parks: The Case of Sarah Mae Flemming," in Burke, Gergel and Kennedy, eds. *Matthew Perry: The Man and His Times*, 81–94; and "Sarah Mae Flemming: Civil Rights Leader," http://scafricanamerican.com/honorees/view/2008/5/, accessed April 1, 2011.

33. *The Columbia State*, March 30, 2003.

34. *The Columbia State*, March 30, 2003; *Chicago Defender*, December 1, 1956 and August 24, 1963; Currie, "Before Rosa Parks," 93–94; and *Sarah Mae Flemming v. South Carolina Electric and Gas Company, Inc.* 239F.2d 277, Fourth Circuit Court of Appeals, November 29, 1956.

35 Flemming married John Brown during her legal proceedings in 1956. See Currie, "Before Rosa Parks," 91.

36. Currie, "Before Rosa Parks," 91. *Chicago Defender*, December 10, 1956, and *New York Times*, April 24, 1956.

37. "Annie Gibson," *Charleston Chronicle*, undated clipping, Avery Research Center Ver-

tical Files; Cecil Williams, *Out-of-the-Box-in-Dixie: Cecil Williams' Photography of the South Carolina Events That Changed America* (Orangeburg, S.C.: Williams Publishing, 2006), 12–14, 163.

38. Minerva Brown, a member of the NAACP Youth Council, eventually participated in Charleston's first sit-ins, in 1960. See William D. Smyth, "Segregation in Charleston in the 1950s: A Decade of Transition," *South Carolina Historical Magazine* 92 (April 1991): 110, 122.

39. Edmund Lee Drago, *Charleston's Avery Center: From Education and Civil Rights to Preserving the African American Experience* (Charleston: The History Press, 2006), 253–54; Stephen Lowe, "*Brown* on Trial: School Desegregation in Charleston, South Carolina, 1960–1964," *The Avery Review* 3 (Spring 2000): 33–56; *The Columbia State,* April 25, 1981, Simkins Collection, Reel 4704; Rebecca L. Miller, "Raised for Activism: Henrie Monteith and the Desegregation of the University of South Carolina," *South Carolina Historical Magazine* 109 (April 2008): 121–45.

40. *The Columbia State,* March 4, 2003. For the 1968 "Orangeburg Massacre," see Jack Bass and Jack Nelson, *The Orangeburg Massacre* (Macon, Ga.: Mercer University Press, 1996).

41. Drago, *Charleston's Avery Center,* 256 and 260–63; Steve Estes, "'I Am Somebody': The Charleston Hospital Strike of 1969," *The Avery Review* 3 (Spring 2000): 8–32; J. H. O'Dell, "Charleston's Legacy to the Poor People's Campaign," *Freedomways* 9 (Third Quarter 1969): 197–211.

8 Black Women Activists in Mississippi during the Civil Rights Era, 1954–1974

Tiyi M. Morris

> "Not needing to clutch for power, not needing the light just to shine on me, I need to be just one in the number as we stand against tyranny."
> —"Ella's Song," by Bernice Johnson Reagon

The modern civil rights movement, 1954–74, was a struggle built upon generations of black activism and the contributions of nationally recognized as well as largely unknown individuals. As demonstrated by recent scholarship, the contributions of the latter group—often local, grassroots activists—were indispensable to the successes of the movement.[1] In this grassroots effort, black women figured prominently as community leaders, particularly in the state of Mississippi. Most often in the position of "bridge leaders," creating and sustaining a local movement and serving as liaison between the masses and the formal leadership, many black women activists have been marginalized and sometimes rendered invisible in traditional civil rights history.[2] This invisibility, however, is a poor indication of the value of their contributions. Historian Charles Payne argues that in the Mississippi Delta during the 1960s, at the height of the movement, black women participated in greater numbers than men.[3] And race uplift took myriad forms, from working within a traditional civil rights organization to creating an autonomous organization to ensure that one's voice and ideas are not overshadowed by black male patriarchy, white paternalism, or bureaucracy.

In demonstrating how ordinary townspeople mobilized to advance the civil rights movement, this essay will highlight some women and organizations among the many whose contributions were vital to the Mississippi movement. On the other hand, as Bernice Johnson Reagon wrote so eloquently in "Ella's Song," many black women activists eschewed the spotlight, understanding that empowering people to action against oppression and attaining equality and justice were a much better reward than recognition.

The battles of the civil rights movement and the stages upon which they were fought are many. Mississippi, in particular, captured the national spotlight with events such as the arrival of the Freedom Riders, the integration of the University of Mississippi by James Meredith, Freedom Summer 1964, and the Mississippi Freedom Democratic Party challenge in Atlantic City, New Jersey. These major battles were the culmination of a long struggle by many people. Often characterized as the worst state in the Union for blacks, Mississippi was notorious for the "tripartite [social, political, and economical] system of oppression" that dominated black life.[4] This system held a firm grip on black life until the 1930s and 1940s, when the economic largesse based on cotton production was substantially reduced. A profitable, yet labor-intensive crop, cotton was a source of wealth primarily because of a cheap work force, which consisted mainly of blacks. After World War II, however, the need for the massive black agricultural force declined with the increased modernization of cotton production. Furthermore, fluctuations in cotton prices put many sharecroppers and farmers out of business. Others turned to less labor-intensive crops. With the loosening of the reins that had confined blacks to agricultural labor came a shift in the sociopolitical system that for so long had defined blacks' position in society. By lessening the possibility of white economic retaliation against social activism, these changes provided an avenue for effective black resistance. The destruction of the cotton-based economy upon which race relations had been structured allowed for positive developments for blacks.[5]

Despite the political impotence and economic hardship that characterized life for many black Mississippians, a few were able to obtain some measure of economic success. A small middle-class cadre of entrepreneurs, teachers, doctors, ministers, farmers, and federal employees (postal and railway workers) emerged, people who could initiate social movements with less fear of economic retaliation from whites. These individuals, some of whom are responsible for the creation of the first Mississippi chapters of the National Association for the Advancement of Colored People, were activists engaged in civil rights activity before the movement became fully entrenched there.[6] And of course women were among the ranks of this cadre, community leaders who fought to improve the lives of their fellow Mississippians.

Before the decades of the modern civil rights movement, women's organizations were preparing black women for the organizing and mobilizing that soon would sweep the state. One such group was the Mississippi State Federation of Colored Women's Clubs (the local affiliate of the National Association of Colored Women, which was founded in 1896). The importance of the MSFCWC to women's activism within the state is twofold: it provided resources for black Mississippians, and for many who participated in the movement it provided their activist beginnings. Furthermore, the MSFCWC was instrumental in demonstrating the potential and promoting the necessity of black women's leadership. When it was founded, in 1903, through the initiative of the Phyllis Wheatley Club of Jackson, the members dedicated themselves to pursuing and upholding the goals of the NACW through "the binding together of our women for social, moral, religious, industrial and educational betterment, with the fundamental object of raising to the highest plane, home, moral, and civil life."[7] Consistent with the NACW motto, "Lifting as we climb," the MSFCWC undertook numerous endeavors to improve the immediate quality of life for black Mississippians. These activities could be interpreted as merely social activism, typical of women's traditional roles, but to do so would be to grossly undervalue their significance. Given the context of the times and the racial climate in which they were active, their undertakings were inherently political in that they challenged the relegation of blacks to separate and inferior resources or, many times, the denial of services altogether. At the same time these women were supporting the black community through institution building and confronting the racist political structure that dominated the South. Their work ran the gamut from successfully petitioning the State Department to include black history in the public grammar-school curriculum and establishing a public library for blacks to providing scholarships for young black women attending college and encouraging black women to vote.[8] Additionally, these women were dedicated to establishing permanent, viable institutions for their communities. Through the efforts of the MSFCWC, Governor Paul Johnson and ultimately the state legislature approved funding for the Mississippi Negro Juvenile Reformatory (later Oakley School), a "state training school for delinquent, colored youth," which began operation in 1943.[9]

One member of the MSFCWC who stands out for her civil rights activism is the tenth president, Ruby E. Stutts Lyells, who served from 1944 to 1948. Born in Anding, Yazoo County, Lyells attended Alcorn State University, Hampton Institute, and the University of Chicago Library School, earning a B.S., an L.S., and an M.A., respectively.[10] Mississippi's "first professionally trained Negro librarian," Lyells was dedicated to black equality, especially in the area of educational opportunity. During the summer of 1954, following the *Brown v. Board of Education* decision, Lyells was one of a group of black leaders who met with Governor Hugh White concerning desegregation in the state. When a black male colleague expressed an acceptance of the governor's proposed segregation and equalization plan, Lyells said the comments were indicative of the internalized oppression that stems from segregation.[11] She was well known for her unwillingness to acquiesce to racist oppression and her penchant for holding other black leaders accountable. Lyells was a model of leadership for black women and men.

At a speech given at the twentieth reunion of Alcorn's class of 1920, Lyells passionately urged her peers to respond to the need for leadership and activism for black equality:

> It is not understandable why Negro leaders generally steer clear of pronouncements which may even remotely be construed as favoring the continuation of segregation. . . . So obvious is the fact that the only practical way to get the things Negroes hope for . . . is to begin working *now* in the present political framework. . . . Basic to cooperation between the races in attacking our problems is the assumption that change is inevitable and whether it is relatively peaceful or violent depends upon the resistance encountered.[12]

This excerpt is characteristic of Lyells' calls for immediate redress of black grievances. Through such leaders this legacy of community activism and responsibility for race uplift was passed on to younger members of the MSFCWC, who would become participants and leaders in Mississippi civil rights efforts.

One battle early in this era focused on equal pay for black teachers. Like the discrepancies in expenditures for black and white schools throughout the state, the disparity between black and white teachers' salaries was clear evidence of the reality of separate and unequal. In 1948, Gladys Noel Bates volunteered to serve as plaintiff in the NAACP suit for equalization of pay for public-school teachers. The daughter of local NAACP leader Andrew J. Noel, a US railway mail clerk, and Susie Hallie Davis, a homemaker, Gladys grew up in a fairly privileged home for a black person growing up in Mississippi in the 1920s and 1930s. Her mother refused to teach her and her older sister how to cook because Mrs. Noel did not want, in any way, to prepare them for the traditional occupation of black women in the South. Instead, Gladys and her four siblings were prepared for college, which each of them would attend. Initially Gladys attended her father's alma mater, Alcorn Agricultural and Mechanical College, to pursue a degree in business administration, but she completed her undergraduate studies at Tougaloo College after having left Alcorn to marry John Bates, the head coach of Alcorn's football team. She did not become the bookkeeper her father had in mind; instead she completed a B.S. in biology, initially hoping to pursue her own dreams of becoming a doctor. Realizing that the limitations imposed on black women likely would prevent her from earning an M.D., she taught school in North Carolina before returning to Jackson and taking a position as a science teacher at Smith Robertson Junior High School in 1944.[13]

As a member of the NAACP, the Progressive Voters League, and the Jackson Teachers Association and as the daughter of an NAACP "founding father," growing up a member of the Youth Council, Bates was practically destined to have a seminal role in shaping the conditions of black life in Mississippi.[14] When the Mississippi Association of Teachers in Colored Schools raised sufficient funds for the NAACP to file the pay-equalization suit, Bates stepped in as plaintiff. Not surprisingly, neither Bates nor her husband (a teacher at nearby Lanier High School) received a contract from the school board. This type of retribution for challenging white supremacy in Mississippi was commonplace, and it kept many of Bates's colleagues from openly supporting or even associating with her. Nevertheless, in spite of the isolation and white intimidation, Bates stood firm for herself and indeed for all black teachers. The Bateses received support from black organizations such as MATCS, which hired Bates in 1950. She remained in their employ until 1960, when, at her brother's suggestion, she and her family relocated to Denver, Colorado, to teach in the Denver public schools.[15]

At the conclusion of the nearly three-year case, in which she was represented by two powerhouses, Constance Baker Motley and Robert Carter, Bates lost on the grounds that the proper chain of command had not been followed and that she had not exhausted the administrative possibilities at her disposal prior to filing the suit.[16] Even so, there was a minor victory. Presiding Judge Sidney Mize declared that discrimination was the cause of the discrepancy in teacher salaries. To give the appearance that they were abiding by separate but equal, some school districts responded by increasing black teachers' salaries.[17] More significant, Bates's use of litigation was a foundational step for the movement in Jackson, signaling the possibility of future success.

Clarie Collins Harvey, one of Bates's contemporaries and, like her, a daughter of Jackson NAACP founding fathers, also provided key leadership for the local movement. Harvey was the daughter of Rev. Malachi C. and Mary Augusta Rayford Collins, a schoolteacher and a member of the MSFCWC. In 1916, Reverend Collins opened a funeral home and an insurance business of which Clarie would later become the owner. In 1943, Clarie wed Martin L. Harvey, dean of Southern University. Although the couple had no children, her "mothering instinct" fueled much of her activism. This activism included participation in the NAACP and the Mississippi Advisory Committee to the US Commission on Civil Rights on the local level and Church Women United, of which she became the first black president in 1971, and Women Strike for Peace on the national and international levels.

Perhaps Harvey's greatest contribution to the Mississippi movement was the creation of a women's organization that provided crucial leadership and mobilization for the movement—Womanpower Unlimited. Founded in May 1961, Womanpower was initially designed to organize and mobilize local black women in support of the Freedom Riders. Upon recognizing the value of its material and emotional support in this endeavor, Womanpower expanded its activism to address other key aspects of the civil rights movement. These endeavors included voter education and registration, in which Womanpower focused specifically on black women's political empowerment. Working independently by securing funds from the Voter Education Project as well as collaboratively with the Southern Regional Council, Womanpower held education and registration classes for all members of the community and canvassed for women specifically to engage in the political process.

In 1964, during the inaugural Freedom Summer, Womanpower members provided crucial material and emotional support for summer volunteers, largely through free food and housing. Womanpower's ability to generate resources for the project in addition to their "othermothering" of the activists was necessary for sustaining this project. As indicated in a letter from one of the summer volunteers to Womanpower:

> There is a very important way, perhaps the most important way, that the Mississippi Project has been able to be so successful. That is that all of the workers have been made to feel here that you are really glad for us to be here.
>
> We want to say something special to these ladies. . . . [T]hey kept us healthy in a very real way, and we are very grateful to them . . . We will miss much more than the food, much more than the vitamins—and we thank you for the real sense of being cared for that you gave us this summer.[18]

As Womanpower membership consisted largely of middle-aged women, like Harvey, they felt a sincere responsibility to take care of the activists, many of whom were young enough to be their children. Members of Womanpower also advanced the movement through school-integration initiatives—canvassing door-to-door to encourage parents to participate in school integration efforts and providing material and emotional support for children (and their families) integrating formerly all-white schools—and by soliciting funds from their national "Chain of Friendship" for all civil rights organizations working within the state.

Harvey created Womanpower as a "safe space" in which black women could contribute to the movement in Jackson without being subjected to the marginalization that often occurred in male-dominated organizations. As a result, these local women sustained the civil rights movement in Mississippi by generating new forms of activism among uninvolved populations, supporting the existing civil rights organizations, and improving the quality of life for members of their community. Additionally, Harvey's activism is significant because through her example she brought legitimacy to middle-class participation in the movement and inspired others to activism. Womanpower Unlimited also holds a prominent position in Mississippi history because it revitalized black women's social and political activism in the state. When the organization eventually disbanded in 1968 as a result of Harvey's belief that they had fulfilled their destiny, many members continued their activism by joining the newly established section of the National Council of Negro Women.

The NCNW was the architect both of Wednesdays in Mississippi (in 1964) and of Workshops in Mississippi (in 1966). The former plan was to foster effective inter- and intra-racial communication among Northern and Southern women in hopes of increasing racial awareness and civil rights activism. The latter, which evolved from WIMS, focused on economic development for poor blacks and whites in the state. The council's work in Mississippi would not have been as successful without the collaboration and leadership of local women such as Harvey, who strategized and provided local resources for WIMS; Annie Devine, who chaired one of the workshops in Mississippi; and Fannie Lou Hamer.

Hamer has received significantly more scholarly attention in recent years than most of the women discussed in this chapter, but her considerable contributions, in partnership with the NCNW, to the improved conditions of black Mississippians deserve recognition here. Living as a sharecropper during both her childhood and her adult life, Hamer was all too familiar with the poverty plaguing rural blacks. Thus, after witnessing the slow impact of political change on the day-to-day life of those in the Mississippi Delta, Hamer undertook efforts to effect immediate change in the lives of poor Mississippians. In 1966, Hamer organized one of the NCNW Workshops in Mississippi, bringing poor black and white women together to provide them skills, such as grant-proposal writing, and information, such as the availability of federal resources, that they needed in order to address their needs arising from poverty.[19] In 1968, with a grant from the NCNW to purchase pigs, Hamer established what she called a Pig Bank to provide poor families with food. Families would receive a pregnant pig and, once the litter was born, would return the mother pig to the bank. When two pigs from the litter became pregnant, those would be given to the bank as well to assist other needy families. By 1973, approximately nine hundred families had benefited from the bank.[20]

Hamer's major project was the Freedom Farm Cooperative in Sunflower County. Freedom Farm was designed to provide families with land and with vegetables to grow on the land. These projects represented the type of community development the NCNW supported and Hamer's role in addressing the immediate conditions of black poverty.[21]

A. M. E. Marshall Logan, a native of Myles, in Copiah County, was another key figure both in Womanpower Unlimited and in the larger Mississippi movement. Like many other women activists, Logan was heavily influenced by her independent, strong-willed father, and she followed in his footsteps. In a 1986 interview, Logan said: "My daddy wasn't afraid of nothing. . . . [H]e wasn't a mean man, he was a kind person and a very religious person, but he never took second step for nobody I don't care who you were and I guess I got that from him. And I've never been afraid of nothing."[22] After marriage in 1943 and moving to Jackson in the late 1950s, Logan became a traveling sales representative for the Michigan based A.W. Curtis, a distributor of George Washington Carver products. At that time, Logan began working with the NAACP and civil rights activism became a prominent component of her life.

Logan recalled that, in the meeting convened at Central Methodist Church to organize Womanpower Unlimited, "Mrs. Harvey said she had one person in mind [for executive secretary] and she didn't want that woman to refuse. All types of people were there PhDs, lawyers, teachers and ministers and I wasn't thinking anything about it at the time that she was talking about me. . . . [and, she said,] 'That's Mrs. A. M. E. Logan,' and I was just knocked off my feet because I'm just an insignificant person in comparison to the [others]."[23] This statement underscores the contributions of many local women who were instrumental in the Mississippi movement. They were not all middle-class professionals or the educated elite, but they did possess the courage, passion for justice, and determination to improve their community and sustain the civil rights struggle.

As executive secretary of Womanpower Unlimited, Logan was often responsible for overseeing and implementing daily tasks. She was central to the overall functioning of Womanpower, and her peripatetic experience became an added bonus for the organization and the civil rights activists. Logan recalls that because she owned a car, she was often the person called upon to transport activists around town. Known for her willingness to house civil rights activists working in the state, she opened her home to dozens of young people.[24] Furthermore, her work as a sales representative, which often took her to the rural areas surrounding Jackson, afforded her the opportunity to disseminate information about the movement and to mobilize women in various parts of the state. Logan's participation became an integral part of her life as she used all possible avenues to support other activists and generate support for the cause of Womanpower and the larger civil rights movement.

Vera Mae Pigee, a native of Coahoma County, was a prominent leader in the county NAACP, alongside Aaron Henry. As secretary of the branch she helped organize in 1953, Pigee encouraged NAACP youth councils to support civil rights activism.[25] The NAACP shied away from direct action as a national policy, but Pigee guided her young activists in this very direction, making the Coahoma County branch the most active in the state.[26] Prior to the arrival of the Student Nonviolent Coordinating Committee in 1961, Pigee was responsible not only for guiding the activism of many Mississippi youth and leading direct-action demonstrations, but also for "othermothering" them, creating an extended family of fictive kin for her daughter.[27] Although Pigee worked formally with the youth, this position also gave her contact with parents, usually mothers, who often were drawn into the movement because of their children's involvement.[28] As the owner of a beauty shop—a central business within the black community—Pigee, like Clarie Collins Harvey, held a position of status and admiration, thereby bringing respectability to movement activism.

Like voter registration, educational equality was a staple of civil rights activism. The all-black town of Harmony, Mississippi, was home to sisters Winson and Dovie Hudson. Winson Hudson's activism began in the 1950s when she worked with Medgar Evers to establish the Leake County NAACP, of which she would become president.[29] As an NAACP leader, she was instrumental in mobilizing voter-registration and school-desegregation efforts in Leake County.[30] In

1962, for example, when the county decided to close the Harmony school and seize the land as part of a school-consolidation process, the Hudson sisters and other members of their community filed desegregation suits.[31]

The Mississippi Freedom Democratic Party, an independent organization founded in 1964 to provide an alternative to the standard Jim Crow Democratic gatherings, was a prime means of challenging black disfranchisement in the state. Not only did the MFDP engage in consciousness-raising among black Mississippians and encourage them to participate in electoral politics, but this "movement-led organization" also cultivated political leadership among black women. Victoria Gray Adams, Annie Devine, Unita Blackwell, and Fannie Lou Hamer were central figures within the Mississippi movement and were part of the guiding force behind the MFDP. Each recognized the power of black participation in electoral politics and pursued this route as a means of black empowerment and institution building.

Raised in Canton, Mississippi, Annie Devine became involved in civil rights activism in the 1950s when she and other local leaders made plans to organize their community. When the Congress of Racial Equality established itself in Canton in 1963, Devine joined full-time, giving up her job as a saleswoman for Security Life Insurance Company.[32] Her job, like that of A. M. E. Logan, required that she travel and interact with many people. In the process she acquired skills and experience that were valuable to the movement. As a civil rights "strategist and policy maker," Devine was essential in organizing, mobilizing, and educating Canton residents.[33] By the time she joined CORE, Devine was in her forties, a mother of four, and a pillar in her community. She could offer advice and guidance to younger activists setting up shop in Canton. Devine's role as a bridge leader, acting as liaison between the community and incoming activists, was recognized when she was elected a state representative for the MFDP.

Victoria Gray was born in Palmer's Crossing, near Hattiesburg. When the movement reached Hattiesburg in the spring of 1962, Gray was among the first who attempted to register to vote. Soon she became an SNCC field secretary, and later that fall, when the SNCC organizers had relocated to the Delta, she became the project director.[34] In this capacity and with the responsibility for conducting citizenship-training classes, Gray became a priceless resource to her community. Not only was she engaging in political mobilization, but for many she also was providing the basic tools of literacy that had been denied so many blacks in the state. As a married mother of three, Gray helped organize the MFDP and was elected a national spokesperson for the 1964 Democratic National Convention, in Atlantic City, New Jersey, and served as president of the

Forrest County Voters League. In 1964 she ran for the US Senate on the MFDP ticket, and in 1965 she, Hamer, and Devine led the MFDP drive to unseat the Congressional representatives on the basis that they had been elected as a result of discriminatory practices.[35]

Born into a family of sharecroppers in the Mississippi Delta, Unita Blackwell grew up in Mississippi, Tennessee, and Arkansas.[36] She also worked as a tomato picker in Florida until 1962, when, in her early thirties, she returned to Mississippi and settled in Mayersville, Issaquena County. In 1964, SNCC representatives attending a Sunday service at Blackwell's church introduced her to the movement. Inspired by their message, she became one of eight who volunteered to attempt to register. This entrance into the movement was the beginning of a journey that would lead her to become the first black woman mayor in Mississippi in 1977. Soon after her attempt to register to vote she became an SNCC field secretary, encouraging blacks in Mayersville to register, and eventually was elected an MFDP delegate. In this leadership role, Blackwell not only organized and registered voters but also challenged the oppression blacks faced in the educational system.

In 1965, after students at Henry Weathers High School were suspended for wearing SNCC buttons, Blackwell spearheaded *Blackwell v. Issaquena Board of Education,* not only in defense of the students' freedom of expression, but also for the desegregation of public schools still operating under the separate and unequal segregation that had been outlawed by *Brown v. Board of Education* in 1954.[37] Outdated textbooks, unequal pay for teachers, and truncated academic years (to accommodate cotton picking) reflected the lack of control black parents had over the quality of their children's education. Blacks had established their freedom of speech rights, and now, under the *Brown* ruling, black students would be able to enroll in previously all white schools in the upcoming school year.[38] Consequently, because Issaquena County had only black schools, approximately fifty black students enrolled in Sharkey County schools in the fall of 1965. Few were able to endure the harassment and intimidation for the entire school year, but integration increased continually over the next few years. Eventually, however, white students enrolled in newly established private schools, and by the time Blackwell's son graduated high school in 1976, the recently integrated schools were overwhelmingly black.[39]

Like Hamer, Blackwell had grown up in an impoverished sharecropping family. And like Hamer, Blackwell became involved in efforts at institution building for her local community. In 1967, Blackwell helped found Mississippi Action for Community Education, a community-development program geared at cultivating indigenous leadership and institution building for Delta communities. There she continued her efforts to shape the social, political, and economic development of black Mississippians. Through activities such as the legal incorporation of Delta towns—which qualified them to receive municipal services (e.g., utilities and affordable housing) and job and investment opportunities—Blackwell and other MACE organizers honed their movement skills and strategies to improve the quality of life for community residents.[40]

Blackwell would also work for the NCNW to improve housing on a statewide level. The NCNW Workshops in Mississippi made them acutely aware of the deplorable housing to which Mississippi's poorest blacks were subjected. In an effort to address this basic need, in 1967 the NCNW pursued funding through the Department of Housing and Urban Development and the Office of Economic Opportunity as well as private enterprises such as the Ford Foundation. The result of their efforts was a federally funded home-ownership program for low-income families called Turnkey III. Two hundred pilot homes were built in Gulfport, Mississippi, and the success led to the development of similar projects in such cities as Raleigh, North Carolina; St. Louis, Missouri; San Antonio, Texas; New Orleans, Louisiana; and Elizabeth City, New Jersey.[41]

Blackwell's activism in these endeavors prepared her to become the mayor of Mayersville in 1977. She brought to this position a rootedness in the community and a grassroots orientation. And in this office she continued to improve the lives of black Mississippians, working to bring to her dispossessed constituents their birthright as American citizens.

In addition to their efforts in their respective communities, Hamer, Devine, Gray, and Blackwell maintained a grassroots focus that proved indispensable to the MFDP during the 1964 Democratic National Convention. Their leadership was legitimized when they were given the national stage as a platform on which to address their grievances. At the same time they refused to legitimize the all-white Democratic Party delegation from Mississippi by accepting Lyndon Johnson's proffered compromise: two at-large seats instead of being seated in lieu of party regulars. The MFDP representatives were not seated, but these grassroots activists propelled the fight for black equality in Mississippi into the national spotlight.

Reflecting on her activism, Unita Blackwell said, "We had no idea that we were changing the whole political future of America." Through their efforts to improve the lives of black Mississippians, these women were doing just that. The impact they had on the social, political, and economic climate of Mississippi cannot be overstated. One of the easiest areas in which to observe this progress is electoral politics. In 1964 there were six black elected officials in Mississippi. By 1970 there were eighty-one black elected officials. And by 2000 this number had increased to 897, of whom 267 were women.[42] These numbers reflect increased black participation in the electoral process—a direct result of the civil rights movement in general and of these women's efforts in particular. Expanded educational opportunities, Head Start programs, improved housing—the way of life taken for granted by many black youth today—all are results of the tireless efforts of these women and many more.

In examining women's activism, it is important to acknowledge their roles as "othermothers" and nurturers and how this shaped their activism and leadership within the movement. Unita Blackwell articulated a desire to get involved for the sake of her child, and Vera Pigee viewed participation in the movement as a form of education for her daughter.[43] Their activism was influenced by a desire to provide better opportunities for their children and a life free of the racism and oppression they themselves had experienced. They were compelled to stand up for children, as Blackwell did when students were suspended from Henry Weathers High School. Similarly, Annie Devine stated, "My kids had missed out on so many things they needed and I couldn't provide. My community had missed out on so many things that we needed, and it was denied, so I had no choice . . . but to get in and try to make a difference."[44] This "mothering" instinct was a key aspect to many women's involvement.

Considering the influence of women's roles as nurturers is not meant to diminish their contributions or relegate their activism to secondary or merely supportive work. Given the context of oppression for black people during this era, women's nurturing arguably can best be understood as a form of resistance against white supremacy and dehumanization. It was equal in importance to the activism of mainstream leaders and central to the survival and progress of the community and freedom movement. Black women's activism has incorporated mothering as a means of addressing the needs of the black community to ensure the survival of the race. According to black feminist scholar Patricia Hill Collins, black women who are community and political activists "work on behalf of the Black community by expressing ethics of caring and personal responsibility . . . [working to help] members of the community . . . attain the self-reliance and independence essential for resistance."[45] It is this ideology that propelled many black women to the front lines of leadership and allowed them to challenge the oppression that permeated Southern black life.

The women whose lives this essay has touched on are part of a tradition of black women's activism premised on the survival of one's community and with the goal of preserving and advancing black culture and society. Although such women often exist on the margins of history, their activism was central to the civil rights struggle and black equality in Mississippi.

Notes

1. See Vicki L. Crawford, Jacqueline A. Rouse, and Barbara Woods, eds. *Women in the Civil Rights Movement: Trailblazers and Torchbearers, 1941–1965* (Bloomington: Indiana University Press, 1990); John Dittmer, *Local People: The Struggle for Civil Rights in Mississippi* (Champaign: University of Illinois Press, 1994); Charles Payne, *I've got the Light of Freedom: The Organizing Tradition and the Mississippi Freedom Struggle* (Berkeley: University of California Press, 1995); J. Todd Moye, *Let the People Decide: Black Freedom and White Resistance Movements in Sunflower County, Mississippi, 1945–1986* (Chapel Hill: University of North Carolina Press, 2004); Emilye Crosby, A *Little Taste of Freedom: The Black Freedom Struggle in Claiborne County, Mississippi* (Chapel Hill: University of North Carolina Press, 2005); Jeanne Theoharis and Komozi Woodard, eds., *Groundwork: Local Black Freedom Struggles in America* (New York: New York University Press, 2005).

2. For a detailed explanation of the concept, see Belinda Robnett, *How Long? How Long? African American Women in the Struggle for Civil Rights* (New York: Oxford University Press, 1997).

3. Charles Payne, "Men Led, but Women Organized: Movement Participation of Women in the Mississippi Delta," in Crawford, Rouse and Woods, eds., *Women in the Civil Rights Movement,* 2.

4. Aldon Morris, *The Origins of the Civil Rights Movement: Black Communities Organizing for Change* (New York: The Free Press, 1984).

5. Payne, *I've Got the Light of Freedom,* 16–19; Doug McAdam, *Political Process and the Development of Black Insurgency, 1930–1970* (Chicago: University of Chicago Press, 1982), 73–77, 81–82.

6. The first chapter of the NAACP in Mississippi was established in Vicksburg in 1918. This branch, along with others founded in subsequent years, disbanded and was rechartered in the 1940s.

7. Geneva Brown Blalock White and Eva Hunter Bishop, eds., *Mississippi's Black Women: A Pictorial Story of Their Contributions to the State and Nation* (Mississippi Bicentennial Commission, 1976), 4.

8. Alferdteen Harrison, *Piney Woods: An Oral History* (Jackson: University of Mississippi Press, 1983), 61; White, *Mississippi's Black Women,* 23.

9. White, *Mississippi's Black Women,* 16.

10. White, *Mississippi's Black Women,* 9.

11. Charles Bolton, *The Hardest Deal of All: The Battle over School Desegregation in Mississippi, 1870–1980* (Jackson: University Press of Mississippi, 2005), 65.

12. Ruby E. Stutts Lyells, "A Look Ahead: What the Negro Wants" in *Vital Speeches* (Mount Pleasant, S.C.: City News Publishing Co., 1949), 661.

13. Gladys Noel Bates, interview by Catherine Jannik, December 12, 1996, University of Southern Mississippi Center for Oral History and Cultural Heritage.

14. Dittmer, *Local People,* 31.

15. Bates, interview by Jannik.

16. Bates, interview by Jannik, 35.

17. Charles C. Bolton, "Mississippi's School Equalization Program, 1945–1954: 'A Last Gasp to Try to Maintain a Segregated Educational System,'" in *The Journal of Southern History* 66, no. 4 (Nov. 2000): 801.

18. Sig to Mrs. Redmond, September 1, 1964, Rosie Redmond Holden Papers, Margaret Walker Alexander Research Center.

19. Dorothy I. Height, *Open Wide the Freedom Gates: A Memoir* (New York: PublicAffairs, 2003), 189.

20. Chana Kai Lee, *For Freedom's Sake: The Life of Fannie Lou Hamer* (Champaign: University of Illinois Press, 1999), 147–48; Deborah Gray White, *Too Heavy a Load: Black Women in Defense of Themselves, 1894–1994* (New York: W. W. Norton), 195–96; Moye, *Let the People Decide,* 155–57.

21. White, *Too Heavy a Load,* 195.

22. A. M. E. Logan, interview by Vicki Crawford, July 16, 1986, personal collection of Vicki Crawford.

23. A. M. E. Logan, interview by Tiyi Morris, September, 2000, Jackson, Mississippi.

24. Logan, interview by Morris.

25. Francoise Hamlin, "Vera Mae Pigee: Mothering the Movement" in Martha H. Swain, Elizabeth Anne Payne, and Marjorie Julian Spruill, eds., *Mississippi Women: Their Histories, Their Lives,* (Athens: University of Georgia Press, 2003), 284; Dittmer, *Local People,* 122.

26. Hamlin, "Vera Mae Pigee," 290.

27. Hamlin, "Vera Mae Pigee," 288.

28. Charles Payne, "Men Led."

29. Dittmer, *Local People,* 256–57.

30. Dittmer, *Local People,* 256–57.

31. Charles Bolton, *The Hardest Deal of All,* 99–100; Winson Hudson, interview by John Rachal, August 31, 1995, University of Southern Mississippi Oral History Program.

32. Vicki Crawford, "Beyond the Human Self: Grassroots Activists in the Mississippi Civil Rights Movement" in Crawford, Rouse, and Woods, eds., *Women in the Civil Rights Movement,* 18.

33. Crawford, "Beyond the Human Self," 20.

34. Dittmer, *Local People,* 181–82.

35. Unita Blackwell, interview by Mike Garvey, April 21, 1977, University of Southern Mississippi, Civil Rights in Mississippi Digital Archive.

36. Unita Blackwell with JoAnne Prichard Morris, *Barefootin': Life Lessons from the Road to Freedom* (New York: Crown Publishers, 2006), 133–35.

37. Blackwell with Morris, *Barefootin,'* 135–39.

38. Blackwell with Morris, *Barefootin,'* 143.

39. Pratt Center for Community Development: Planning, Building, and Educating for

Change. "Mississippi Action for Community Education (MACE) Greenville, Miss." Pratt Center for Community Development, http://prattcenter.net.

40. Height, *Open Wide the Freedom Gates,* 195–97.

41. David A. Bositis, *Black Elected Officials: A Statistical Summary, 2000* (Washington, DC: Joint Center for Political and Economic Studies, 2002), 18, 22.

42. Jenny Irons, "The Shaping of Activist Recruitment and Participation: A Study of Women in the Mississippi Civil Rights Movement," in *Gender and Society,* 12, no. 6 (December 1998): 703; Hamlin, "Vera Mae Pigee," 288.

43. Irons, "The Shaping of Activist Recruitment," 702.

44. Patricia Hill Collins, *Black Feminist Thought: Knowledge, Consciousness, and the Politics of Empowerment,* 2nd ed. (New York: Routledge, 2000), 189–90.

9 Black Women in the North Carolina Civil Rights Movement

Dwonna Naomi Goldstone

In September 1961, Willena Cannon was an eighteen-year-old freshman at the Agricultural and Technical College of North Carolina, in Greensboro. Originally from Mullins, South Carolina, Cannon had arrived some eighteen months after four African American students from North Carolina A&T sat down at Woolworth's in downtown Greensboro and ordered coffee.[1] When the waitress told the four young men that Woolworth's did not "serve Negroes," they remained seated until closing time that day, and the next day they returned with more A&T students. The sit-ins continued until Woolworth's eventually shut down its lunch counter rather than serve black customers. Within two months, however, the sit-in tactic had spread to fifty-four cities in nine states. After six months of protests, Woolworth's manager C. L. Harris agreed it was time to allow African Americans to eat at the lunch counter. Still, by the time Willena Cannon arrived in Greensboro, only Woolworth's and Kress's served black customers at their lunch counters. There was more work to do to integrate downtown Greensboro.[2]

Though the news of the sit-ins had not reached Mullins (such news was often suppressed), Cannon got involved with the student movement shortly after her arrival on the A&T campus. "All that struggle in '60 meant only that we could go and eat at Woolworth's and sit on those uncomfortable little stools," she recalled. African Americans were prohibited from eating at other places, such as K&W Cafeteria, which, she said, "had good food and nice tables." Those African Americans who wanted to eat at K&W had to "go to a window and buy the food and then walk down the street to eat it." Watching how whites treated black Americans caused Cannon "a lot of pain" and placed a heavy burden on her. By joining the protests, Cannon said, she "got rid of that burden completely."[3] That fall, A&T students focused their sit-in protests on two places: K&W Cafeteria and the Carolina Theater, where African Americans were relegated to the balcony. Some four thousand black students arrived at K&W Cafeteria, where police officers greeted the protesters and threatened them with jail. The students sat on the corner of Elm and Market Streets, a major intersection downtown, and filled the roads, "making a huge cross, blocking downtown Greensboro." "Then came the paddy wagons," Cannon remembered. "I was afraid. . . . But after a while, even if they treat us like dogs, we've got to stand up and fight. Even if you have to die." Even after a paddy-wagon fender pushed the students back, they remained resolute and continued the protest until the police arrested many of them, filling up the Greensboro jail and other makeshift holding spots. Many of these students risked being expelled from college and having a permanent criminal record, but they were fully prepared to make the sacrifice. "The things I did as a student—the sit-ins—felt so good. It was a taste of freedom," Cannon said. "Any time we won, it did something to me."[4]

The work of African American women in the civil rights movement continues to gain attention in both academic and nonacademic settings; indeed, this book sets the stage for identifying, exploring, and celebrating the contributions of these black women. The protests and civil disobedience demonstrations in which Cannon and other African American women participated in the years following the return of black soldiers from the battlefields of World War II are often left out of the stories of the modern civil rights movement and its leaders. Yet these events are important not just because they encapsulate what the women did but also because early "activism, leadership, and courage created the militant community-based activist infrastructure that was necessary for a later mass movement to thrive."[5] As sociologist Belinda Robnett notes, black women served an important role in recruiting and mobilizing people for demonstrations. Because many African Americans—especially in rural areas—believed that joining the movement would get them killed or would "[stir] up trouble in their communities," civil rights activists employed "specific methods of recruitment" in order to "persuade the masses to risk their lives for the movement." The purveyors of the message were most often women.[6] This was true in North Carolina, where the physical and psychological strength of African American women served them both in leadership and in behind-the-scenes roles in a civil rights movement that would not have been successful without them.

The February 1, 1960, Greensboro sit-ins are one such example. Generally the story is told from the perspective of the four male North Carolina A&T students who sat down at the Woolworth's lunch counter and waited to be served. But African American women from Bennett College served as the "foot soldiers for the sit-in movement by providing pickets, marchers, and canvassers."[7] In fact, during the sit-in movement, "as much as forty percent of Bennett College's student body was in the local jail, and they accounted for more than half the students being held at that time in the city."[8] These Bennett College women took their leadership cues from Dr. Willa B. Player, the school president from 1955 to 1966.[9] Not only did Player participate in the "organizational meetings to plan, strategize, and inspire each other," but when she was unable to attend, she supported the students by "making space available on the Bennett College campus for the meetings."[10] President Player always thought about the students first. Thus she rejected a planned November 1959 sit-in because "the disruption ... would occur at the end of the semester when many students were leaving for the holiday break." And in 1963, when several students were arrested after a demonstration to force the desegregation of public accommodations in Greensboro, President Player refused to order Bennett students back to campus, choosing instead to send them their course materials and personal necessities. After a sit-in at the mayor's office, Player again refused to order her students back to campus. "They are part of this protest," Player declared, "and as long as they are willing to stand up for their beliefs until the problem is properly resolved, I'm not looking for an exceptional way to get them out of something that is very difficult, but very important."[11]

African American women at Bennett College did not begin their activism with the February 1960 lunch-counter sit-ins. In the 1930s, Bennett students picketed Greensboro movie theaters refusing to show movies that portrayed blacks and whites as equals. In 1951, Bennett students worked with the Greensboro Citizens Association to register voters. Nine years later they formed "Operation Door Knock" for the same purpose. When the men from North Carolina A&T staged their sit-in on February 1, they worked without the women on the frontlines. Three days later, however, women were among the protesters occupying the seats at the Woolworth's lunch counter. Within a week of the sit-ins, Gloria Brown of Bennett College and Ernest Pitt of North Carolina A&T became co-chairs of a newly formed Student Executive Committee for Justice, whose charge was "to set strategy, to keep the students informed about the demonstrations, and to recruit new protesters." As the sit-ins expanded, so did the charge of this group; they began to coordinate carpools and provide replacement protesters.[12] The SECJ also expanded its sit-ins to include the lunch counter at the Kress store, which was down the street from Woolworth's. During an April 22, 1960, demonstration, several Bennett College students were arrested along with others from North Carolina A&T.

The role of women in efforts to desegregate public and private spaces during the civil rights movement in North Carolina is not unlike that of women in other Southern states and cities. As a scholar of the movement recently noted, "Women took civil rights workers into their homes of course, but women also canvassed more than men, showed up more frequently at mass meetings and demonstrations and more frequently attempted to register to vote."[13] And, even if women were not in charge of organizing the demonstration, they were often active participants. On May 19, 1963, in Durham, North Carolina, for example, approximately five thousand African Americans—most of them women and girls—participated in what would be the largest mass demonstration in the city's history. Gathering in the parking lot of Howard Johnson's—the last segregated motel in Durham—students from North Carolina College and Hillside High School sang "We Shall Overcome," "We're Going to Eat Those Twenty-eight Flavors," and other freedom songs to protest segregation at the motel. When the police ordered the protesters to leave immediately, they refused, after which the police "backed up a bus and gunned the engine, blasting exhaust fumes over the edge of the assembled mass of humanity." When the students still refused to leave, the police "jerked, dragged and tossed [demonstrators] to the pavement, especially the female students."[14] Some 700 were arrested that day, and because the city jail only held 120, police were forced to house the students on three floors in the courthouse. The protests proved successful, though: Howard Johnson's eventually agreed to integrate its motel.

As the demonstration at Howard Johnson's suggests, black women often participated in demonstrations but were not necessarily leaders. On the other hand, many NAACP youth chapters had female presidents as early as 1956.[15] For example, North Carolina College student Guytana Horton was president of the statewide NAACP intercollegiate division, and Nancy Grady was president of an active NAACP chapter at DeShazor's Beauty College in Durham.[16] Ella Baker was another prominent face in the fight to overturn Jim Crow segregation. A native North Carolinian, Baker worked tirelessly as a grassroots organizer sometimes in a leadership capacity, but most often behind the scenes. Historian Barbara Ransby notes that over the course of Baker's life in the civil rights movement—from the 1930s until her death in 1986—she "participated in over thirty organizations and campaigns ranging from the Negro cooperative movement during the Depression to the Free Angela Davis campaign of the 1970s."[17]

Perhaps Baker's most important contribution to the movement was as the first national director of the Southern Christian Leadership Conference and then as founder of the Student Nonviolent Coordinating Committee and an advisor during its first six years. Baker was not a student (she was fifty-eight years of age) when she founded SNCC, but, according to Ransby, she "became a key source of support, guidance, and stability for the youthful leaders." Helping to "convene the founding meeting," Baker also "garnered space and resources, drafted many of the group's early documents, and advised its leaders on strategy, structure, and life." Most important, however, Baker served as a model for the young SNCC leaders. Many would adopt her political philosophy, which was based upon "militant antiracism, grassroots popular democracy, a subversion of traditional class and gender hierarchies, and a long-term vision for fundamental social and economic change."[18]

Some black women assumed both formal and informal leadership roles. Others just felt compelled to challenge customs designed to keep African Americans "in their place." One such person was Shirley Ramsey. In 1963, at age nineteen, Ramsey became one of the first African American cashiers in the Duke University dining halls. Three years later, on May 9, 1966, a white supervisor asked her to cut pies during lunch. Ramsey refused but agreed to bus tables in the men's dining hall that afternoon. The next day, asked again to cut pies instead of working at the cash register, Ramsey again refused. This time she was fired. An active member of Local 77 of the American Federation of State, County, and Municipal Employees, Ramsey used the grievance procedure to file a claim charging racial discrimination and demanding her job back. The grievance panel rejected her complaint at the final step because white cashiers now were being assigned work previously relegated only to black women. "Supervisors complied with Miss Ramsey's request [that white women share the work]," Local 77 wrote, "but fired her for making it."[19] Still, Ramsey's actions encouraged other black women to challenge racial discrimination at their campus jobs.

Iola Woods, a black maid who mostly cleaned dormitories, followed Ramsey's example. When Woods had been a Duke University employee for more than twenty-five years, a new workload policy required that she "clean twelve dormitory rooms, empty trash from an additional twelve, and clean two dorm bathrooms in one hour and twenty minutes' time." After receiving numerous complaints from its members, Local 77 met with Duke personnel directors to discuss workloads, but the loads were not reduced. On October 24, 1966, forty-two maids filed a grievance demanding that their workloads be reduced. All forty-two were turned down at the second or third steps. Only Woods and Dafine Evans continued to pursue their grievance. Evans eventually found a job outside the University, and Woods's request was rejected at the final stage. In response to the maids' work schedule, Duke University faculty and students established an official committee to "assist workers in their struggle." Calling themselves the Students, Faculty, and Friends of Local 77, the group wrote an open letter to the Duke community, requesting that "a student-faculty group . . . provide education and consultation in technical matters, assist with public information, help with fund raising, and serve to focus on public opinion around specific issues."[20] Eventually, after African American workers filed several more grievances, which led to picketing on campus, Duke University agreed to establish a new grievance panel. This new policy was brought about because one black woman refused to cut pies during lunch.

In addition to being in the front lines of demonstrations intended to integrate local school systems, black women served other important roles in North Carolina school-desegregation cases. Historian Christina Greene argues that "parental fears of retaliation against sons for real or imagined contact with white females" explains in part why African American girls made up the majority of "students desegregating Durham schools in the early years."[21] Throughout North Carolina and other parts of the South in the 1950s, white people's desires to maintain strict racial lines were based in part on their fears of miscegenation. Though this fear applied mainly to relationships between black boys and white girls, "few issues had the same power to send the defenders of the Lost Cause into a frenzy as did the volatile mixture of race and sex."[22] Thus, in the years following the 1954 Supreme Court decision in *Brown v. Board of Education,* white opponents of school integration often used miscegenation as their "rallying cry."

The first students to desegregate North Carolina schools were often subjected to physical and psychological abuse, a situation worsened by the fact that white adults often failed to intervene or to discipline the white offenders. In 1959, the first year of integration at Durham High School, African American Andree McKissick and her sister Joycelyn were the victims of racial taunts and harassment. As Andree walked to her English class, twelve white boys surrounded her and spat on her, but the teacher refused to discipline the boys because the "episode had occurred outside of her classroom." Joycelyn also experienced many racial incidents during her tenure at Durham High School. A student emptied a fountain pen on her new yellow dress, others tripped her in the hallway and shoved her into lockers, and yet another pushed her head into a toilet.[23]

As the civil rights movement continued into the late 1960s and early 1970s, some African American women used what they had learned in the movement to pursue feminist goals. Frustrated by the unwillingness of leaders to place black women in more prominent roles, African American women such as Anna Pauline (Pauli) Murray publicly linked issues of race and gender to advance the cause of both. Born in Baltimore, Maryland, and raised in Durham by her grandparents, Murray argued that black women had "an equal stake in women's liberation and black liberation." "By asserting a leadership role in the growing feminist movement," Murray argued, "the black woman can help to keep it allied to the objectives of black liberation while simultaneously advancing the interests of all women." One of Murray's most important contributions to the cause of civil rights and women's rights was to "use her experience and authority as a black woman to demonstrate that race and sex discrimination were inextricably linked." To this end, Murray campaigned to add sex discrimination to Title VII of the Civil Rights Act of 1964, writing in a letter to Lady Bird Johnson that "opponents of the amendment tended to intimidate women from speaking out on this issue on the ground that by doing so they will endanger the larger civil rights legislation. As both a Negro and a woman," she continued, "I feel this point of view is erroneous." When Title VII passed with the sex discrimination amendment intact, Murray then turned her efforts to making sure the amendment was enforced. In a March 1966 letter to Richard Graham, head of the Equal Employment Opportunity Commission, Murray wrote: "Unless the sex provision is vigorously enforced and the relationship between the two types of discrimination, race and sex, fully recognized, only half of the Negro population is protected."[24]

Murray's involvement with the women's rights movement began with her work for the President's Commission on the Status of Women. After arguing that the Equal Rights Amendment was an unnecessary constitutional amendment because "the Supreme Court could be persuaded to apply the equal-protection clause of the Fourteenth Amendment," Murray became acquainted with Dorothy Kenyon, a white feminist and longtime executive board member of the American Civil Liberties Union. Murray joined the ACLU executive board in 1965, and she played a key role in the ACLU decision in 1970 to establish a Women's Rights Project. Murray also helped found the National Organization for Women, though she left the organization a few years later. In explaining her decision to leave, Murray said that at a NOW conference she saw "no Catholic sisters, no women of ethnic minorities other than about five Negro women, and obviously no women who represent the poor." For Murray, her desire to advance the status of African Americans, women, and workers meant she was unable to "be fragmented into Negro at one time, woman at another, or worker at another."[25] With an executive board made up of leaders from the labor movement and from the black-freedom struggle, the ACLU afforded Murray a greater opportunity to work for the needs of all disadvantaged groups, so she focused her efforts on it.

Murray's contribution to the civil rights movement in North Carolina actually began in November 1938, some thirty years before her fight to ensure that gender was a protected category in the Civil Rights Act of 1964. At twenty-eight years of age and living in New York City, Murray applied to do graduate work in the Sociology Department at the all-white University of North Carolina in Chapel Hill. After being told that "members of your race are not admitted to the university," Murray wrote to UNC President Frank Porter Graham: "How much longer, Dr. Graham is the South going to withhold elementary human rights from its black citizens? How can Negroes, the economic backbone of the South for centuries, defend our institutions against the threats of fascism and barbarism if we too are treated the same as the Jews of Germany?"[26] For many historians, Murray's application for admission "serves as a model for civil rights strategy" prior to the movement of the 1950s and 1960s. Unlike other civil rights demonstrators, Murray worked not as part of an organization but as an individual woman, using varying tactics, constituencies, and degrees of radicalism to forward her causes. To garner support for her admission to UNC, Murray wrote a letter to the *Daily Tar Heel,* the student newspaper at UNC; she wrote a letter to FDR, which she released to the black press; and she wrote a letter to First Lady Eleanor Roosevelt. Eleanor Roosevelt responded, telling Murray that she understood "perfectly" but that "great changes come slowly." "I think they are coming," she wrote, "and sometimes it is better to fight hard with conciliatory methods."[27]

Murray contacted the NAACP to take her case and was referred to Thurgood Marshall. However, because Murray was considered a resident of New York and not of North Carolina, the NAACP refused to take her case, arguing that the state of North Carolina had no legal responsibility to admit her or to provide a requisite graduate education for African Americans in accordance with the Supreme Court's 1938 decision in *Missouri ex rel. Gaines* v. *Canada*—a "galling disappointment" for Murray.[28] Later she attended Howard University School of Law, where she first experienced sex discrimination. "The racial factor was removed . . . and the factor of gender was exposed," Murray recalled.[29] She dedicated her life to fighting for racial and gender equality: going to jail rather than accept segregated seating, providing grassroots leadership for the March on Washington, and helping found the Equal Employment Opportunity Commission. Yet, even as historians reconsider the importance of women like Murray, her contributions to both movements are often lost. She was unable to sue the University of North Carolina, but she believed that her activism was "part of a tradition of continuous struggle, lasting nearly twenty years, to open the doors of the state university to Negroes." "Each new attempt was linked with a previous effort," she said. "Once begun, this debate would not be silenced until the system of enforced segregation was outlawed everywhere in the land."[30]

Reclaiming and retelling the contributions of black North Carolina women in the civil rights movement gives historians a new way to look at the intersection of race and gender in the South and challenges "the orthodoxy of southern political history." Historian Glenda Gilmore argues that the time has come to "re-vision the southern political narrative from other angles" in order to "take into account the plethora of sources on African American and women's history." By doing this, she says, we can "test new ideas about the junctures of public and private space in political culture."[31] What these demonstrations also show is that younger generations of African American women in North Carolina and throughout the United States refused to be as tolerant of the slow pace of social change as previous generations had been. And for many of these women, participation in the movement—both in and behind the scene—gave them a sense of empowerment and marked the beginning of an era that no longer privileged race over gender. As Paula J. Giddings writes, "In times of racial militancy, Black women threw their considerable energies into that struggle—even at the expense of their feminist yearnings. However," she continues, "when militancy faltered, Black women stepped forward to demand the rights of their race from the broader society, and their rights as women from their men."[32] This, of course, was true for African American women in North Carolina during the civil rights movement years, and it continues to be true for us today. We must tell these stories because, as Giddings notes, it is black women who "hold the key to the future of America."[33]

Notes

1. The four North Carolina A&T students were Ezell Blair, Franklin Eugene McCain, Joseph Alfred McNeil, and David L. Richmond.

2. See Miles Wolff, *Lunch at the 5 & 10* (Chicago: Elephant Paperbacks, 1990).

3. Sally Avery Bermanzohn, *Through Survivors' Eyes: From the Sixties to the Greensboro Massacre* (Nashville: Vanderbilt University Press, 2003), 53.

4. Bermanzohn, *Through Survivors' Eyes,* 54.

5. Christina Greene, *Our Separate Ways: Women and the Black Freedom Movement in Durham, North Carolina* (Chapel Hill: University of North Carolina Press, 2005), 32.

6. Belinda Robnett, "African-American Women in the Civil Rights Movement, 1954–1965: Gender, Leadership, and Micromobilization," *The American Journal of Sociology* 101, no. 6 (May 1996): 1663.

7. William Chafe, *Civilities and Civil Rights: Greensboro, North Carolina, and the Black Struggle for Freedom* (New York: Oxford University Press, 1980), 180.

8. Linda Beatrice Brown, *Long Walk: The Story of the Presidency of Willa B. Player at Bennett College* (North Carolina: Bennett College 1998), 173.

9. Player, who had received her doctorate from Teacher's College at Columbia University in 1948, rose through the ranks at Bennett, first as a French professor, then as director of admissions, and finally as vice president in charge of instruction there. When she was appointed president, Player became the first African American woman to lead a four-year college in the United States.

10. Brown, *Long Walk,* 172.

11. Brown, *Long Walk, 172.*

12. Chafe, *Civilities and Civil Rights,* 117–18.

13. Charles Payne, *I've Got the Light of Freedom: The Organizing Tradition and the Mississippi Freedom Struggle* (Berkeley: University of California Press, 1995), 266, 425.

14. Greene, *Our Separate Ways,* 63.

15. Erik Ludwig, "Closing in on the 'Plantation': Coalition Building and the Role of Black Women's Grievances in Duke University Labor Disputes, 1965–1968," *Feminist Studies* 25, no. 1 (Spring 1999): 79.

16. Greene, *Our Separate Ways,* 96.

17. Barbara Ransby, "Behind-the-Scenes View of a Behind-the-Scenes Organizer: The Roots of Ella Baker's Political Passions," in Bettye Collier-Thomas and V. P. Franklin, eds., *Sisters in the Struggle: African American Women in the Civil Rights–Black Power Movement* (New York: New York University Press, 2001), 42.

18. Ransby, "Behind-the-Scenes View," 43.

19. Ransby, "Behind-the-Scenes View," 81.

20. Ransby, "Behind-the-Scenes View," 82.

21. Greene, *Our Separate Ways,* 73.

22. Greene, *Our Separate Ways,* 73. For other books on miscegenation, see Elise Lemire, *"Miscegenation": Making Race in America* (Philadelphia: University of Pennsylvania Press, 2003); Glenda Elizabeth Gilmore, *Gender and Jim Crow: Women and the Politics of White Supremacy in North Carolina, 1896–1920* (Chapel Hill: University of North Carolina Press, 1996); Grace Elizabeth Hale, *Making Whiteness: The Culture of Segregation in the South, 1890–1940* (New York: Vintage, 1999); Charles F. Robinson II, *Dangerous Liaisons: Sex and Love in the Segregated South* (Fayetteville: University of Arkansas Press, 2006); and Scott Malcolmson, *One Drop of Blood; The American Misadventure of Race* (New York: Oxford University Press, 2001).

23. Greene, *Our Separate Ways,* 74–75.

24. Susan M. Hartmann, "Pauli Murray and the Juncture of Women's Liberation and Black Liberation," *Journal of Women's History* 14, no. 2 (Summer 2002): 74.

25. Hartmann, "Pauli Murray," 75.

26. Glenda Elizabeth Gilmore, "Admitting Pauli Murray," *Journal of Women's History* 14, 2 (2002): 62.

27. Gilmore, "Admitting Pauli Murray," 64.

28. In this 1938 decision, the US Supreme Court ruled that the State of Missouri was in violation of the Fourteenth Amendment by denying African Americans the same educational opportunities as white Americans within the state.

29. Hartman, "Pauli Murray," 74.

30. Gilmore, "Admitting Pauli Murray," 65. For an additional book on Pauli Murray's life, see Pauli Murray, *Song in a Weary Throat: The Autobiography of a Black Activist, Lawyer, Priest and Poet* (Knoxville: University of Tennessee Press, 1989).

31. Glenda Gilmore, "But She Can't Find Her [V.O.] Key," *Feminist Studies* 25, no. 1 (Spring 1999): 137.

32. Paula Giddings, *When and Where I Enter: The Impact of Black Women on Race and Sex in America* (New York: Bantam Books, 1984), 7.

33. Giddings, *When and Where I Enter*, 357.

10 Southern Black Women in the Louisiana Civil Rights Era, 1954–1974

Shannon L. Frystak

In March 1953, in what appeared to be a harbinger of events to come, the Baton Rouge, Louisiana, city council passed an ordinance allowing blacks and whites to board city buses on a first-come, first-served basis, ostensibly ending segregation in public transportation. Whites would sit from front to back and blacks from back to front, and black and white passengers were not permitted to sit in the same seat, according to state law requiring the separation of passengers on inner-city routes. Since 1949, when the city outlawed sixty black-owned buses that served the black community, members of that community had been forced to contribute financially to a public-transportation system that excluded them from equal participation. The city council decision was primarily an attempt to make the Baton Rouge Bus Company—a monopoly—operate more efficiently, but many, both black and white, saw it as another move toward greater civil rights for blacks.[1]

When the Baton Rouge Bus Company issued a directive ordering its bus drivers—all of whom were white—to comply with the council decision, ninety-five drivers staged a strike, protesting the end of segregated seating. Accusing the local NAACP chapter of instigating the new ordinance, the striking bus drivers argued that it created a situation "in which Negroes seated in the front seats of the buses refused to move to make room for white passengers." The drivers called for a return to a system in which seats in the back of the bus were reserved for black passengers and in the front for whites. With all of its bus drivers on strike, the public transportation system ground to a halt, leaving twenty thousand daily commuters, two-thirds of them African American, hitching rides, using taxis, or walking.[2] For four days the bus drivers met with the city council.

On a Wednesday, the bus drivers' wives, some with their children, marched to the parish courthouse to persuade the council to return to the status quo. The women "stressed that they and their children were suffering because of the strike and urged the council to rescind the seating ordinance." On Friday, June 19, 1953, Louisiana Attorney General Fred S. LeBlanc ruled that the ordinance was "in conflict with the state statute requiring that separate seats or compartments be provided for white and colored races," thus the ordinance did "not comply with state law."[3]

That same day the strike, which had kept all Baton Rouge citizens off the buses, turned into a boycott by the African American community, keeping the buses nearly empty. In response to a radio plea by a member of the United Defense League, "a Negro inter-civic club organization," black citizens rallied in support of a boycott and stayed off the buses. The UDL promised free rides throughout the city, and true to their word, the next day Baton Rouge's black citizens provided cars and taxis, "cruising the bus routes flaunting large signs reading 'Free Rides.'" In some areas of the city, black female domestics were picked up at their homes and taken to work. The few blacks who did ride the bus, apparently unaware of the boycott, were approached and told not to ride. The drivers on two empty buses noted that on any given day approximately 98 percent of their usual passengers were black. The UDL considered the boycott "virtually 100 percent effective as far as Negro passengers are concerned."[4]

With Rev. T. J. Jemison as its acting president, the United Defense League served as the boycott's parent organization. Fannie Washburn, a housewife and a member of the local voters league, served as the lone female on the executive board. However, black community women were an integral part of the success of both the UDL and the boycott. Community leaders held a mass meeting after the first day; all in attendance agreed to continue the boycott. After the second day, a mass rally was held in which the UDL collected more than $1,000 to sustain the boycott. As Reverend Jemison presciently stated, "Baton Rouge will go down in the annals of history as an example of cooperation among Negroes." With "Operation Free Lift" in full swing, by the fifth day, the manager of the bus company announced that the company was losing as much as $1,600 a day. The UDL continued to hold nightly mass meetings with an estimated four thousand in attendance. By week's end, the manager of the bus company called the boycott 100 percent effective, stating that the company's situation was worsening and that if the "no riding" policy continued, it would force the company out of business.[5]

On June 24, 1953, the bus company and the UDL agreed to a new ordinance, which the city council adopted the next day. Similar to the original one passed by the city in March, it allowed blacks to sit on a first-come, first-served basis, but it also reserved a limited number of seats at the front of the bus for whites and at the back for blacks. R. Gordon Kean, Jr., attorney for the Parish of East Baton Rouge, said that the bus drivers had carried both black and white passengers for twenty years without any problems and that "during this time, the drivers have enjoyed pleasant relations with their passengers of both races." He hoped "that this relationship will continue to be pleasant." The UDL agreed to accept the new ordinance "under strong protest." However, they also announced that with strong financial support—having collected close to $7,000 at the weeklong mass rallies—they intended to pursue a lawsuit sponsored by the local NAACP. Consistent with its legal strategy to end Jim Crow in the South, and aided by New Orleans attorneys A. P. Tureaud and Louis Berry, the NAACP sought to test the validity of the attorney general's ruling and the constitutionality of Louisiana's laws governing segregation in public transportation.[6] That evening, after a mass rally with some eight thousand blacks in attendance at a heavily guarded Memorial Stadium, the seven-day bus boycott officially ended. Participants shouted "Stay off, stay off" and "Walk, walk," even as Reverend Jemison urged the black community to return to the buses. Jemison offered further encouragement, stating, "Justice is on our side . . . and, brother, it's on the way."[7]

In Baton Rouge, as in Montgomery and elsewhere across the South, black women, historically the majority of public-transportation patrons, had experienced harassment and intimidation daily at the hands of white drivers. As a consequence of the boycott, the "private misery" endured by many black women became "a public issue and a common enemy." After the black community mobilized, women were no longer alone in their daily battle for dignity.[8] And the Baton Rouge Bus Boycott provided a model for the much longer and more newsworthy Montgomery Bus Boycott, spearheaded and sustained in large part by Montgomery's black and white women. The Montgomery Improvement Association used the Baton Rouge boycott as the model for its free transportation system, mass meetings, and organizing of community leaders. The ministers of Montgomery, including Martin Luther King, Jr., even consulted with the leaders of the Baton Rouge movement before initiating mass action in that city.[9]

The civil rights organizations in Baton Rouge, as in most communities, were led mainly by men, and by black ministers in particular. In 1955, Reverend Jemison quickly assumed the role that Martin Luther King, Jr., had in Montgomery, negotiating a settlement with the bus company and, at nightly mass meetings, encouraging the city's black residents to stay off the buses. The church—historically the nucleus of protest activity—claimed a particularly strong following among women. As in Montgomery, women supported the Baton Rouge boycott by working as drivers or organizers or by simply remaining off the buses. Mrs. Alemnia Freeman, a black Baton Rouge resident, drove for the free ride system: "When the bus boycott come along in 1953, I was happy with that. We met with Mr. Matthews and Reverend Jemison and others. We had meetings, and I was available to get out and drive up and down the road, take people wherever they needed to go. It was like a daily job."[10] Another female driver said, "We got the bus people on the run and can hold out as long as they can."[11]

Domestics who refrained from riding were crucial to the success of the boycott. Reverend Jemison said, "I watched women who had cooked and cleaned the houses of white folks all day having to stand up on a long bus ride."[12] Now they refused even to ride. Patricia Robinson's parents participated in the bus boycott when she was a young girl. She recalled stories of her mother walking to work daily. "We started it," her mother stated, "We were in the forefront with our bus boycott." According to Robinson, her grandmother "talked about how they would stand on a different corner cause you couldn't stand on the regular bus corner . . . and somebody would pick them up and take them to work, come back and pick them up from work and take them home."[13] Indeed, without the organized dedication of Baton Rouge's African American female community, the mass action would not have succeeded.

Louisiana's African Americans, like black citizens of other states in the Deep South, found themselves contending with the socially, economically, and politically repressive Jim Crow system that defined mid-twentieth-century America. Even in New Orleans, arguably the most prominent and, in many respects, integrated city in Louisiana, African Americans were forced to contend with some of the worst forms of systemic and systematic racism. So vile was this treatment that, in the early 1960s, a group of black men established the Deacons for Defense and Justice, an armed resistance organization dedicated to ensuring the safety of Louisiana's black communities. Even in this environment, however, Louisiana produced some of the movement's most noteworthy and respected activists. And as in other Southern states, African American women were indispensable members of the civil rights movement in Louisiana.

In Louisiana, black women were significant actors in a tradition of dissent that existed well before what many historians term the beginning of the modern civil rights movement in the 1950s. In October 1924, for instance, police arrested a New Orleans female schoolteacher for moving into a house that she had purchased on a "white" block. The NAACP defended her, but a local judge upheld the state's segregated-housing ordinance. A few days later, when another African American woman apparently was undeterred by the court's ruling, police arrested her "for attempting to interfere with an officer" when she refused to stop construction on a house she had purchased in a predominantly white neighborhood.[14]

By 1930 the Louisiana NAACP had established nine branches that included prominent black women members. In Alexandria, for instance, Georgia Johnson presided over the NAACP attack on the system of unequal voting rights. In Baton Rouge and in Orleans Parish, respectively, Viola Johnson and Rosana Aubert worked with the NAACP legal team to end segregation in the public school system. In communities throughout the state, black women worked with the national NAACP to challenge discrimination in teachers' pay and to advocate equal treatment in teachers' unions. Thus by the 1950s, when the civil rights movement "proper" had begun, African American women were primed for more vigorous and direct challenges to the racial status quo. The 1953 Baton Rouge Bus Boycott only highlights the significant contributions made by Louisiana's black female community.

Little more than a year after the events in Baton Rouge, African American women in New Orleans sought justice on behalf of their children. At the end of every school year, thousands of Orleans Parish schoolchildren participated in the McDonogh Day (subsequently renamed Founders Day) ceremony, which honored John McDonogh, a white slaveholder who bequeathed most of his fortune for "the purpose of educating both sexes of all classes and castes of color." For African American children the event did more than simply pay respect to the man who had helped fund their education. It also paid homage to a man who, according to the *Louisiana Weekly,* was "hated and abused" by white New Orleanians for the charitable way he treated the African Americans who "worked" for him.[15]

In February of 1954, four African American women—Ethel Young (president of the PTA council of New Orleans), Emily Davis Thomas (principal of McDonogh 24 and representative of the Orleans Parish Principals Association), Veronica B. Hill (president of the League of Classroom Teachers and national vice-president of the American Federation of Teachers), and Mrs. E. Belfield Spriggins (a teacher at McDonogh 35)—met with the Orleans Parish School Board to challenge the way the McDonogh Day parade was organized. Since its inception, white schoolchildren had assembled, marched in a processional, and laid flowers at McDonogh's monument in Lafayette square while black schoolchildren were forced to stand, sometimes in sweltering humidity and unbearable heat, waiting their turn until all the white children had paraded by the monument.

The women expressed their dismay that by the time the African American children reached McDonogh's monument, the noted dignitaries in attendance and most "interested spectators" had already left. In addition, they cited the "extra hardship on colored children . . . due to the lack of toilet facilities for [their] group." "For those of our children who understand the significance of this parade," they continued, "it is a most humiliating experience. For the rest, the parade only serves to condition them before they are old enough to think, to second class citizenship." On behalf of black Louisiana parents and their children, Young, Thomas, Hill, and Spriggins requested an end to the decades-old discrimination against black schoolchildren so that the McDonogh Day Parade could "stand at last as a symbol of true American democracy."[16]

In response to their request that the schools parade in alphabetical order according to school district, the Orleans Parish School Board cited Louisiana's segregation laws, adding that it was forced to "go along" with the admonition of the police superintendent not to alter the format of the parade. Dr. Clarence Scheps, president of the school board, further noted: "We live in a community in which segregation is the law and we would not be doing our duty if we did not abide by the law. We operate under the law and will continue. It cannot be done or will not be done." In early May, a number of black civic, educational, and religious associations, including the New Orleans branch of the NAACP, the Louisiana State Conference for Labor Education, and Teamsters Local 965 called for a boycott of the McDonogh Day ceremonies. The NAACP asked all local school principals not to "impede aroused parents who refuse to permit their children to become a part of any mass demonstration fostering second class citizenship." It would, they added, be better to keep the "children home rather than see them participate in such an open display of segregation." Local civil rights leaders appeared on local radio stations and sent more than ten thousand letters to parents urging them to keep their children home that day.[17]

On Friday May 7, 1954, thousands of black schoolchildren stayed home during the McDonogh Day ceremonies. Citing only "token Negro participation," the local black newspaper called the protest the most "unified action ever undertaken by local Negroes." Among blacks who nevertheless participated in the mass demonstration were a number of middle-class women, including the original petitioner Ethel Young, the retiring principal of the all-black Valena C. Jones School, Fannie C. Williams, and the PTA president at Jones, Mrs. Simon

Marine. Williams said she "had been attending these ceremonies for some time," and as this was the last year before she retired she did not, as an American citizen, "want to miss this opportunity."[18]

School board president Clarence Scheps expressed his regret that "all Negro children did not participate in the ceremonies, because it means a great deal to them." Ethel Young countered that "the parents have spoken and gone on record as not approving of the second-class citizenship demonstration accorded their children at the biased McDonogh Day ceremonies." Marine added that she was "not discouraged. I worked hard for them not to go and I am greatly disappointed that even four children from my school had to go." The following year another mass boycott was called; not one African American child attended the ceremony.[19]

On May 17, 1954, ten days after the initial McDonogh Day boycott, the US Supreme Court ruled, in *Brown v. Board of Education,* that separate was "inherently unequal." Following this decision, the South saw the rise of white "massive resistance" campaigns. And because the South, like the rest of the nation, was in the midst of the Cold War, many of its residents were subjected to an extremist, anti-subversive campaign. People associated with civil rights were labeled "nigger loving communists" or worse. But even within this climate, Louisiana women sought to create a more just and democratic society. By refusing to let their children participate in the McDonogh Day ceremonies, they taught them, and the Orleans Parish school system, how to challenge white supremacy.

In the 1950s, black women also challenged voting restrictions across the state. The Louisiana NAACP, most of whose members were black, middle-class women, led the state in voter-registration efforts. In 1954, with fifty branches and more than 12,500 members, it was the largest civil rights organization in the state. As national NAACP leader Gloster Current noted in 1959, "When the NAACP began to organize in the South, much of the organizing was done by women." The NAACP not only encouraged its members to vote but also worked register African Americans by teaching them how to achieve equal citizenship rights.[20]

With the 1956 gubernatorial campaign approaching, the NAACP Steering Committee launched a massive voter-registration effort utilizing a "telephone pyramid project to increase the voting power of the Negro throughout the city." A network of middle-class black women from various organizations aided the voter-registration project. Ethel Young and the PTA council directed the program and were assisted by the nurses at Flint-Goodridge Hospital, one of only a few facilities in New Orleans that served the African American community.

Mrs. Elizabeth Drake of J. H. Rutter Rex Manufacturing Company, "personally accompanied a number of [her] employees to the registrar's office." One member of the NAACP Committee on Registration said of the women working on the west side of the city, "I think they have encouraged more new registrants during the drive than we have even though we have a larger potential."[21]

Both Oralean Davis (sister of A. L. Davis, a prominent New Orleans minister) and her daughter, Joyce Davis, were NAACP members, and both worked on voter registration efforts in the city. The Davises recalled registering black New Orleanians in "leaps and bounds."[22] And Leontine Goins Luke, a founding member of the Ninth Ward Civic League (created in the 1930s to educate and register voters), had a similar recollection: "It really was a marvelous effort. We held registration in the schools because they made it hard at the registration office. They not only give you some type of test, but then they wanted the people to recite the preamble to the constitution. Then they wanted them to bring a letter from the head of the household to verify that they were the person they said they were."[23]

By 1954, 25,524 African Americans were registered to vote in New Orleans, approximately 25 percent of the eligible voting-age public. The Ninth Ward boasted the second-largest number in the city. Considering the repressive political climate during these years, the results of work by women such as the Davises and Luke are significant.[24]

The NAACP was not the only organization involved in the registration effort. The Young Women's Christian Association of New Orleans, which had integrated in 1934, also took part in the campaign. Katie Wickham, an African American member of the NAACP, led the YWCA in a thirty-day registration drive. With the aid of Mrs. Venice Spraggs, a former nationally known newspaperwoman and member of the National Democratic Committee, Wickham contacted "key women in every town in the state" to assist in getting people to register "regardless of race, color, or religion." Out of this effort, and because the local League of Women Voters had yet to integrate, Wickham and other African American women founded the Metropolitan Women's Voters' League. Katie Wickham was its first chair, and women dominated the executive committee.[25]

In the more rural areas of the state, black voters confronted myriad obstacles when attempting to register. Yet, despite the difficulties, African American Louisianians, women in particular, continued to press for full citizenship. In April 1954, Sherman Williams, Wesley Harris, Florence Harris, Mabel Johnson, and Leola Enoch filed suit against the Registrar of Voters in Rapides Parish. The original petitioners, Florence Harris and Mabel Johnson, contacted the

NAACP for assistance after attempting to register "on several occasions." They believed that they had filled out their applications correctly and "were denied registration because they could not read and interpret the constitution to the satisfaction" of the registrar, James McCulley. On February 2, 1953, when Wesley and Florence Harris and Florence's mother, Mabel Johnson, again attempted to register, the registrar refused Florence Harris and Johnson because they had applied "on other occasions." When Wesley Harris asked McCulley why he would not register the two women, McCulley "became angry and hostile and forced Wesley Harris to surrender his registration certificate, which [he] then destroyed," disqualifying Harris "on the grounds that he was 'sassy.'" McCulley then ordered Harris out of his office. Fellow plaintiff Leola Enoch, who had attempted to register to vote "on at least four or five occasions," believed that she also had filled out her application correctly. McCulley rejected her on the grounds that she "could not answer the questions about the state and federal constitution" to his satisfaction. The petitioners argued that McCulley refused to register them "simply and solely on account of their race and color."[26]

The female petitioners were resolute in their determination to obtain their voting rights. After filling out six cards "incorrectly," Leola Enoch "finally executed a satisfactory card," but she subsequently was asked to read "a portion of the constitution dealing with religious freedom." Literacy tests, historically used to disfranchise blacks, worked this time. Enoch either "could not or did not comply, and accordingly, was refused a certificate of registration." Two white witnesses testified that they, too, had filled out their registration cards incorrectly and were denied registration. Thus, no discrimination was involved.[27]

The case went before the US District Court for the Western District of Louisiana. The justices opined that the plaintiffs had not established that McCulley "administered the registration laws of Louisiana as to discriminate against Negroes" and that "no evidence was evoked from the five plaintiffs themselves to show that the white people received better or different treatment." The judges reasoned that the plaintiffs were not allowed to register "because they could not interpret the constitution to the satisfaction of the defendant." They pointed out that some three hundred whites as well as eight hundred blacks were denied registration for the same reasons. Judge Hunter continued:

> Unless the court goes completely beyond the record, we do not see how we could decide that the administration of the laws by the defendant penalized Negroes any more than it did other citizens. We have reached our conclusions with an acute and sustained awareness of our duty to protect the constitutional rights of

> all. But we are not at liberty to impose on state and local authorities our conception of what constitutes a proper administration of their offices, so long as there is no discrimination and the laws are equally administered.

The NAACP filed a notice of appeal to the US Supreme Court on January 3, 1955.[28]

Harris and Enoch are typical of Louisiana's black female constituents in the incredible persistence of their efforts to obtain voting rights. In 1959 a black woman in Caddo Parish arrived at the registrar's office and, when asked to establish her identity, produced receipts from a doctor, a mail carrier, and a hospital. The white registrar accepted none as proof of identity. Nor would he accept, when she returned later that day, written evidence of her identity from friends and neighbors. When she returned the following day, the registrar informed her that she must bring in a registered voter to prove her identity; she returned with a registered African American voter only to be rebuffed that she must produce a registered *white* voter. She did just that, returning with a white storeowner as well as a white notary. Still, the registrar rejected both as sufficient evidence of the woman's identity. After these endless complications, and only after flexing such power and resoluteness, did the registrar let her to register to vote.[29]

Registering to vote in the South, thought by many a white Southerner to signal overt defiance of one's place in Southern society, could bring with it substantial economic and social risk. In Caddo Parish, blacks who attempted to register "were cut off the welfare rolls . . . [and] had difficulty selling their crops and things."[30] And yet, despite the seemingly insurmountable obstacles they faced in the registration process, African American women attempted to register to vote in increasing numbers through the 1960s as voter registration drives, particularly in the rural parishes, intensified.[31]

Although the movement waned in intensity at the end of the 1950s, the 1960s would bring a tenacious new generation of activists. In February 1960 the student-led sit-in movement swept the South, and Louisiana students quickly joined the fray. In Baton Rouge, seven student organizers, including Janette Houston, a junior at Southern University, asked Rev. T. J. Jemison to informally address SU students in hopes of getting them "excited about" participating in sit-ins.[32] Houston, one of the lead organizers, had a history of bucking the system. As a child she refused to sit in the "Negro" section of the bus. During her junior high and high school years, her defiance apparently surfaced so frequently that the bus drivers often simply drove her directly to the jailhouse. "It happened so much," recalls Houston, "my dad just got tired of it. He said 'I think I would do better just buying you a damn bus.'" Houston also refused to drink from the "colored" water fountains and remembers employees at Kress and Woolworth's "putting me out" for drinking from the white fountain and using white restrooms. Before the sit-ins, Houston had "led a few revolts on campus." In particular, she fought to get better cafeteria food after she discovered from her research that Louisiana State University, the white university in Baton Rouge, had larger allotments for food, libraries, and other amenities. By the time the sit-ins began, in February, Houston was primed for protest. At SU she became one of the seven student leaders, distributing flyers to the dormitories and organizing support.[33]

On March 28, 1960, as Houston walked to class, a fellow student informed her that the sit-in was about to take place. The students met at the men's dormitory and headed downtown, where Houston, freshman Jo Ann Morris, and five other students sat-in at the Kress lunch counter. The waitresses told Houston that she and the others would have to stand at the black lunch counter, which, Houston recalled, was covered with crickets. She refused and sat directly between two whites, who "started jumping up and running like I had the plague."[34] Police immediately arrested the group, charged them with disturbing the peace, and placed them in segregated jails. That evening the black community held a mass rally in support of the jailed students and called for a boycott of downtown stores over the Easter holiday. The following day, nine more students sat in, two at Sitman's Drugstore and seven, including Sandra Ann Jones and Mary Briscoe, at the Greyhound bus station. Again, they were arrested, but this time the students remained in jail for almost a week awaiting a court hearing. On March 30, three thousand five hundred students marched downtown to the state capitol and held an hour-long prayer vigil. Seventeen students, including the speaker—Major Johns—were expelled from the university. Eventually, more than one thousand five hundred SU students either were expelled or left the university.[35]

Although the sit-in movement in Baton Rouge ground to a halt after the student expulsions, organizers throughout the state continued their support for the SU student protesters. One such organization was the Consumers' League of Greater New Orleans, a black organization founded in 1959 in the wake of the assault by the Louisiana State Legislature on the integrated membership of the NAACP. The CLGNO was organized to fight the employment discrimination practiced by merchants on Dryades Street, the main shopping district for the city's African American community. On April 12, 1960, the CLGNO held a march on Dryades Street, denouncing the merchants' unwillingness to employ blacks *and* in support of the sit-ins. In what was heralded as a "double feature night," five expelled student leaders from SU, Houston among them, joined a mass meeting at the end of the march.[36]

As in other civil rights organizations, a significant number of the CLGNO members were African American women. Longtime activists Millie Charles and Madelon Cochrane, both members of the NAACP in the 1950s, joined the CLGNO when the Louisiana State Legislature forced the NAACP to cease operating in the state. Millie Charles began her activism when she challenged Louisiana State University to integrate its graduate school in 1956. For a time she was the only black student in the LSU School of Social Work. Later, in the 1950s, she worked with the NAACP on voter registration and with the CLGNO during the boycotts. Madelon Cochrane helped the CLGNO organize meetings and picket stores, lunch counters, and restaurants, and often she was arrested. Cochrane stressed the importance of women to the CLGNO: "Would you believe they listened to us then because they knew the backbone of this organization was women. We were there. Avery [Alexander] would call and say, 'Madelon, we need a meeting, such and such a thing has happened.' And I would call at 3pm and say we need to be at the Y at 5:00 p.m. and these people were there and it was mostly women. Maybe eight to ten men, but all the rest were women. We were the organizers."[37]

By May of 1960 the CLGNO had achieved only limited success. The number of African Americans hired by Dryades Street merchants had increased only nominally, and the lunch counters and restaurants had not desegregated. By that summer, however, a group of young black students working with the CLGNO decided on direct-action protests in New Orleans by sitting in. Local black college students Rudy Lombard, Jerome Smith, and Oretha Castle Haley, and a white student, Hugh Murray, had joined the CLGNO protests in April during the Easter holiday. As word of the sit-ins in Baton Rouge and across the country spread, New Orleans students came together to press for more direct action. Haley recalled, "Of course the same systematic problem of segregated lunch counters and other segregated facilities existed in New Orleans as in other places in the South." Finding themselves without support from older, more-established black activists in the city, the students organized themselves into a small cadre with the intention of beginning direct-action demonstrations in the city and then affiliated themselves with the Congress of Racial Equality. Most of the founding members of CORE were strong, militant African American women such as Haley, her sister Doris Castle, sisters Jean, Alice, and Shirley Thompson, Julia Aaron, Doratha Smith, Katrina Jackson, Joyce Taylor, Ruthie

Wells, and Sandra Nixon. Within a year, Haley became president of the New Orleans chapter.[38]

Having a woman lead such a high-profile organization deviated somewhat from the predominantly male-led character of the civil rights movement. In Louisiana, however, women often were appointed or elected to such positions. In 1954, for instance, a widowed mother of six and longtime civil rights activist, Doretha Combre, was named president of the Louisiana State Conference of NAACP branches, with overwhelming support, when the previous male president retired. In accepting the appointment, Combre betrayed lingering traditional views. "This is a position I did not seek or desire," she said. "I feel it is a job for a man. Since you elected me unopposed surely you see some good in me and my ability. It is my desire and determination to do all the good I can at all times for the advancement of my people."[39] In 1959, Combre was elected to a three-year term on the NAACP National Board of Directors, one of just three female members of the board.[40]

Thus, Haley was not the first woman to hold a prestigious position in the movement, but many of the successes in the state, and in the New Orleans movement in particular, occurred during her tenure as president of the New Orleans chapter of CORE. For example, she participated in one of the most significant Supreme Court decisions of the movement, *Lombard, et al. v. Louisiana,* in which the Supreme Court overturned a lower-court ruling that violated the Fourteenth Amendment. When the national CORE announced its intent to begin the Freedom Rides, Oretha's parents' home became Freedom Ride central and the unofficial CORE headquarters. Under Oretha's leadership, in early 1962, following battles between members regarding interracial relations, the New Orleans chapter of CORE purged its white members—three years before the call for Black Power arose and other civil rights organizations took similar action. Amidst much local and national internal dissension, Haley continued leading citywide marches and demonstrations to protest Jim Crow racism.

In the late spring of 1964, Haley left her position as president of the New Orleans CORE and joined the local staff of CORE in Monroe Parish as acting field secretary. In addition she worked with the national organization as a scout for the Fourth and Fifth Congressional Districts assessing the needs of black residents in those areas of the state. When she moved on to Ouachita Parish to work in voter-registration clinics, Haley found herself under constant surveillance and harassment by the local police. Despite the dangers, she continued her fieldwork, canvassing and directing a number of local offices. By November 1964 the national CORE office was so impressed with her leadership abilities that they hired her as field director for all of northern Louisiana, a position held by only one other woman in CORE.[41]

Oretha Castle Haley was not the only black woman in Louisiana to hold such prominent positions in CORE. In 1961 the national CORE appointed seasoned activist Mary Hamilton as their second female field secretary and the first woman to organize in the South. Although she worked in almost every state in the Deep South, Hamilton eventually settled in Louisiana, first working on voter registration in West Feliciana Parish, a particularly dangerous part of the state, and in 1962 rebuilding the New Orleans CORE chapter, which was still reeling from the purge of some of its members. Hamilton eventually concentrated her organizing efforts on Plaquemines Parish, working on voter registration. In 1963, Hamilton became CORE's first female Southern Regional Director. While working in Louisiana, Hamilton vigorously fought a contempt-of-court conviction she received for refusing to answer a county solicitor in Alabama when he addressed her as "Mary." Eventually the case found its way to the US Supreme Court, which overturned her conviction. This important decision struck "a blow at the practice in some Southern courtrooms of addressing Negroes by their first names."[42]

When the civil rights movement "proper" ended and segued into the era of the Great Society, black women such as Oretha Castle Haley transferred the skills they had learned and used in the movement to War on Poverty initiatives, bettering public education, and the fight for equality in the state. As historian Kent Germany notes in his work on the Great Society and New Orleans, Haley was a pioneer and a leader in citywide community efforts during the late 1960s and early 1970s. According to Germany, by 1970 Haley was "probably the most influential female activist in New Orleans."[43]

A number of other black women continued (and continue) exerting a profound influence on civil rights in Louisiana. In 1972, with Haley's assistance, Dorothy Mae Taylor became the first female state legislator. Leontine Goins Luke became a board member of the local chapter of the NAACP. Most notably, the Black Nationalist Virginia Collins, hails from Louisiana. Collins found her radical roots in 1938, when she joined the Southern Conference for Human Welfare, an interracial organization working for social, racial, and economic justice, which racial conservatives quickly targeted as a communist front group. She later joined the Women's International League for Peace and Freedom. Throughout her life she has worked to "promote quality education for black children, political power through the vote, and equal access to public accommodations." Collins changed her name to Dara Abubakari in the early 1970s when she became involved with the Republic of New Africa, in which she served as Vice President of the South, fighting for "land and nationhood for Black people in America."[44] Today, known as Mother Dara Abubakari, she continues her work on behalf of African Americans, and women in particular.

In a state that prides itself on its unique culture, cuisine, and musical heritage, Jim Crow racism and discrimination made Louisiana indistinguishable from any other state in the Deep South. And as in the struggle for human dignity waged in other Southern states, African American women were indispensable to the success of the black liberation struggle in Louisiana. Their leadership took many forms: they joined civil rights organizations; they created interracial alliances for the betterment of their children; they doggedly fought for the right to vote and for equal access to public accommodations; and they marched, sang, picketed, and sat in. In the late 1960s, when the movement waned, they used their talents to exert profound change in areas such as public education, housing, crime, and police brutality. And in the wake of Hurricane Katrina, African American female Louisianians have fought to reclaim their communities and their lives. One of the many lessons taught by Katrina is that the South, indeed, the nation, has a long way to go toward realizing what the civil rights movement sought to achieve in the 1950s and 1960s. However, the numerous ordinary and extraordinary actions of Louisiana's black female constituency certainly contributed to the much-altered status of race relations in the state today.

Notes

1. "City Transportation System Closed Down; Drivers Object to Ordinance over Passenger Seating," *Baton Rouge State-Times,* June 15, 1953, East Baton Rouge Parish Library, Baton Rouge, La.

2. "City Transportation System Closed Down," "Councilmen Air Views on Strike of Bus Drivers—Two Indicate Prompt Council Action; Bus Service Still Out," and "Prospects Dim for Settlement of Bus Strike—Council, Company, Union Hold Fruitless Conference on Issue," *Baton Rouge State-Times,* June 15, 16, and 17, 1953.

3. "Buses May Move Before Nightfall—Union Attorney Expects Settlement Today, Company Stands Pat" and "Buses Roll But Boycott is Started—Very Few Negro Patrons Seen on Buses; Private Cars Cruise City Flaunting Large 'Free Ride' Signs," *Baton Rouge State-Times,* June 18 and 19, 1953.

4. "Buses Roll but Boycott Is Started" and "Bus Boycott Continues as Parley Fails—Negro Leaders, City and Bus Company Officials Unable to Reach Agreement; Firm May Reduce Service," *Baton Rouge State-Times,* June 19 and 20, 1953.

5. "BR Negros May Petition," "To Propose New Bus Ordinance—Details Are Not Announced; Negroes Are Maintaining Boycott," and "Bus Case to Be Aired on Radio—Mc-

Connell to Cite Council Views; 'Free Rides' Continue," *Baton Rouge States-Times,* June 21, 22, and 23, 1953.

6. "Bus Ordinance Set For Action—Compromise Proposal Accepted with Protest; Test Suit Planned" and "Enact Bus Emergency Ordinance—Negroes Expected to Return to Buses Tomorrow Following Mass Meeting Tonight; Eject Student at Council Meeting," *Baton Rouge State-Times,* June 24 and 25, 1953.

7. "Bus Boycott Is Lifted, Traffic Is Sub-Normal—Action in Test Case Anticipated; Car Pools Operating," *Baton Rouge State-Times,* June 26, 1953.

8. Aldon D. Morris, *The Origins of the Civil Rights Movement: Black Communities Organizing for Change* (New York: The Free Press, 1984), 49.

9. Morris, *The Origins of the Civil Rights Movement,* 24–25, 56, 58, 64–65.

10. Alemia Freeman, quoted in "Baton Rouge Bus Boycott: The People," LSU Special Exhibit website http://www.lib.lsu.edu/special/exhibits/e-exhibits/boycott/thepeople.html.

11. "Bus Boycott Continues" and "BR Negroes May Petition For Separate Bus System," *Baton Rouge State-Times,* June 20 and 21, 1953.

12. Rev. Theodore Jefferson Jemison, quoted in "Baton Rouge Bus Boycott: The People," LSU Special Exhibit website, http://www.lib.lsu.edu/special/exhibits/e-exhibits/boycott/thepeople.html.

13. Patricia Robinson, interview by Erin Porche, n.d., listed on LSU Special Exhibit website, http://www.lib.lsu.edu/special/exhibits/e-exhibits/boycott/thepeople.html.

14. "Race Zoning Law Is Ruled Against in District Case" and "Segregation City Law Invalid," *New Orleans Times-Picayune,* n.d., and "Race Segregation Law Is Upheld," *New Orleans States-Item,* March 2, 1925, NAACP Papers, II, D.

15. "McDonogh Day Bias Ironic," *Louisiana Weekly,* May 8, 1954, Amistad Research Center, Tulane University, New Orleans, Louisiana, (hereinafter cited as ARC).

16. "Three Groups Unite To Protest McDonogh Day Discrimination," *Louisiana Weekly,* February 6, 1954.

17. "Tell Children to Stay Away from Celebration," *Louisiana Weekly,* May 8, 1954.

18. "United Action Marred By Only Two Exceptions," *Louisiana Weekly,* May 15, 1954.

19. "Not to Bow to McDonogh Day 'Jim Crow,'" *Louisiana Weekly,* May 7, 1955. See also Arnold R. Hirsch, "Simply a Matter of Black and White: The Transformation of Race and Politics in Twentieth-Century New Orleans" in Arnold R. Hirsch and Joseph Logsdon, eds., *Creole New Orleans: Race and Americanization* (Baton Rouge: Louisiana State University Press, 1992), 281.

20. "Annual Report, 1955," NAACP New Orleans Papers, Earl K. Long Library, University of New Orleans, New Orleans, Louisiana, and Gloster Current, "Women in the NAACP," *The Crisis,* April 1959.

21. "Committee on Registration Busy Buzzing Phones with 'Are You a Registered Voter?'" *Louisiana Weekly,* September 1954. At the time, the employees of the Ruters Rex Clothing Company were on strike for better wages and working conditions.

22. Oralean and Joyce Davis, interview by Kim Lacy Rogers, May 19, 1979, Rogers–Stevens Collection, ARC.

23. Leontine Goins Luke, interview by Kim Lacy Rogers, n.d., Rogers–Stevens Collection, ARC.

24. "Registration of Negroes in the City of New Orleans," NAACP Report, July 9, 1954, NAACPNO Papers. There were 14,172 black men and 11,352 black women registered.

25. "Women Vote Conscious Organize Voters League" and "MWVL To Open Vote Registration Drive in Ward 10," *Louisiana Weekly,* January 8 and March 5, 1955. Note that fourteen board members were women, four were men, and all were African American.

26. *Sherman Williams, Wesley Harris, Florence Harris, Mabel Johnson, and Leola Enoch v. James H. McCulley, Registrar of Voters for Rapides Parish, Civil Action # 4541,* NAACP Papers, File 212, "Voting, Louisiana, 1954–55," Library of Congress, Washington DC.

27. *Williams et al. v. McCulley.*

28. Opinion in *Williams et al. v. McCulley.*

29. Margaret Price, *The Negro and the Ballot in the South* (Atlanta: Southern Regional Council Publication, 1959), 19.

30. Dr. C. D. Simkins, cited in Morris, *The Origins of the Civil Rights Movement,* 111.

31. Price, *The Negro and the Ballot in the South,* 21, 70–71.

32. "Chronology of Southern University Demonstrations, 7 March–1 April 1960," cited in Adam Fairclough, *Race and Democracy,* 269, and in Janette Harris (Houston), interview by Mary Hebert, January 9, 1994, Special Collections, Louisiana State University, Baton Rouge, Louisiana.

33. Harris, interview by Hebert, January 9, 1994, Special Collections, Louisiana State University.

34. Harris, interview by Hebert, January 9, 1994, Special Collections, Louisiana State University.

35. Major Johns and Ronnie Moore, "It Happened in Baton Rouge: A Real Life Drama of Our Deep South Today" (New York: Congress of Racial Equality, April 1962), Copy on file in Special Collections, Hill Memorial Library, Louisiana State University, Baton Rouge, and "Jail Sixteen in La. Sit-Down," *Louisiana Weekly,* April 2, 1960.

36. "Protest March Hits Dryades St. Stores" and "Reinstatement for Eighteen SU Expelled Students Sought," *Louisiana Weekly,* April 16, 1960.

37. Madelon Cochrane, interview by author, December 11, 2001; Raphael Cassimere, interview by author, March 2, 2003. No collection of manuscripts or papers exists for the Consumers League of Greater New Orleans. Information on its activities was culled from newspaper articles, NAACP records, and interviews.

38. Oretha Castle, interview by James M. Mosby, Jr., May 26, 1970, Ralph Bunche Civil Rights Documentation Project, Moorland-Spingarn Center, Howard University, Washington, DC.

39. "Name Mrs. Combre NAACP State Conference Proxy," *Louisiana Weekly,* November 20, 1954.

40. "Mrs. Combre Named to NAACP Nat'l Board," *Louisiana Weekly,* January 17, 1959. By 1959 the NAACP boasted 108 female branch presidents and 669 female branch secretaries of 850 throughout the country.

41. Louisiana Citizenship Education Program, July 20, 1964, CORE papers; Field Re-

port, December 13, 1964–January 24, 1965, submitted by Oretha Castle, "Castle's Projected Schedule for February–March 1965," n.d., CORE papers, and Field Report, January 19, 1965, CORE 6th Congressional District Papers, State Historical Society of Wisconsin, Madison, Wisconsin.

42. Employee Record of Mary Hamilton, n.d., CORE Papers—Addendum, Reel 22, 129, Howard University Library, "Court Backs Negro's Bid To Be Addressed as 'Miss,'" *The Baltimore Sun,* March 31, 1964, Southern Conference Educational Fund papers, Box 2, Folder 11, State Historical Society of Wisconsin, Madison, Wisconsin.

43. Kent Germany, *New Orleans after the Promises: Poverty, Citizenship, and the Search for the Great Society* (Athens: University of Georgia Press, 2005), 84–86, 254–56.

44. Maria Hernandez, "Life of Virginia Collins," http://cat.xula.edu/unmasked/articles/428. See also Evelyn Kakano Glenn, "Cleaning Up/Kept Down: A Historical Perspective on Racial Inequality in "Women's Work," *Stanford Law Review* 43, no. 6 (July 1991): 1333–56; Simone M. Caron, "Birth Control and the Black Community in the 1960s: Genocide or Power Politics?" *Journal of Social History* 31, no. 3 (Spring, 1998): 545–69; and Dara Abubakari, "The Black Woman Is Liberated in Her Own Mind," in Gerda Lerner, ed., *Black Women in White America: A Documentary History* (New York: Vintage, 1972), 585.

11 African American Women in the Tennessee Civil Rights Movement

Bobby L. Lovett

The civil rights movement carried out in Tennessee by black women and men has a complex and an expansive history, but it has always has been about gaining socioeconomic equality and human and civil rights for African Americans. The movement, which reached its acme following World War II, had its beginnings in antebellum times. In 1780, most black residents of Tennessee were slaves who had arrived with white Tennessee settlers. When Tennessee became a state, in 1796, nearly 20 percent of its residents were African Americans. Each was counted as a person for the purpose of state representation in Congress, and the state constitution made no mention of the fact that slaves were property or, indeed, of slavery. Tennessee's free black citizens had civil rights and could vote until they were disfranchised in the state constitution of 1835.[1] As a consequence, some free blacks relocated to Ohio and Canada. For example, Sally Thomas, a quasi-independent slave laundress and operator of a Nashville boarding house, helped one of her three boys escape to the North and bought the freedom of her youngest. After 1838, because numerous escaped slaves also were fleeing the state, Tennessee newspapers carried hundreds of announcements offering rewards for their return.[2]

The modern civil rights movement in Tennessee had its origins in the Civil War, when 26 percent of Tennesseans were black. And from the beginning, many black Tennessee activists were women. In 1881, for example, Julia B. Hooks, a teacher, suffered arrest and a $5 fine for disorderly conduct for defiantly sitting in a whites-only section of a downtown Memphis theater.[3] In December 1884, Ida B. Wells, another Memphis schoolteacher, sued a local railroad for forcing her into Jim Crow seating. (A lower court ruled in her favor, but the decision was overturned by the Tennessee Supreme Court.[4]) When three black grocers accused of rape were taken from a Memphis jail and shot to death by a mob, Wells used the newspaper she edited, the *Memphis Free Speech and Headlight*, to condemn the accusation of rape and to assert that the men had been killed because they were competing too successfully against nearby white businesses. While Wells was out of town, her newspaper office was destroyed. Warned not to return, she relocated to Chicago and in 1892 published *Southern Horrors: Lynch Law in All Its Phases.* Frederick Douglass joined Wells in a national anti-lynching campaign, and in 1909 she became a founder of the National Association for the Advancement of Colored People.[5]

Native Memphian Mary Eliza Church-Terrell was prominent among black women who used social and civic clubs, benevolent societies, church auxiliaries, and professional training to promote black uplift and racial equality and to gain woman's suffrage. A founding member of NAACP, she also became president of the National Association of Colored Women's Clubs of America, which held its first convention in Nashville in 1897. The NACWCA challenged "racism, discrimination, and segregation" and fostered racial advancement.[6]

Black women in Tennessee pooled their financial resources to support the struggle for civil rights. When Tennessee implemented a Jim Crow streetcar law in 1905, for example, black citizens boycotted the cars in the major cities. Nashville blacks formed the Union Transportation Company to establish their own streetcar lines, and women were major stockholders. But even when those resources were not available, courageous women strove to meet the needs of victims of civil injustice. At this time, Tennessee paid pensions to former Confederate soldiers and their widows but left former slaves destitute. In an effort to meet this need, Callie House, a former slave from Rutherford County, organized and gave thirty years of her life to the National Ex-Slave Mutual Relief, Bounty and Pension Association, whose purpose was to enlist support for a federal slave-pension bill.[7]

Meharry Medical College graduates Francis M. Kneeland, Josie Wells, and Emma R. Wheeler helped bring better health care, nutrition, and medicine into Tennessee's urban black communities at a time when the state and white professionals refused to treat black citizens.[8] J. Frankie Pierce became a leader in juvenile delinquency reform for young black girls, and the state reform-school campus that she convinced state officials to establish a for black girls endured from 1923 to 1979.[9] In 1919 and 1920, Mattie E. Coleman, Nettie Langston-Napier, and J. Frankie Pierce led the effort to organize the black woman's suffrage movement in Tennessee. Sallie Hill Sawyer, Ethel Benson Beck, Harriett Hale, Julia Hooks, Josephine Groves-Holloway, Saint Mary Magdalena L. Tate, Lula Crim, and Mrs. W. D. (Anne) Weatherford were leaders in gaining social-welfare improvements, juvenile and day-care centers, YWCA units, and Girl Scouts of America camps for black citizens.[10] When the first NAACP chapters were formed in Memphis (1917) and in Nashville (1919), women gladly graced the first membership rosters. Black women participated in the biracial Southern Women and Race Cooperation Conference held in Memphis in 1920 for the anti-lynching campaign. (The association addressed an ongoing problem: by 1950, two hundred Tennesseans, including women, would be lynched.[11]) Marcus Garvey's Universal Negro Improvement Association—which advocated black separatism and self-help as alternatives to begging whites for freedom and equality—established Tennessee chapters. Minerva Alexander of Chattanooga served as a UNIA reporter and co-organizer.[12] Art teacher Francis Elizabeth Thompson at Tennessee Agricultural and Industrial State College was part of the late 1920s movement to infuse black studies into the curricula at black colleges so that the "New Negro" could proudly counter white claims that the Negro was uncreative, inferior, and unfit to participate in American prosperity.[13]

Blacks ratcheted up their civil rights movements. In 1942, following *Michaels v. University of Tennessee,* the state established a graduate school at Tennessee A & I State College. A woman received the first master's degree in June 1944.[14] On April 14–16, 1940, when the Southern Conference for Human Welfare—which worked to repeal the poll tax and Jim Crow laws—convened its second biannual meeting in Chattanooga, children organized by the Chattanooga Teachers Union, mostly black women, performed musicals at conference receptions.[15] In January 1946, Mary McLeod Bethune of Florida (who, along with Eleanor Roosevelt, was a founding member of the SCHW) arrived in Nashville to help with SCHW fund-raising. The sororities at Tennessee A & I hosted Bethune on campus, and J. Frankie Pierce, head of the Tennessee Federation of Colored Women's Clubs, hosted Bethune's tour of local black churches and mobilized other black women in this cause.

When a white male store clerk in Columbia, Tennessee, struck Gladys Stephenson, the mother of a black World War II veteran, in the face during a dispute over the repair of a radio, the son beat the attacker. On February 25, 1946, black men in Columbia armed themselves and defended the community against white men intent on lynching blacks. The NAACP sent lawyers to town, where they successfully defended twenty-four black men accused of wounding police officers. The Columbia race riot spurred increased NAACP membership. Black women in Nashville helped lead the drives.[16]

After 1950, black women played even more visible roles in the Tennessee civil rights movement. Roberta Church entered politics and in 1952 became the first black woman to win the executive committee seat for the Tennessee Republican Party. She then campaigned for the Republican presidential candidate, Dwight D. Eisenhower, and for the next thirty years gained federal patronage positions. Following *Brown v. Board of Education,* the district federal court in east Tennessee ordered that, beginning in September 1946, Clinton High School be desegregated. Lillian and Shirley Willis, Gail A. Epps, Jo Ann Allen, and Regina Turner were among the first eleven Negro students. Regina Turner's mother, Louise Turner, readied a gun and a dog to defend the house. Bobby L. Cain, Theresa Caswell, Minnie A Dickey, and Alva McSwain graduated from CHS.[17] The NAACP headquarters pushed Tennessee branch offices to organize massive voter registration drives. Women, especially in the Memphis branch (NAACP's largest) but also in Nashville, often won prizes for the most voters registered *and* the most NAACP membership subscriptions.[18]

Black women increasingly gained community support for their activist behavior. Black activists—especially children of black World War II veterans—specifically targeted Jim Crow. But they became impatient with NAACP legal tactics, which seemed to be dismantling Jim Crow much too slowly. In September 1957, Nashville, the state capital, began one-grade-at-a-time desegregation of elementary schools. Alice Smith told interviewers about telephone threats, about policemen assigned to guard the alley behind her home, and about how she and husband, Kelly, made the decision to let their child, Joy, be among the first Negro first-graders to integrate Nashville public schools.[19] By 1958, black college students felt angry enough to start public protests, sit-in demonstrations, and civil-disobedience tactics.[20] Black women, who, by the 1950s, outnumbered black men in Tennessee's historically black colleges and universities, played major roles as "foot soldiers."

In December 1955, before the Montgomery, Alabama, bus boycott drew national attention, African Americans in Tennessee had begun demonstrating against segregated streetcars. More than 70 percent of female black workers in Tennessee cities were domestics, and they had to ride the buses to and from their work in white homes. Even on intercity buses, blacks rode in the back. Blanche Pettus Rudolph, the mother of Wilma G. Rudolph, the famous Olympian, suffered this humiliation when she transported Wilma back and forth to Meharry

Hubbard Hospital for polio treatment.[21] In January 1954 a Memphis bus driver moving a resistant black woman to the back to accommodate more white riders, exclaimed, "There is still segregation in Tennessee." A few days later a Memphis bus driver pulled a pistol on another defiant black woman, telling her, "A nigger on my bus gets off at the back door."[22] These women involved their neighborhood clubs. Willa McWilliams, for example, with others of the Bluff City and Shelby County Council of Civic Clubs in northeast Memphis began protests against the segregated city bus system.

Women were prominent among Tennessee delegates attending the NAACP national conventions, which inspired their activism, and after attending the Tennessee NAACP Statewide Conference in Memphis in September 1959, they returned home fired up against Jim Crow.[23]

The most insulting Jim Crow practice in Tennessee was the segregation of downtown lunch counters, restaurants, theaters, water fountains, restrooms, parks, public recreational facilities, city auditoriums, employment, and the like—anything to remind working middle- and upper-class African Americans that they all were "blacks," devoid of standing and without full citizenship. Black customers often bought ill-fitting clothes, hats, and shoes because store owners forbade them from trying on merchandise before buying it. A "white" could be poor, corrupt, nasty, and ignorant but still was white. As used in this manner, the term transcended class and cast all blacks as dirty, diseased, ignorant, and inferior. Anti-civil rights signs read, "Keep Memphis down in Dixie" and "Nigger, don't you wish you were white?"[24]

James M. Lawson, Jr., who came to Nashville in 1958, brought nonviolent tactics to Tennessee, which enabled women to participate in public civil rights demonstrations. Diane Nash of Fisk University was among the small group who attended Lawson's first workshops. By November 1959 they were putting into practice some test sit-in demonstrations at downtown lunch counters. The test demonstrations broke off during the college holiday break. On February 1, 1960, word arrived that nine black students from the Agricultural and Technical College of North Carolina had been arrested for sit-in demonstrations in Greensboro. So that the spontaneous movement in North Carolina would not die, Lawson's group launched demonstrations. They sent scouts to count lunch-counter seats in order to hold reserves at First Colored Baptist Church who could replace demonstrators as they were arrested, maintaining control of the seats until the restaurants capitulated.

The Nashville sit-ins began on Monday, February 13, 1960, and became the most disciplined and successful sit-in demonstrations. A national television network filmed the sit-ins, and the film was used to train demonstrators in other cities. After a mass march from Tennessee A & I State University, Fisk University, and Meharry Medical College to the Davidson County Courthouse protesting the recent bombing of the home of civil rights attorney Z. Alexander Looby, Diane Nash boldly asked the mayor if he believed racial segregation was wrong, and in front of the crowd and the cameras, he responded "Yes." Nashville began desegregation on May 10, 1960. The *Nashville Tennessean* photographed Diane Nash, another young woman, and two male students peacefully eating lunch at a desegregated downtown lunch counter. Diane Nash had become head of the Nashville Student Movement when, as often happened, the designated male leader did not show up for a workshop or a meeting. In *Walking with the Wind: A Memoir of the Movement,* John Lewis recalled that Diane Nash was the leader of the NSM.[25]

Black women civil rights activists sometimes accepted the protective company of black male activists and male leadership. During peaceful marches and demonstrations, black males took the outside edges, protecting the women. Without fear of criminal punishment or shame—as in the days of slavery—white men threatened the black women with physical and sexual violence. White male policemen with clenched fists and batons would as soon strike a black woman—as in the days of slavery—as hit a Negro man. As a consequence of the white legacy of violence toward blacks, the civil rights movement became brutal and bloody. Elizabeth Harbour-McClain and her brother, William Harbour, both students at Tennessee A & I State College, were two of the "Horrible Seven" who formed the core of the sit-in demonstrators. When other demonstrators lost interest and drifted away, the seven continued the Nashville public protests against racial discrimination. When the sit-ins reached Chattanooga, Shirley Jones, Imogene Leslie, Betty Raines, Edna Sanders, and Wanders Wells were among its leaders. Josephine Maxey-Derrick was a chief plaintiff in the Chattanooga school-desegregation suit. Ann Robinson was among sit-in leaders in Knoxville. Cathy White and Acie McFarland were leaders in desegregating Lebanon, as were women in Jackson and other towns.[26]

Diane Nash, like many other black women demonstrators, held to the principles of nonviolence. She preferred filling up jails, refusing bail, doing the time, and refusing to join demonstrators who sought bail and release as soon as they were arrested. Nash and three others showed their faith by answering the call to join the "Rock Hill Nine" on the chain gang in South Carolina in February 1961. Later Septima Clark of the Highlander Folk School in Monteagle and Ella Baker, the administrator at the SCLC headquarters in Atlanta, sponsored a meeting of black college student representatives at Shaw University, North Carolina, on April 15–17, 1961, to organize a regional organization, the Student Nonviolent Coordinating Committee. Diane Nash became SNCC's director of projects to sustain activism.[27]

Even in the black churches, women received subordinate positions in the institutional leadership. Women did much of the hard work; men became leaders and spokesmen to the outside world. Most churches excluded women as deacons, trustees, and ministers. Even the First Colored Baptist Church of Nashville, with its great civil rights legacy and liberal theology, did not ordain women ministers until 1980. In heavily black west Tennessee, the NAACP held the leadership position in the civil rights movement, but by the early 1960s the SCLC had preacher-dominated chapters in Chattanooga, Knoxville, Memphis, and Nashville. Women were heavily represented on the membership rosters of these organizations, but the Congress of Racial Equality, the Fellowship of Reconciliation, and smaller grassroots organizations, which shared civil rights projects in Tennessee cities, included fewer local black women. Septima Clark of Highlander Folk School criticized chauvinist and sexist practices in SCLC offices. SNCC was accused, too, but in November 1964 it approached gender-based problems by distributing *SNCC Position Paper: Women in the Movement,* which acknowledged giving women subordinate roles in its daily work. The paper provoked discussion.[28] One respondent, Diane Nash, said she had little resentment that women had to work behind men because she knew that women also played important roles in the leadership and the offices. Women went "south to present a united front to white authorities; consequently, they suppressed their differences with the [black] male leadership."[29]

After 1946 the federal government began taking steps to improve America's racial image. And soon thereafter, African American women in sports were helping to dismantle America's Jim Crow society. Members of he Tennessee State women's track and field teams, the Tigerbelles, competed in the Olympics in 1948. They won four bronze medals and one silver in 1956. And in 1959, at the Pan American Games, they swept the relays. In the 1960 Olympics, America's entire women's relay team was represented by one institution, Tennessee A & I State University, and the track team, including twenty-year-old Wilma G. Rudolph, stunned the nation and the world by taking home four gold medals. Rudolph, who received three of those medals (including one that she and her teammates won in the relay) was invited to the White House to meet President John F. Kennedy, and she participated in many parades and ceremonies. Rudolph and her teammates still could not eat at most restaurants or sit on the main floor of a movie theater in vast parts of America, but the triumphant black legacy in sports helped soften the hearts of many segregationists.[30]

The Freedom Rides were one of the greatest expressions of black female leadership, but black men and white male reporters, writers, and authors usurped its public presentation. The stories and recollections favored male leadership, and the reporters, writers, and authors gave white participants disproportionate visibility. In May 1961 the Congress of Racial Equality (which had grown out of nonviolent protests against Jim Crow practices in Chicago and Washington DC) launched the Freedom Rides project using pairs of black and white volunteers to take interstate bus rides from DC through the Southern states to arrive in New Orleans by May 17—the seventh anniversary of *Brown v. Board of Education.* The two buses did well until they reached Anniston, Alabama. There the Ku Klux Klan ambushed the buses and burned one. After airlifting the survivors to New Orleans, CORE, fearful that students might die in future confrontations, announced the end of the Freedom Rides.

But a black woman restarted the project. From Nashville, Diane Nash telephoned James Farmer to say that if a few violent whites could stop the Freedom Ride project, the civil rights movement might die and that therefore SNCC would take over the Freedom Rides. Nash and fellow SNCC leaders consulted with Kelly Miller Smith (pastor of First Baptist Church, Capitol Hill) and the executive committee of the National Christian Leadership Council, and finally the adult civil rights leaders gave in to Diane and the students who insisted they were going to Birmingham to continue the Freedom Rides project. The NCLC gave Diane and the students their support and $900. Nash recruited ten local college students, including three females and two whites, and they took a bus to Birmingham. When they arrived, the Birmingham police arrested them, called the white students' parents to come and get them, and took the black students to the state line. During that ride, Catherine Burks, a graduating senior at Tennessee A & I, invited Police Commissioner Eugene "Bull" Connor to the Fisk campus "for breakfast" and, when they exited the car, said sweetly, "We will be back." Catherine Burks was the hero of the ride to the state line.

In the darkness of night the students made their way to a rural home and convinced its elderly black occupants to let them in. There they telephoned Nash, who told them to stay put until someone came to get them. Nash recruited Leo Kwame Lillard, a Tennessee A & I senior, who borrowed a large automobile from a white parent at George Peabody College and drove in search of the stranded students. When he found them, he drove them back to the Birmingham bus station. There the students, and ten newly arrived riders, sat at the station singing freedom songs until their bus arrived. When the bus reached Montgomery, a white mob brutally ambushed its riders.[31] Dr. Martin Luther King, Jr., together with Farmer and other CORE leaders, rushed to Montgomery and there vetoed Nash's dangerous proposal to march downtown. On May 21 a white mob attacked a black church in which Dr. King was conducting a mass rally. When the mob threatened to burn the church with the people inside, President John F. Kennedy persuaded the governor of Alabama to send state troops to truck the churchgoers to their homes. President Kennedy opposed the demonstrations, but Nash and the Freedom Riders refused to stop. After J. Edgar Hoover's FBI agents refused to stop the violence, Kennedy sent hundreds of federal marshals to protect the riders. When the project resumed on May 24, SNCC leaders blamed Kennedy for making a deal with racist authorities in Mississippi, permitting them to arrest some three hundred arriving riders. In November 1961 the Interstate Commerce Commission outlawed segregated interstate transportation.[32]

In August 1961, Nash and a few hard-core student activists attended a workshop for college students held at Highlander, returned to Nashville, and just to keep the faith, held one more demonstration against segregated holdouts in downtown Nashville. When Nash and the students were arrested, they decided to do the time rather than pay the fine.

SNCC next launched voter-registration drives in Mississippi. When she was arraigned in a Mississippi court, the pregnant Nash told the judge she would serve a two-year sentence and have her baby in jail rather than pay a fine for expressing her constitutional rights. Declaring, "You people are crazy," the judge let them go.[33] Newspaper stories likely led to the expulsion of eighty-three Freedom Riders and sit-in students from Tennessee A & I, but Pauline Knight, a graduating senior, filed *Pauline Knight et al. v. State Board of Education, Governor Buford Ellington, et a*l. US (1961), and the federal district court ordered that the students be reinstated.[34]

Maxine Atkins-Smith was an enduring civil rights leader in Tennessee. Born Maxine Atkins in 1929, she attended Memphis public schools, Spelman College, and Middlebury College in Vermont, where she received a master's degree. Beginning in 1957 and continuing through the next several decades, she and her husband, Vasco (a Meharry-trained dentist and a military veteran), reared their family while she served faithfully and tirelessly in leadership capacities at the Memphis branch of the NAACP. Smith was executive secretary of the Memphis branch for more than twenty years. Black Republicans and Democrats worked tirelessly to get black men elected in the city elections of 1959, but they met a crushing disappointment when black voters did not respond as expected. In

March 1960, Smith and the Memphis NAACP shifted their support to local sit-ins by Lemoyne College students who first targeted the segregated public libraries. The national office was not yet on board with sit-in tactics, but it soon bought into the Memphis movement.[35]

Beginning in 1961, Atkins-Smith helped lead the desegregation of local public schools. She and Vasco were among the individuals designated to drive thirteen black children to school on the first day and then to pick them up. When she was involved in the Memphis garbage strike, she was injured and jailed. She was an invited guest at the April 4, 1968, dinner that Martin Luther King Jr., failed to attend. On September 24, 1969, she and the NAACP devised the "Black Monday" protest. Black citizens boycotted the classrooms every Monday until the at-large election process for school-board members was changed to allow black representation in specific districts. After a November 10 march protesting the school-board election process, Ralph Abernathy of the SCLC, Atkins-Smith, Vasco, and other local leaders of the boycott were arrested. When the Black Monday boycott threatened to bankrupt the Memphis public schools (whose state funding depended on per-pupil daily attendance), the school board sued the black leaders for $10 million. Ultimately, however, the board relented. It included two blacks as sitting advisors to the board and agreed to state legislation allowing the election of members by districts. Blacks gained three of nine school-board seats.

In 1971, Atkins-Smith gained election to the board. There, after *Swann v. Charlotte-Mecklenburg Board of Education* (in which the US Supreme Court allowed busing to desegregate public schools), she pushed for busing among Memphis public schools. In the Memphis NAACP annual report for 1971, she said: "The NAACP wants it understood that we are wholeheartedly behind busing. Whites have barred us legally and illegally from certain residential areas by restrictive zoning, by outright exclusion, by violence, and by pricing us out of certain housing markets because of discrimination in employment. . . . Therefore busing white children into black areas and black children into white areas is the only means by which black children can receive quality education. . . . Neighborhood schools have not been accepted in the South, where children have been bused past a nearby school to maintain Jim Crow."[36] Atkins-Smith blasted segregationists, white supremacists, and hypocrites who continued to defy *Brown:* "To set the record straight, we could care less about your children going to school with our children. But as long as you control the public tax dollars, as long as you control the schools; as long as you control the legislature, the judicial and business processes in the state, your past actions indicate that you will short-change . . . our children."[37] By January 22, 1973, Memphis was busing 13,006 students to achieve some racial balance. In response, white families fled the Memphis public schools. By 1978, although the county system remained predominantly white, Memphis public schools were 73 percent black. Smith said, "This we must realize is not the democracy we purport ourselves to be."[38] The school-desegregation suit *Northcross v. Memphis Schools,* US (1961) ended by consent decree in 1984. Subsequently, in the Memphis NAACP Annual Report for 1989, Smith said, "The need for creative and progressive change in our educational delivery becomes more and more persistent."[39]

Maxine Atkins-Smith's efforts went beyond school desegregation and reached into the spheres of economic and employment discrimination. She and Vasco, other leaders, and the NAACP lawyers fought and won a four-year battle to force city officials to desegregate city facilities, including parks, swimming pools, the zoo, the fairgrounds, and the municipal auditorium. *Watson v. Memphis,* US (1964) set a precedent, forcing all Jim Crow cities to desegregate public facilities. In the process, she was again injured, humiliated, and jailed by the police. Nevertheless, she and other leaders persuaded a local bank president to close his bank on Martin Luther King Day.[40] Atkins-Smith and the Memphis NAACP began petitions to force the city's largest employers and national corporations to include local blacks among those they hired, trained, and promoted. She spearheaded efforts to get Dr. W. W. Herenton elected the first black Memphis school superintendent, and in 1991 she helped him become the city's first elected black mayor. The national NAACP named a school desegregation forum in her honor. She was appointed to the Tennessee Board of Regents, which governed several public colleges and universities. One observer said, "We even saw Maxine help reform and refine corporate strategy and marketing." Maxine Atkins-Smith's "thunder has inflamed rivals and inspired supporters . . . made her . . . the most loved and the most despised woman in Memphis. She has been spat on and bowed to, cursed and applauded, called everything from crusader to fiend."[41]

Other black Tennessee women fought also. Viola McFerren, for example, supported her husband, John, in a rural Tennessee civil rights movement. In 1959–61, the McFerrens, who were small farmers in Fayette County, west Tennessee, became leaders in a movement to register rural African Americans to vote. In 1959 the predominantly black Haywood and Fayette Counties had only a few hundred black voters on the rolls. When whites installed and maintained a brutal Jim Crow system, using economic isolation and even lynching to intimidate black citizens, NAACP leaders fled to Chicago and Memphis. Whites owned 75 percent of the land, and they employed blacks as maids, child nurses, tenants, sharecroppers, and day laborers. Haywood and Fayette Counties maintained segregated school systems. Most blacks lived in poverty, and none held elective office. In 1959, John and Viola McFerren, Becky Douglass, June Dowdy, Minnie Jameson, and others started a voter-registration drive in Fayette and Haywood Counties. The McFerrens used their home and a small store they operated to help organize and maintain the County Civic and Welfare League in both counties.

In Fayette and Haywood Counties, the powerful white minority emulated nearby Mississippi, where whites, although they were the minority in many counties, maintained control by means of economic discrimination, constant fear, and terrorism.[42] Black voter registrants were made to stand outside the Fayette and Haywood County courthouses in the hot sun while white employees, without fear of punishment, poured coffee and pepper from the roof. Local law-enforcement authorities and newspapers named leaders of the County Civic and Welfare League the way that runaway slaves had been listed in 1836. John McFerren and others drove to Washington to beg the US Justice Department, Civil Rights Division, to intervene. Then, because they lacked money for a hotel or for food, they immediately returned to Tennessee. By using bogus traffic violations, the sheriff began arresting black people whose names appeared on the list of registered voters. Store owners and banks began denying loans and credit to black customers and farmers. Viola McFerren could buy food and medicine for her baby only by going outside the county—sometimes thirty miles to Memphis. When Ted Poston, an awarding-winning reporter for the *New York Post,* wrote a series of articles that brought the northern press to town, whites became resentful. Their cotton gins refused service to Negro farmers. They cut off gasoline to Negro-owned automobiles and tractors. McFerren and others had to go to Memphis and convince a wholesaler to deliver gas to the McFerren store. The wholesaler agreed provided that the blacks would drive the truck into dangerous Fayette County. When the truck arrived, there was a festive scene as blacks arrived from all over to fill up their cars, trucks, and machines. When Odell Sanders, a black merchant, and his wife, Marge, a beautician, aided voter-registration efforts, they lost customers because their store had no supplies on the shelves. Even so, by 1962 the number of black registered voters in Fayette County had increased significantly. Soon local blacks joined county commissions, school boards, and town councils.[43]

When black citizens began boycotts and Saturday marches in downtown Somerville, the seat of Fayette County, Viola McFerren was among those arrested. On June 11, 1963, President Kennedy addressed the nation, saying that all citizens had civil rights that must be respected and proposing a new civil rights bill to Congress. On August 28, civil rights organizations held a march on Washington to pressure Congress to pass the legislation. Women in Chattanooga, Memphis, and Nashville, including Delores Wilkinson, of the First Colored Baptist Church, helped organize the bus caravans to Washington, and they prepared signs and posters on site. In Washington the male organizers of the march introduced Diane Nash as one of the outstanding women of the civil rights struggle, but no woman was invited as a major speaker. Congress enacted the Civil Rights Act in 1964 and the Voting Rights Act in 1965.[44]

The new civil rights acts revitalized the school-desegregation movement. The US Justice Department intervened in *McFerren and United States v. County Board of Education of Fayette County, Tennessee.* Black students began demonstrations around the courthouse and the white high school, and the whites began boycotting classes. Somebody firebombed the McFerren store, but Viola McFerren continued her leadership activities by going to Washington, DC, with others to obtain federal housing and business grants for local blacks. And she helped organize boycotts of local businesses to gain better treatment and employment of blacks.[45]

In 1967, Dorothy L. Brown became the first black woman elected to the Tennessee General Assembly. A Pennsylvania native, she was a graduate of historically black Bennett College and Meharry Medical College. She established a private practice in Nashville and became the first black woman to practice surgery in the South. In her daily operations, Brown had seen women endure unwanted pregnancies, and she used her political power to address this problem. Her bill to legalize abortions when pregnancy was the consequence of rape or incest and threatened a woman's life drew the opposition of fellow legislators. "The roof fell in when I dropped that bill in the hopper. One of the leaders of the powerful rural bloc in the House came to me and said: 'If you don't withdraw that bill within the next hour, this will be your first and last term.'" The bill was rejected. She left the House in January 1969 when defeated by Avon N. Williams, Jr., for a newly districted senate seat. In 1977 she said, "I am sure, to this day, it was because of the abortion issue." Nevertheless, she continued, "I must 'Run to Live,' and I must seek to serve in as many different areas of endeavor as I can."[46]

Inez Crutchfield of Nashville served the Davidson County Democratic Party for decades. She often used her own resources to attend national meetings to make sure the black voice was heard in Democratic Party circles. She never ran for a larger elective office. Nashville native Mary Frances Berry became a member of the US Commission on Civil Rights after she prepared a preliminary draft of *Constitutional Aspects of the Right to Limit Childbearing* for the commission. In 1975 Berry graduated from Nashville public schools, attended Fisk and Howard universities before completing PhD and JD degrees at other universities. She became a college professor and administrator at notable American universities and published several books. Because she believed that the Commission was the conscience of the nation on civil rights, Berry refused to compromise. When President Ronald Reagan fired her, she sued and won reinstatement.[47]

Lois M. DeBerry, a graduate of LeMoyne College, became one of the most powerful black woman politicians. She and the Tennessee Caucus of Black State Legislators were a vocal force in the continuing civil rights movement in Tennessee. In 1973, DeBerry was elected to the state House of Representatives from Memphis. By 1974 the newly chartered Tennessee Black Caucus offered its first Annual Legislative Retreat at Paris Landing. DeBerry headed the retreat, which was designed to draw hundreds of political leaders, community leaders, and high school and college students to a remote site to discuss a legislative agenda that addressed black concerns and needs. The Sunday morning session ended with various task forces or committees recommending resolutions and bills to be filed at the next General Assembly. The caucus became a civil rights forum in itself by cosponsoring bills to make affirmative-action remedies for discrimination available in Tennessee Chancery Courts, to allow the Tennessee Human Rights Commission to hold hearings on alleged violations of civil rights by policemen, to revise the Tennessee housing-discrimination law to conform with amendments to the federal Fair Housing Act, to establish a Martin Luther King Day Task Force, and to authorize bond issues for facilities to be built at Tennessee State University, the state's public historically black university. The Black Caucus also successfully championed appropriations that aided private HBCUs.

In fact they submitted so many bills that there was a failed attempt by white legislators to impose a rule of no more than nine bills per senator.[48]

By 2004, five judges, ten county commissioners, and thirteen elected school-board members in Tennessee were black women. Mary Mills, a Franklin teacher and school principal and a Williamson County commissioner, worked tirelessly in the fields of black historic preservation and local politics to make certain that African American issues were equally addressed in one of Tennessee's wealthiest counties. Henri Brooks from Memphis served in the House of Representatives for about ten years before moving on to elective office in Memphis-Shelby County. A tough, hard-working legislator, she demanded that black citizens have a proportional voice on Tennessee's capitol hill. She pushed black issues, including the creation of a black granite "Middle Passage" monument commemorating African slaves who lost their lives coming to America via the Atlantic. The monument is on the south side of the state capitol near memorials to former slave owners. White supremacists issued threats against Brooks, and extra security was needed in the legislative sessions.

In May 1968, in an effort to stop white state officials from using discriminatory policies and financial practices to keep Tennessee State University unequal to white public universities, Rita Sanders-Geier, a history instructor at Tennessee A & I, along with fellow black and white plaintiffs filed *Geier v. Governor of Tennessee et al.* In 1977 the federal district judge ordered the precedent-setting merger of predominantly white University of Tennessee at Nashville with Tennessee State University. *Geier v. Governor of Tennessee* was among the first federal court cases to apply *Brown v. Board of Education* to the desegregation of higher education. In Washington, DC, NAACP plaintiffs filed *Adams v. Richardson* against the federal government for failure to enforce provisions of the 1964 Civil Rights Act against Jim Crow states that maintained segregated higher education that was harmful to the public HBCUs. *Adams, Geier,* and other higher-education desegregation cases filed over the next thirty-four years forced the nineteen former Jim Crow states to develop long-range plans to upgrade public HBCUs and desegregate the student body, staffs, and faculty of traditionally white institutions. *Geier* continued through 2004 and in so doing helped dismantle the worst vestiges of Jim Crow higher education in Tennessee. In 2007, when she retired as a lawyer and a federal employee, Rita Geier returned to Tennessee as a distinguished fellow at the University of Tennessee at Knoxville.[49]

In 1991, Rosetta Irvin Miller-Perry continued a strong black newspaper tradition in Tennessee when she became founder, editor, and publisher of the weekly *Tennessee Tribune.* Miller-Perry's *Tribune* headed black newspaper efforts to place civil rights issues before the communities of Tennessee. A native of Pennsylvania, she had worked for the US Civil Rights Commission and the US Equal Employment Commission before settling in Memphis and then Nashville, where she founded the Nashville Black Chamber of Commerce to promote economic issues and businesses in behalf of the African American Community. The *Tennessee Tribune* included issues such as immigration laws that affected Hispanics as well as blacks. Miller-Perry became a member of American History

Makers, which aimed to "provide living proof that African American history did not begin or end with the civil rights movement."[50]

Because Tennessee experienced black enslavement and, following the American Revolution, an intensification of racism against free blacks, a continuous civil rights movement was essential following statehood, and the success of that movement has depended on the sacrifices of black women. As they enlisted in the male-dominated movements between 1865 and the 1990s, African American women became prominent activist leaders. And when male leadership in the African American communities declined (for a variety of cancerous reasons, especially in the core cities), black women had no choice but to assume the leadership. They often did this in desperate efforts to save their communities and especially their men and children. Maxine Smith said:

> My life in the movement has been judged by many over the years, and perhaps the writer who once described me as "Maxine, the most loved and the most hated" got it right. I doubt that most people who hated me for my outspoken and never-ending advocacy for true equality will change their perspective . . . but I hope they will understand more fully what drove me to the lengths I had to go for my people. I was decidedly an activist, and I have no regrets. . . . All around me I see the fruits of the civil rights movement. . . . I know the transformation of Memphis took not only the laudable actions of the core group with whom I labored but also the courage of every Black person who picketed with us, who went to jail with us, who supported us in countless ways; I was only one of many committed to the cause.[51]

Notes

1. Bobby L. Lovett, *The African American History of Nashville, Tennessee, 1780–1830: Elites and Dilemmas* (Fayetteville: University of Arkansas Press, 1999), 1–45, 20. At about that time, several northern states also disfranchised their free black citizens. Regardless of color, women could not vote in Tennessee. Bobby L. Lovett, *The Civil Rights Movement in Tennessee: A Narrative History* (Knoxville: University of Tennessee Press, 2005), 1–345; Linda T. Wynn, "Mary Church Terrell (1863–1954)," in Bobby L. Lovett and Linda T. Wynn, *Profiles of African Americans in Tennessee* (Nashville: Annual Local Conference on Afro American Culture and History, 1996), 128–30.

2. Benjamin Drew, ed., *Refugees from Slavery: Autobiographies of Fugitive Slaves in Canada* (Mineola, N.Y.: Dover Publications, 2004; reprint of 1855 edition), xxvii; Walter T. Durham, *The Underground Railroad in Tennessee to 1865: A Report by the State Historian* (Nashville: Tennessee Historical Society, 2008), 1–85; E. Raymond Evans, *Chattanooga:*

Tennessee's Gateway to the Underground Railroad (Chattanooga, Tenn.: African American Museum, 2005), 1–10; "'Runaway Slave,' *Nashville Republican Banner,* September 9, 1842," in John Hope Franklin and Loren Schweninger, *Runaway Slaves: Rebels on the Plantation* (New York: Oxford University Press, 1999), 151, 177; Ira Berlin, *Many Thousands Gone: The First Two Centuries of Slavery in North America* (Cambridge: Belknap/Harvard University Press, 1998), 265; Lovett, *African American History of Nashville,* 41–45; US Census Bureau, *Preliminary Report to Congress on the Eighth Census, 1860* (Washington, DC: US Census Bureau, 1862), 1–50; Herschel Gower and Jack Allen, eds., *Pen and Sword: The Life and Journals of Randal W. McGavock* (Nashville: Tennessee Historical Commission, 1959), 373, 385, 387.

3. James B. Jones, Jr., *Every Day in Tennessee History* (Winston-Salem, N.C.: John F. Blair, 1996), 50; A. E. and Roberta Church, *The Robert R. Churches of Memphis: A Father and Son Who Achieved* (Ann Arbor, Mich.: Edwards Brothers, 1974), 42; "Mary Church Terrell, 1863–1954, Feminist, Activist," in Roberta Church, Robert Walter, and Charles W. Crawford, eds., *Nineteenth Century Memphis Families of Color 1850–1900* (Memphis: Burkes Book Store, 1987), 90–94; Kenneth W. Goings and G. L. Smith, "'Duty of the Hour': African American Communities in Memphis, 1862–1923," in Carroll Van West, ed., *Tennessee History: The Land, the People, and the Culture* (Knoxville: University of Tennessee Press, 1998), 224–42.

4. Miriam DeCosta-Willis, ed., *The Memphis Diary of Ida B. Wells: An Intimate Portrait of the Activist as a Young Woman* (Boston: Beacon Press, 1995), i–xiii; and Linda T. Wynn, "Ida B. Wells Barnett (1862–1930)," 1232–38, and Alice A. Deck, "Zora Neale Hurston (1891–1960)," 543–48, in Jessie Carney Smith, ed., *Notable Black American Women,* vol. 1 (Detroit: Gale Research, 1992).

5. Wynn, "Ida B. Wells Barnett"; DeCosta-Willis, ed., *The Memphis Diary of Ida B. Wells,* 2, 161.

6. Lester C. Lamon, *Black Tennesseans, 1900–1930* (Knoxville: University of Tennessee Press, 1977), 213; B. L. Lovett, "Nashville: Civic, Literary, and Mutual Aid Associations"; Nina Mjagkij, *Organizing Black America: An Encyclopedia of African American Associations* (New York: Routledge, 2001), 351–54.

7. Mary F. Berry, *My Face Is Black Is True: Callie House and the Struggle for Ex-Slave Reparations* (New York: Knopf, 2005), 1–120; Susan L. Gordon, "'Colored Men's Applications for Pension," in West, ed., *The Tennessee Encyclopedia of History and Culture* (Nashville: Rutledge Hill Press and Tennessee Historical Society, 1998), 191; Pamela Palmer, ed., *The Robert R. Church Family of Memphis: Guide to Papers with Selected Facsimiles of Documents and Photographs* (Memphis: John W. Brister Library and Memphis State University Press, 1979), 9, 1, 22, Carton 2, Folder 1, item 11 on Mary Church Terrell, Douglass 12: 31; Beverly G. Bond and Janann Sherman, *Images of America: Beale Street* (Charleston, S.C.: Arcadia Publishing, 2006), 36, 38; Church, Walter, and Crawford, eds., *Nineteenth Century Memphis Families of Color,* 117.

8. Church, Walter, Crawford, eds., *Nineteenth Century Memphis Families of Color,* 54.

9. All the following profiles are found on the specified pages in Lovett and Wynn, *Profiles of African Americans in Tennessee:* Virginia Edmondson, "J. Frankie Pierce and the Tennessee Vocational School for Colored Girls" (102–103); L. T. Wynn, "Ida B. Wells-Barnett" (137–

38); Roberta Church and Ronald Walter, "Robert Reed Church, Sr." (34–36); Carrie R. Hull and Linda T. Wynn, "Blue Triangle YWCA (1919–1974)" (8–10); L. T. Wynn, "Bethlehem Centers of Nashville" (7–8); and Robert J. Booker, "James Garfield Beck and Ethel Benson Beck" (67–68).

10. Rosalyn Terborg-Penn, *African American Women in the Struggle for the Vote, 1850–1920* (Bloomington: Indiana University Press, 1998), 154–60, 162; Peter J. Ling and Sharon Monteith, *Gender in the Civil Rights Movement* (New Brunswick, N.J.: Rutgers University Press, 1999), 234; Bettye Collier-Thomas and V. P. Franklin, eds., *Sisters in the Struggle: African American Women in the Civil Rights–Black Power Movement* (New York: New York University Press, 2002), 53, 191, 199, 200; Lovett, *The African American History of Nashville,* chap. on politics.

11. NAACP, *Thirty Years of Lynching in the United States, 1889–1918* (New York: NAACP, 1919), 1–120; John Hope Franklin and Alfred A. Moss, Jr., *From Slavery to Freedom: A History of Negro Americans,* 6th ed. (New York, Alfred A. Knopf, 1988), 319–23.

12. Robert A. Hill, ed., *The Marcus Garvey and Universal Negro Improvement Association Papers* (Berkeley: University of California Press): November 1927–August 1940 (1991), 7: 672, 995, 1002; September 1924–December 1927 (1989), 6: 165 (n. 5), xxxix, 578–79, 580–82, 583 (nn. 3, 4), 584–87.

13. Darlene Clark Hine, William C. Hine, and Stanley C. Harrold, *African Americans: A Concise History,* 2nd ed. (Upper Saddle River, N.J.: Prentice Hall, 2005), 372–79.

14. Hasia R. Diner, *A Time for Gathering: The Second Migration, 1820–1880,* vol. 2 in *The Jewish People in America* (Baltimore: Johns Hopkins University Press, 1992), 1–236.

15. Chattanooga *Free Press,* April 16, 1942.

16. Lovett, *Civil Rights Movement in Tennessee,* 17, 41, 58, 136; Carroll Van West, "Columbia Race Riot, 1846," in West, ed., *The Tennessee Encyclopedia,* 191–92.

17. June N. Adamson, "Few Black Voices Heard: The Black Community and the 1956 Desegregation Crisis in Clinton," in Carroll Van West, ed., *Trial and Triumph: Essays in Tennessee's African American History* (Knoxville: University of Tennessee Press, 2002), 334–49.

18. Berry, *My Face Is Black Is True;* Church, Walter, and Crawford, eds., *Nineteenth Century Memphis Families of Color,* 20–25, 90–94; Palmer, ed., *The Robert R. Church Family Papers,* register, Series 5, Sara Roberta Church, Series 10, photographs.

19. Marcia Riggs, ed., *The Kelly Miller Smith Papers* (Jean and Alexander Heard Library, Vanderbilt University, Nashville, Tenn., 1989), register, files on SNCC and Diane Nash; Dale A. Johnson, ed., *Vanderbilt Divinity School: Education, Contest, and Change* (Nashville: Vanderbilt University Press, 2001), 1–130, 234–64.

20. David Halberstam, *The Children* (New York: Fawcett Books, 1998), 1–250.

21. Bobby L. Lovett, "Wilma Glodean Rudolph," *The Scribner Encyclopedia of American Lives: Notable Americans Who Died between 1994 and 1996* (New York: Charles Scribner's Sons, 2001), 4: 469–71.

22. Lovett, *Civil Rights Movement in Tennessee,* 108, 116.

23. Lovett, *Civil Rights Movement in Tennessee,* 116–25.

24. Lovett, *Civil Rights Movement in Tennessee,* 403.

25. David J. Garrow, *Bearing the Cross: Martin Luther King, Jr., and the Southern Christian Leadership Conference* (New York: William Morrow and Co., 1986), 202, 625; Charles

M. Payne, *I've Got the Light of Freedom: The Organizing Tradition and the Mississippi Freedom Struggle* (Berkeley: University of California Press, 1995), 71, 97, 107, 419; Andrew Young, *An Easy Burden: The Civil Rights Movement and the Transformation of America* (New York: Harper Collins Publishers, 1996), 126.

26. John Lewis, *Walking with the Wind: A Memoir of the Movement* (New York: Simon and Schuster, 1998), 172, 185, 91–95, 122, 182, 184–85, 189, 212, 265, 342, 418. Each of the following profiles is found on the specified pages in West, *Trial and Triumph:* Cynthia Griggs Fleming, "White Lunch Counters and Black Consciousness: The Story of the Knoxville Sit-Ins" (367–89); Linda T. Wynn, "Toward a Perfect Democracy: The Struggle of African Americans in Fayette County to Fulfill the Unfulfilled Right of the Franchise" (390–419); and Beverly G. Bond, "Every Duty Incumbent upon Them: African American Women in Nineteenth-Century Memphis" (203–225).

27. John M. Glen, "Highlander Folk School," in West, ed., *The Tennessee Encyclopedia of History and Culture,* 423–25.

28. Manning Marable and Leith Mullings, eds., *Let Nobody Turn Us Around* (Lanham, Md.: Rowman & Littlefield, 2003) 423–25, 175, 190, 197, 312, 359.

29. Vickie L. Crawford, Jacqueline A. Rouse, and Barbara Woods, eds., *Women in the Civil Rights Movement: Trailblazers and Torchbearers, 1941–1965* (Bloomington: Indiana University Press, 1993), 194.

30. Bobby L. Lovett, "Wilma Glodean Rudolph," in Kenneth T. Jackson, ed., *The Scribner Encyclopedia of American Lives, Notable Americans Who Died Between 1994 and 1996* (New York: Charles Scribner's Sons, 2000), 4: 469–71; Mary L. Dudziak, *Cold War Civil Rights: Race and the Image of American Democracy* (New York: Oxford University Press, 2000), 1–250; Dwight Lewis and Susan Thomas, *A Will to Win* (Nashville: Cumberland Press, 1983), 1–120.

31. Lovett, *Civil Rights Movement in Tennessee,* 158–227.

32. Lovett, *Civil Rights Movement in Tennessee,* 158–227.

33. Lovett, *Civil Rights Movement in Tennessee,* 158–227.

34. Arsenault, *Freedom Riders,* 533–87. Nearly half the Freedom Riders were whites, who also suffered harassment

35. Lovett, *Civil Rights Movement in Tennessee,* 90–93, 118, 194–95, 196–98, 202, 214, 216, 221, 227, 285, 290, 331, 345, 353–54, 360–62, 404–5, 431–32, 435, 441, 443.

36. Lovett, *Civil Rights Movement in Tennessee,* 90–93, 118, 194–95, 196–98, 202, 214, 216, 221, 227, 285, 290, 331, 345, 353–54, 360–62, 404–5, 431–32, 435, 441, 443.

37. Lovett, *Civil Rights Movement in Tennessee,* 90–93, 118, 194–95, 196–98, 202, 214, 216, 221, 227, 285, 290, 331, 345, 353–54, 360–62, 404–5, 431–32, 435, 441, 443.

38. Lovett, *Civil Rights Movement in Tennessee,* 63, 85–90, 116–17, 133–45.

39. Lovett, *Civil Rights Movement in Tennessee,* 90–93, 118, 194–95, 196–98, 202, 214, 216, 221, 227, 285, 290, 331, 345, 353–54, 360–62, 404–405, 431–32, 435, 441, 443.

40. Sherry L. Hoppe and Bruce W. Speck, *Maxine Smith's Unwilling Pupils: Lessons Learned in Memphis's Civil Rights Classroom* (Knoxville: University of Tennessee Press, 2007), 232–33.

41. Hoppe and Speck, *Maxine Smith's Unwilling Pupils,* appendices and interviews 242–83; Lamon, *Black Tennesseeans,* 115.

42. David Goldfield, *Still Fighting the Civil War: The American South and Southern History* (Baton Rouge: Louisiana State University Press, 2002), 1–255.

43. Lovett, *Civil Rights Movement*, 278–79.

44. Raye Springfield, *The Legacy of Tamar: Courage and Faith in an African American Family* (Knoxville: University of Tennessee Press, 2000), 155–77; Reavis Mitchell and J. Carney Smith, "Diane Nashville (1938–): Civil Rights Activist, Educator," in Smith, ed., *Notable Black American Women*, 796–800.

45. Lamon, *Blacks in Tennessee*, 86–88; Richard A. Couto, *Lifting the Veil: A Political History of Struggles for Emancipation* (Knoxville: University of Tennessee Press, 1994), 1–202; Springfield, *The Legacy of Tamar*, 1–120; Paul H. Bergeron, Stephen V. Ash, and Jeanette Keith, *Tennesseans and Their History* (Knoxville: University of Tennessee Press, 1999), 310–12; Robert E. Corlew, *Tennessee: A Short History*, 2nd ed. (Knoxville: University of Tennessee Press, 1981), 553, 576–79.

46. Lois L. Dunn, "Dorothy ('D.') Brown," in Smith, ed., *Notable Black American Women*, 1: 114–16; Lovett, *Civil Rights Movement in Tennessee*, 206, 292, 297, 300.

47. G. R. McNeil, "Mary Frances Berry (1938–)," Smith, ed., *Notable Black Women:* 81–86; Kenneth O'Reilly, *Nixon's Piano: Presidents and Racial Politics from Washington to Clinton* (New York: The Free Press, 1995), 372.

48. Lovett, *Civil Rights Movement in Tennessee*, 295–334.

49. Lovett, *Civil Rights Movement in Tennessee*, 371–401.

50. Don Aucoin, "An ambitious project collects the stories of a variety of African-American trailblazers," *Boston Globe*, April 14, 2003, B7.

51. Hope and Speck, *Maxine Smith's Unwilling Pupils*, 232–33.

Selected Bibliography

Bruce A. Glasrud and Merline Pitre

Alexander, Shana. "Visit Bogalusa and You Will Look For Me." *Life* (July 2, 1965): 28.

Allen, Walter R. "The Social and Economic Statuses of Black Women in the United States." *Phylon* 42, no. 1 (March 1981): 26–40.

Anderson-Bricker. "'Triple Jeopardy': Black Women and the Growth of Feminist Consciousness in SNCC, 1964–1975." In *Still Lifting, Still Climbing: Contemporary African-American Women's Activism,* edited by Kimberly Springer, 49–69. New York: New York University Press, 1991.

Babb, Ellen. "'We Took the Leadership Anyway': Women's Social Activism during the Civil Rights Era in St. Petersburg." In *Making Waves: Female Activists in Twentieth-Century Florida,* edited by Jack E. Davis and Kari Frederickson, 293–311. Gainesville: University Press of Florida, 2003.

Baker, Liva. *The Second Battle of New Orleans: The Hundred-Year Struggle to Integrate the Schools.* New York: Harper Collins Publishers, 1996.

Baker, R. Scott. *Paradoxes of Desegregation: African American Struggles for Educational Equity in Charleston, South Carolina, 1926–1972.* Columbia: University of South Carolina Press, 2006.

Barnett, Bernice McNair. "Invisible Southern Black Leaders in the Civil Rights Movement: The Triple Constraints of Gender, Race, and Class." *Gender and Society* 7 (June 1993): 162–82.

Bartley, Melinda. "Southern University Activism, 1960–63, Revisited." Master's thesis, Southern University, 1971.

Bates, Daisy. *The Long Shadow of Little Rock: A Memoir.* Fayetteville: University of Arkansas Press, 1987.

Beil, Gail K. "Four Marshallites' Roles in the Passage of the Civil Rights Act of 1964." *Southwestern Historical Quarterly* 106 (July 2002): 1–14.

Blackwelder, Julia Kirk. "Ladies, Belles, Working Women, and Civil Rights." In *The South for New Southerners,* edited by Paul D. Escott and David R. Goldfield, 94–113. Chapel Hill: University of North Carolina Press, 1991.

Blumberg, Rhoda Lois. "Women in the Civil Rights Movement: Reform or Revolution." *Dialectical Anthropology* 15 (1990): 133–39.

———. "Rediscovering Women Leaders of the Civil Rights Movement." In *Dream and Real-*

ity: *The Modern Black Struggle for Freedom and Equality,* edited by Jeannie Swift, 19–28. Westport, Conn.: Greenwood Press, 1991.

Brandenstein, Sherilyn. "Prominent Roles of Black Womanhood in *Sepia Record,* 1952–1954." Master's thesis, University of Texas at Austin, 1989.

———. "*Sepia Record* as a Forum for Negotiating Women's Roles." In *Women and Texas History: Selected Essays,* edited by Fane Downs and Nancy Baker Jones, 143–57. Austin: Texas State Historical Association, 1993.

Brinkley, Douglas. *Rosa Parks: A Life.* New York: Penguin, 2005.

Brown, Cynthia Stokes, ed. *Ready from Within: Septima Clark and the Civil Rights Movement.* Navarro, Cal.: Wild Tree Press, 1986.

Brown, Millicent Ellison. "Civil Rights Activism in Charleston, South Carolina, 1940–1970." PhD diss., Florida State University, 1997.

Broyles, William. "The Making of Barbara Jordan." *Texas Monthly* 4 (October 1976): 33–47.

Bryan, Dianetta Gail. "Her Story Unsilenced: Black Female Activists in the Civil Rights Movement." *Sage: A Scholarly Journal on Black Women* 2 (Fall 1988): 60–64.

Bryant, Ira B., Jr. *Barbara Charline Jordan: From the Ghetto to the Capitol.* Houston: D. Armstrong Company, 1977.

Buell, Emmette Harold. "The Politics of Frustration: An Analysis of Negro Political Leadership in East Baton Rouge Parish, 1953–1966." Master's thesis, Louisiana State University, 1967.

Burka, Paul. "Major Barbara [Jordan]." *Texas Monthly* 24 (March 1996): 88–89, 110–11.

Burrow, Rachel Northington. "Juanita Craft." Master's thesis, Southern Methodist University, 1994.

Calloway-Thomas, Carolyn, and Thurmon Garner. "Daisy Bates and the Little Rock School Crisis: Forging the Way." *Journal of Black Studies* 26 (May 1996): 616–28.

Cantarow, Ellen, and Susan Gushee O'Malley. "Ella Baker: Organizing for Civil Rights." In *Moving the Mountain: Women Working for Social Change,* edited by Ellen Cantarow, Susan Gusheee O'Malley, and Sharon Hartman Strom. Old Westbury, N.Y.: Feminist Press, 1980.

Chafe, William. *Civilities and Civil Rights: Greensboro, North Carolina, and the Black Struggle for Freedom.* New York: Oxford University Press, 1980.

Chalfen, Michael. "The Way Out May Lead In: The Albany Movement beyond Martin Luther King, Jr." *Georgia Historical Quarterly* 79 (1995): 560–98.

Chappell, Marisa, Jenny Hutchinson, and Brian Ward. "'Dress modestly, neatly . . . as if you were going to church': Respectability, Class, and Gender in the Montgomery Bus Boycott and the Early Civil Rights Movement." In *Gender and the Civil Rights Movement,* edited by Peter J. Ling, and Sharon Monteith, 69–100. New York: Garland Publishing, 1999.

Charron, Katherine Mellen. "We've Come a Long Way: Septima Clark, the Warings, and the Changing Civil Rights Movement." In *Groundwork: Local Black Freedom Movements in America,* edited by Jeanne Theoharis and Komozi Woodard, 116–39. New York: New York University Press, 2005.

Clark, Lottie Montgomery. "Negro Women Leaders of Florida." Master's thesis, Florida State University, 1947.

Clark, Septima Poinsette. *Echo in My Soul.* New York: Dutton, 1962.

Collier-Thomas, Bettye, and V. P. Franklin, eds. *Sisters in the Struggle: African American Women in the Civil-Rights-Black Power Movement.* New York: New York University Press, 2001.

Craft, Juanita. *A Child, the Earth, and a Tree of Many Seasons: The Voice of Juanita Craft.* Dallas: Halifax Publishing, 1982. Ann Fears Crawford and Crystal Sasse Ragsdale. "Congresswoman [Barbara Jordan] from Texas." In *Women in Texas: Their Lives, Their Experiences, Their Accomplishments,* 296–307. Burnet, Tex: Eakin Press, 1982.

Crawford, Vicki L. "We Shall Not Be Moved: Black Female Activists in the Mississippi Civil Rights Movement, 1960–1965." PhD diss., Emory University, 1987.

———. "Grassroots Activists in the Civil Rights Movement." *Sage* 2 (Fall 1988): 24–29.

———. "Beyond the Human Self: Grassroots Activists in the Mississippi Civil Rights Movement." In *Women in the Civil Rights Movement: Trailblazers and Torchbearers, 1941–1965,* edited by Vicki L. Crawford, Jacqueline Anne Rouse, and Barbara Woods, 13–26. Bloomington: Indiana University Press, 1993.

———. "Race, Class, Gender, and Culture: Black Women's Activism in the Mississippi Civil Rights Movement." *Journal of Mississippi History* 58 (Spring 1996): 1–21.

———. "African American Women in the Mississippi Freedom Democratic Party." In *Sisters in the Struggle: African American Women in the Civil Rights-Black Power Movement,* edited by Bettye Collier-Thomas and V. P. Franklin, 121–38. New York: New York University Press, 2001.

———. "Coretta Scott King and the Struggle for Civil and Human Rights: An Enduring Legacy," *Journal of African-American History* 92 (Winter 2007): 106–17.

Crawford, Vicki L., Jacqueline Anne Rouse, and Barbara Woods, eds. *Women in the Civil Rights Movement: Trailblazers and Torchbearers, 1941–1965.* Bloomington: Indiana University Press, 1993.

Crosby, Emilye. "Common Courtesy: The Civil Rights Movement in Claiborne County, Mississippi." PhD diss., Indiana University, 1995.

Curry, Constance, ed. *Deep in Our Hearts: Nine White Women in the Freedom Movement.* Athens: University of Georgia Press, 2000.

Curtin, Mary Ellen. "Reaching for Power: Barbara C. Jordan and Liberals in the Texas Legislature, 1966–1972." *Southwestern Historical Quarterly* 108 (October 2004): 211–31.

Dallard, Shrylee. *Ella Baker: A Leader behind the Scenes.* Morristown, N.J.: Silver Burdett Press, 1990.

Davis, Jack E., and Kari Frederickson, eds. *Making Waves: Female Activists in Twentieth-Century Florida.* Gainesville: University Press of Florida, 2003.

Decker, Stefanie. "Mama, Activist, and Friend: African-American Women in the Civil Rights Movement in Dallas, Texas, 1945–1998." Master's thesis, Oklahoma State University, 1998.

———. "Women in the Civil Rights Movement: Juanita Craft Versus the Dallas Elite." *East Texas Historical Journal* 39.1 (2001): 33–42.

———. "African American Women in the Civil Rights Era, 1954–1974." In *Black Women in Texas History,* edited by Bruce A. Glasrud and Merline Pitre, 159–76. College Station: Texas A&M University Press, 2008.

Deirenfield, Kathleen Murphy. "One 'Desegregated Heart': Sarah Patton Boyle and the Crusade for Civil Rights in Virginia." *Virginia Magazine of History and Biography* 104 (Spring 1996): 251–84.

De Jong, Greta. *A Different Day: African American Struggles for Justice in Rural Louisiana, 1900–1970.* Chapel Hill: University of North Carolina Press, 2002.

Dittmer, John. *Local People: The Struggle for Civil Rights in Mississippi.* Urbana: University of Illinois Press, 1994.

Due, Tananarive, and Patricia Stephens Due. *Freedom in the Family: A Mother-Daughter Memoir of the Fight for Civil Rights.* New York: Ballantine Books, 2003

Dugas, Carroll J. "The Dismantling of De Jure Segregation in Louisiana, 1954–1974." PhD diss., Louisiana State University, 1989.

Dulaney, W. Marvin, ed. *Born to Serve: A History of the Woman's Baptist Educational and Missionary Convention of South Carolina.* Atlanta: Publishing Associates, 2006.

Erenrich, Susie, ed. *Freedom Is a Constant Struggle: An Anthology of the Mississippi Civil Rights Movement.* Montgomery, Alabama: Black Belt Press, 1999.

Evans, Sara. "Women's Consciousness and the Southern Black Movement." *Southern Exposure* 4, no. 4 (Winter 1977): 10–18.

———. *Personal Politics: The Roots of Women's Liberation in the Civil Rights Movement and the New Left.* New York: Knopf, 1979.

Fairclough, Adam. *Race and Democracy: The Civil Rights Struggle in Louisiana, 1915–1972.* Athens: University of Georgia Press, 1995.

Feingold, Miriam. "Chronicling the Movement." *Reviews in American History* (March 1974): 152.

Fields, Mamie Garvin with Karen Fields. *Lemon Swamp and Other Places: A Carolina Memoir.* New York: Free Press, 1983.

Fleming, Cynthia Griggs. "White Lunch Counters and Black Consciousness: The Story of the Knoxville Sit-Ins." *Tennessee Historical Quarterly* 49 (Spring 1990): 40–52.

———. "Black Women Activists and the Student Nonviolent Coordinating Committee: The Case of Ruby Doris Smith Robinson." *Journal of Women's History* 3 (Winter 1993): 65–81.

———. "'More Than a Lady': Ruby Doris Smith Robinson and Black Women's Leadership in the Student Nonviolent Coordinating Committee." In *Hidden Histories of Women in the New South,* edited by Virginia Bernhard, Betty Brandon, Elizabeth Fox-Genovese, Theda Perdue, and Elizabeth Hayes Turner, 204–23. Columbia: University of Missouri Press, 1994.

———. *Soon We Will Not Cry: The Liberation of Ruby Doris Smith Robinson.* Lanham, Md.: Rowman and Littlefield, 1998.

———. "Black Women and Black Power: The Case of Ruby Doris Smith Robinson and the Student Nonviolent Coordinating Committee." In *Sisters in the Struggle: African American Women in the Civil-Rights-Black Power Movement,* edited by Bettye Collier-Thomas and V. P. Franklin, 197–213. New York: New York University Press, 2001.

———. *In the Shadow of Selma: The Continuing Struggle for Civil Rights in the Rural South.* Lanham, Md.: Rowman and Littlefield, 2004.

Frear, Yvonne. "Juanita Craft and the Struggle to End Segregation in Dallas, 1945–1955." In

Major Problems in Texas History, edited by Cary D. Wintz and Sam W. Haynes, 429–36. Boston: Houghton Mifflin Company, 2002.

———. "Juanita Craft." In *Black Women in America: An Historical Encyclopedia.* 2nd edition, edited by Darlene Clark Hine, 317–18. Brooklyn: Carlson Publishing Company, 2005.

———. "Generation v. Generation: African Americans in Texas Remember the Civil Rights Movement." In *Myth, Meaning and Historical Meaning in Texas,* edited by Greg Cantrell and Elizabeth Hayes Turner. College Station: Texas A&M University Press, 2007.

Frystak, Shannon L. "'With All Deliberate Speed': The Integration of the League of Women Voters of New Orleans, 1953–1963." In *Searching for Their Places: Women in the South across Four Centuries,* edited by Thomas H. Appleton, Jr. and Angela Boswell, 261–83. Columbia: University of Missouri Press, 2003.

———. "Elite White Female Activism and Civil Rights in New Orleans." In *Throwing Off the Cloak of Privilege: White Southern Women Activists in the Civil Rights Era,* edited by Gail S. Murray, 181–203. Gainesville: University Press of Florida, 2004.

———. "'Woke Up This Morning with My Mind on Freedom': Women and the Struggle for Black Equality in Louisiana." PhD diss., University of New Hampshire, 2005.

———. "From Southern Lady to Steel Magnolia: Newcomb Women and the Civil Rights Movement in New Orleans." In *Lives of Learning in a Southern Setting: The Education of Women at Newcomb College,* edited by Susan Tucker and Beth Willinger, 320–33. Baton Rouge: Louisiana State University Press, 2007.

———. "A Dissenting Tradition: Women and the Black Struggle for Equality, 1924–1968." In *Louisiana, Race, and Civil Rights,* edited by Michael S. Martin. Baton Rouge: Louisiana State University Press, 2009.

———. "Katrina and the Social Construction of Race in New Orleans." In *Louisiana, Race, and Civil Rights,* edited by Michael S. Martin. Baton Rouge: Louisiana State University Press, 2009.

———. "Oretha Castle Haley (1933–1987): 'Ain't Gonna Let Nobody Turn Me Around.'" In *Louisiana Women,* edited by Janet Allured, 303–23. Athens: University of Georgia Press 2009.

———. *Our Minds on Freedom: Women and the Struggle for Black Equality in Louisiana, 1924–1967.* Baton Rouge: Louisiana State University Press, 2009.

Garrow, David, ed. *The Walking City: The Montgomery Bus Boycott, 1955–1956.* Brooklyn, N.Y.: Carlson Publishing, 1989.

Germany, Kent B. "Making a New Louisiana: American Liberalism and the Search for the Great Society in New Orleans, 1964–1974." PhD diss., Tulane University, 2001.

Gilliam, Stefanie Lee. See Decker, Stefanie.

Glasrud, Bruce A. "Jim Crow's Emergence in Texas." *American Studies* 15 (1974): 47–60.

———. "Women." *African Americans in the West: A Bibliography of Secondary Sources,* 145–54. Alpine, Tex.: SRSU Center for Big Bend Studies, 1998.

Glasrud, Bruce A., and Laurie Champion. "Women." *Exploring the Afro-Texas Experience: A Bibliography of Secondary Sources about Black Texans,* 161–68. Alpine, Tex.: SRSU Center for Big Bend Studies, 2000.

Glasrud, Bruce A., and Merline Pitre, eds. *Black Women in Texas History.* College Station: Texas A&M University Press, 2008.

Glasrud, Bruce A., and James M. Smallwood, eds. *The African American Experience in Texas: An Anthology.* Lubbock: Texas Tech University Press, 2007.

Gooch, Jane P. "Barbara C. Jordan: Her First Forty Years; a Rhetorical Analysis." Master's thesis, Baylor University, 1977.

Grant, Joanne. *Ella Baker: Freedom Bound.* New York: John Wiley, 1998.

Greene, Christina. "'We'll Take Our Stand': Race, Class, and Gender in the Southern Student Organizing Committee, 1964–1969." In *Hidden Histories of Women in the New South,* edited by Virginia Bernhard, Betty Brandon, Elizabeth Fox-Genovese, Theda Perdue, Elizabeth Hayes Turner, 173–203. Columbia: University of Missouri Press, 1994.

———. *Our Separate Ways: Women and the Black Freedom Movement in Durham, North Carolina.* Chapel Hill: University of North Carolina Press, 2005.

Gyant, LaVern. "African American Women's Contributions to Nonformal Education during the Civil Rights Movement, 1954–1964." EdD diss., Pennsylvania State University, 1990.

———. "Passing the Torch: African American Women in the Civil Rights Movement." *Journal of Black Studies* 26 (May 1996): 629–47.

Gyant, LaVern, and Deborah Atwater. "Septima Clark's Rhetorical and Ethnic Legacy: Her Message of Citizenship in the Civil Rights Movement." *Journal of Black Studies* 26 (May 1996): 577–92.

Haines, Herbert H. *Black Radicals and the Civil Rights Mainstream, 1954–1970.* Austin: University of Texas Press, 1988.

Harrison, Alisa Y. "'Ain't Gonna Let Nobody Turn Me Round': The Southwest Georgia Freedom Movement and the Politics of Empowerment." Master's thesis, University of British Columbia, 2001.

———. "Women's and Girls' Activism in 1960s Southwest Georgia: Rethinking History and Historiography." In *Women Shaping the South: Creating and Confronting Change,* edited by Angela Boswell and Judith N. McArthur, 229–58. Columbia: University of Missouri Press, 2006.

Hill, Lance. *The Deacons for Defense: Armed Resistance and the Civil Rights Movement.* Chapel Hill: University of North Carolina Press, 2004.

Hill, Robert A., ed. *The Marcus and Universal Negro Improvement Association Papers.* 7 vols. Berkeley: University of California Press, 1990.

Hirsch, Arnold R. "Simply a Matter of Black and White: The Transformation of Race and Politics in Twentieth-Century New Orleans." In *Creole New Orleans: Race and Americanization,* edited by Arnold Hirsch and Joseph Logsdon, 262–319. Baton Rouge: Louisiana State University Press, 1992.

Hoffman, Edwin D. "Genesis of the Modern Movement for Equal Rights in South Carolina, 1930–1939." *Journal of Negro History* 44 (October 1959): 346–69.

Inger, Morton. "The New Orleans School Crisis of 1960." In *Southern Businessmen and School Desegregation,* edited by Elizabeth Jacoway and David R. Colburn, 82–97. Baton Rouge: Louisiana State University Press, 1982.

Jeffries, Hasan Kwame. "Organizing for More Than the Vote: The Political Radicalization of Local People in Lowndes County, Alabama, 1965–1966." In *Groundwork: Local Black Freedom Movements in America,* edited by Jeanne Theoharis and Komozi Woodard, 140–64. New York: New York University Press, 2005.

Johnson, Ben F., III. *Arkansas in Modern America, 1930–1999.* Fayetteville: University of Arkansas Press, 2000.

Johnson, Joan Marie. "'Drill Into Us the Rebel Traditions': The Contest over Southern Identity in Black and White Women's Clubs in South Carolina, 1898–1930." *The Journal of Southern History* 66 (August 2000): 525–62.

Jones, Cherisse R. "Loyal Women of Palmetto: Black Women's Clubs in Charleston, South Carolina, 1916–1965." Master's thesis, College of Charleston, 1997.

Jones, Maxine D. "'Without Compromise or Fear': Florida's African American Female Activists." *Florida Historical Quarterly* 77 (Spring 1999): 475–502.

Jones, Maxine D., and Kevin M. McCarthy. *African Americans in Florida.* Sarasota, Fla.: Pineapple Press, 1993.

Jordan, Barbara, and Shelby Hearon. *Barbara Jordan: A Self-Portrait.* Garden City: Doubleday, 1979.

Kirk, John A. "Daisy Bates, the National Association for the Advancement of Colored People, and the 1957 Little Rock School Crisis: A Gendered Perspective." In *Gender and the Civil Rights Movement,* edited by Peter J. Ling and Sharon Monteith, 17–40. New York: Garland Publishing, 1999.

———. *Redefining the Color Line: Black Activism in Little Rock, Arkansas, 1940–1970.* Gainesville: University Press of Florida, 2002.

Kirk, Rita G. "Barbara Jordan: The Rise of a Black Woman Politician." Master's thesis, University of Arkansas, 1978.

Lau, Peter *F. Democracy Rising: South Carolina and the Fight for Black Equality since 1865.* Lexington: The University Press of Kentucky, 2006.

Lee, Chana Kai. *For Freedom's Sake: The Life of Fannie Lou Hamer.* Urbana: University of Illinois Press, 2000.

———. "Anger, Memory, and Personal Power: Fannie Lou Hamer and Civil Rights Leadership." In *Sisters in the Struggle: African American Women in the Civil-Rights-Black Power Movement,* edited by Bettye Collier-Thomas and V. P. Franklin, 139–70. New York: New York University Press, 2001.

Lefever, Harry G. *Undaunted by the Fight: Spelman College and the Civil Rights Movement, 1957–1967.* Macon, Ga.: Mercer University Press, 2005.

Lewis, John. *Walking with the Wind: A Memoir of the Movement.* New York: Simon and Schuster, 1998.

Lindsay, Beverly. "The Role of African-American Women in the Civil Rights and Women's Rights Movements in Hinds County and Sunflower County, Mississippi." *Journal of Mississippi History* 53 (August 1991): 229–39.

———. "African American Women and *Brown:* A Lingering Twilight or Emerging Dawn?" *Journal of Negro Education* 63 (Summer 1994): 430–42.

Ling, Peter J., and Sharon Monteith, eds. "Local Leadership in the Early Civil Rights Movement: The South Carolina Citizenship Education Program of the Highlander Folk School." *The Journal of American Studies 29* (1995): 399–422.

———. "Gender and the Civil Rights Movement." In *Gender and the Civil Rights Movement,* edited by Peter J. Ling and Sharon Monteith, 1–16. New York: Garland Publishing, 1999.

———. *Gender and the Civil Rights Movement.* New York: Garland Publishing, 1999.

Lockett, Raymond J. "A History of Black Leadership and Participation in Local Politics in St. Mary Parish, 1950–1970." Master's thesis, Southern University, 1971.

Lofton, Paul S. "'Calm and Exemplary': Desegregation in Columbia, South Carolina." *Southern Businessmen and Desegregation,* edited by Elizabeth Jacoway and David Colburn. Baton Rouge: Louisiana State University Press, 1982.

Lovett, Bobby L. *The Civil Rights Movement in Tennessee: A Narrative History.* Knoxville: University of Tennessee Press, 2005.

Ludwig, Erik. "Closing in on the 'Plantation': Coalition Building and the Role of Black Women's Grievances in Duke University Labor Disputes, 1965–1968." *Feminist Studies* 25 (Spring 1999): 79–94.

Machtinger, Barbara. "Women and the Freedom Struggle in the Twentieth Century." In *Teaching the American Civil Rights Movement: Freedom's Bittersweet Song,* edited by Julie Buckner Armstrong, Susan Hult Edwards, Houston Bryan Roberson, and Rhonda Y. Williams, 47–54. New York: Routledge, 2002.

McCroskey, Vista. "Barbara Jordan." In *Profiles in Power: Twentieth-Century Texans in Washington,* edited by Kenneth E. Hendrickson, Jr., and Michael L. Collins, 175–95. Arlington Heights, Ill.: Harlan Davidson, 1993.

McFadden, Grace Jordan. "Septima P. Clark and the Struggle for Human Rights." In *Women in the Civil Rights Movement: Trailblazers and Torchbearers, 1941–1965,* edited by Vicki L. Crawford, Jacqueline Rouse, and Barbara Woods, 85–97. Bloomington: Indiana University Press, 1993.

McNeil, Genna Rae. "'Joanne Is You and Joanne Is Me': A Consideration of African American Women and the 'Free Joan Little' Movement, 1974–75." In *Sisters in the Struggle: African American Women in the Civil-Rights-Black Power Movement,* edited by Bettye Collier-Thomas and V. P. Franklin, 259–79. New York: New York University Press, 2001.

McWhorter, Diane. *Carry Me Home: Birmingham, Alabama: The Climatic Battle of the Civil Rights Revolution.* New York: Simon & Schuster, 2001.

Mills, J. Thornton. "Challenge and Response in the Montgomery Bus Boycott of 1955–1956." *Alabama Review* 33 (July 1980): 163–235.

Mills, Kay. *This Little Light of Mine: The Life of Fannie Lou Hamer.* New York: Dutton, 1993.

Morris, Aldon. *The Origins of the Civil Rights Movement: Black Communities Organizing for Change.* New York: Free Press, 1984.

Morris, Tiyi. "Local Women and the Civil Rights Movement in Mississippi: Re-visioning Womanpower Unlimited." In *Groundwork: Local Black Freedom Movements in America,* edited by Jeanne Theoharis and Komozi Woodard, 193–214. New York: New York University Press, 2005.

Moynihan, Daniel Patrick. *The Negro Family: The Case for National Action.* Washington, DC: United States Department of Labor, 1965.

Mueller, Carol. "Ella Baker and the Origins of Participatory Democracy." In *Women in the*

Civil Rights Movement: Trailblazers and Torchbearers, 1941–1965, edited by Vicki L. Crawford, Jacqueline Anne Rouse, and Barbara Woods, 51–70. Bloomington: Indiana University Press, 1993.

Muller, Mary Lee. "New Orleans Public School Desegregation." *Louisiana History* 17 (Winter 1976): 69–88.

Murray, Gail S., ed. *Throwing Off the Cloak of Privilege: White Southern Women Activists in the Civil Rights Era.* Gainesville: University Press of Florida, 2004.

———. "White Privilege, Racial Justice: Women Activists in Memphis." In *Throwing Off the Cloak of Privilege: White Southern Women Activists in the Civil Rights Era,* edited by Gail S. Murray, 204–29. Gainesville: University Press of Florida, 2004.

Murray, Hugh T., Jr. "The Struggle for Civil Rights in New Orleans in 1960: Reflections and Recollections." *Journal of Ethnic Studies* 6 (Spring 1978): 25–41.

Myrick-Harris, Clarissa. "Behind the Scenes: Doris Derby, Denise Nicholas and the Free Southern Theater." In *Women in the Civil Rights Movement: Trailblazers and Torchbearers, 1941–1965,* edited by Vicki L. Crawford, Jacqueline Anne Rouse, and Barbara Woods, 219–32. Bloomington: Indiana University Press, 1993.

———. "Mirror of the Movement: The History of Free Southern Theater as a Microcosm of the Civil Rights and Black Power Movements, 1963–1978." PhD diss., Emory University, 1988.

Nasstrom, Kathryn. "Women, the Civil Rights Movement, and the Politics of Historical Memory in Atlanta, 1946–1973." PhD diss., University of North Carolina, 1993.

———. "Down to Now: Memory, Narrative, and Women's Leadership in the Civil Rights Movement." *Gender and History* 11 (1999): 113–44.

Norrell, Robert I. *Reaping the Whirlwind: The Civil Rights Movement in Tuskegee.* New York: Alfred A. Knopf, 1985.

Oldendorf, Sandra B. "The South Carolina Sea Island Citizenship Schools, 1957–1961." *Women in the Civil Rights Movement: Trailblazers and Torchbearers, 1941–1965,* edited by Vicki L. Crawford, Jacqueline Anne Rouse, and Barbara Woods, 169–82. Bloomington: Indiana University Press, 1993.

Olson, Lynne. *Freedom's Daughters: The Unsung Heroines of the Civil Rights Movement from 1830 to 1970.* New York: Simon and Schuster, 2001.

O'Neill, Stephen. "From the Shadow of Slavery: The Civil Rights Years in Charleston." PhD diss., University of Virginia, 1994.

Parks, Rosa, with Jim Haskins. *Rosa Parks: My Story.* New York: Scholastic, 1992.

Parks, Rosa, with Gregory J. Reed. *Quiet Strength: The Faith, the Hope, and the Heart of a Woman Who Changed a Nation.* Grand Rapids, Mich.: Zondervan Publishing House, 1994.

Payne, Charles M. "Ella Baker and Models of Social Change." *Signs* 14 (1989): 885–99.

———. *I've Got the Light of Freedom: The Organizing Tradition and the Mississippi Freedom Struggle.* Berkeley: University of California Press, 1995.

Phillips, Lela Bond. *The Lena Baker Story.* Atlanta: Wings Publishing, 2001.

Pinsky, Robert. "On 'Eve Tempted By the Serpent' by Defendente Ferrari, and in Memory of Congresswoman Barbara Jordan of Texas." *Salmagundi* 113 (Winter 1997): 174–75.

Pitre, Merline. "Black Houstonians and the 'Separate But Equal' Doctrine: Carter W. Wesley versus Lulu B. White." *The Houston Review* 12.1 (1990): 23–36.

———. "Barbara Charline Jordan." In *Black Women in America: An Historical Encyclopedia,* edited by Darlene Clark Hine, Elsa Barkley Brown, and Rosalyn Terborg-Penn, vol. 1, 658–59. Brooklyn: Carlson Publishing Company, 1993.

———. "White, Lulu Belle Madison." In *The New Handbook of Texas,* edited by Ron Tyler, Douglas E. Barnett, Roy R. Barkley, Penelope C. Anderson, and Mark F. Odintz, vol. 6, 929. Austin: Texas State Historical Association, 1996.

———. *In Struggle against Jim Crow: Lulu B. White and the NAACP, 1900–1957.* College Station: Texas A&M University Press, 1999.

———. "Building and Selling the NAACP: Lulu B. White as an Organizer and Mobilizer." *East Texas Historical Journal* 39 (2001): 22–32.

———. "Lulu B. White, The NAACP, and the Fight against Segregation in Houston." In *Major Problems in Texas History,* edited by Cary D. Wintz and Sam W. Haynes, 419–36. Boston: Houghton Mifflin Company, 2002.

———. "In Retrospect: Darlene Hine's *Black Victory.*" In Darlene Clark Hine, *Black Victory: The Rise and Fall of the White Primary in Texas,* 25–40, rev. ed. Columbia: University of Missouri Press, 2003.

———. "Lulu B. White and the Integration of the University of Texas, 1945–1950." In *African American Women Confront the West, 1600–2000,* edited by Quintard Taylor and Shirley Ann Wilson Moore, 293–308. Norman: University of Oklahoma Press, 2003.

———. "Lulu B. White and the Civil Rights Movement in Houston, Texas, 1939–1957." In *Invisible Texans: Women and Minorities in Texas History,* edited by Donald Willett and Stephen Curley, 192–203. Boston: McGraw Hill, 2005.

———. "Lulu B. White." In *Black Women in America: An Historical Encyclopedia.* 2nd ed., edited by Darlene Clark Hine, vol. 3. Brooklyn: Carlson Publishing Company, 2005.

Pratt, Robert A. "A Promise Unfulfilled: School Desegregation in Richmond, Virginia, 1956–1986." *Virginia Magazine of History and Biography* 99 (October 1991): 415–48.

Pratt, Susan Norma. "We Are Here: Activism among Black El Paso Women (1955–1965)." Master's thesis, University of Texas at El Paso, 2001.

Prestage, Jewel L., and Carolyn Sue Williams." Blacks in Louisiana Politics." In *Louisiana Politics: Festival in a Labyrinth,* edited by James Bolner, 285–317. Baton Rouge: Louisiana State University Press, 1982.

Rabby, Glenda. *The Pain and the Promise: The Struggle for Civil Rights in Tallahassee, Florida.* Athens: University of Georgia Press, 1999.

Randolph, Lewis, and Gayle T. Tate. *Rights for a Season: The Politics of Race, Class, and Gender in Richmond, Virginia.* Knoxville: University of Tennessee Press, 2003.

Ransby, Barbara. "Behind-the-Scenes View of a Behind-the-Scenes Organizer: The Roots of Ella Baker's Political Passions." In *Sisters in the Struggle: African American Women in the Civil Rights–Black Power Movement,* edited by Bettye Collier-Thomas and V. P. Franklin, 42–57. New York: New York University Press, 2001.

———. *Ella Baker and the Black Freedom Movement: A Radical Democratic Vision.* Chapel Hill: University of North Carolina Press, 2003.

Reagon, Bernice Johnson. "Ella's Song." Washington, DC: Songtalk Publishing Co., 1981.

Riley, Glenda. "African Daughters: Black Women in the West." *Montana: The Magazine of Western History* 38 (Spring 1988): 14-27.
———. "African American Women in the West." In *A Place to Grow: Women in the American West,* 43–57, 262–66. Arlington Heights: Harlan Davidson, 1992.
Robinson, Jo Ann Gibson. *The Montgomery Bus Boycott and the Women Who Started It,* edited by David J. Garrow. Knoxville: University of Tennessee Press, 1987.
Robnett, Belinda. "African American Women in the Civil Rights Movement, 1954–1965: Gender Leadership and Micro-Mobilization." *American Journal of Sociology* 101 (1996): 1661–93.
———. *How Long? How Long? African-American Women in the Struggle for Civil Rights.* New York: Oxford University Press, 1997.
———. "Women in the Student Nonviolent Coordinating Committee: Ideology, Organizational Structure, and Leadership." In *Gender and the Civil Rights Movement,* edited by Peter J. Ling and Sharon Monteith, 131–68. New York: Garland Publishing, 1999.
Rogers, Kim Lacy. "Humanity and Desire: Civil Rights Leaders and the Desegregation of New Orleans, 1954–1966." PhD diss., University of Minnesota, 1982.
———. "'You Came Away with Some Courage': Three Lives in the Civil Rights Movement." *Mid-America* 71 (October 1989): 175–94.
———. *Righteous Lives: Narratives of the New Orleans Civil Rights Movement.* New York: New York University Press, 1993.
———. "Life Questions: Memories of Women Civil Rights Leaders." *The Journal of African American History* 87 (Summer 2002): 355–68.
Rogers, Mary Beth. *Barbara Jordan: American Hero.* New York: Bantam Books, 1998.
Rollins, Judith. *All Is Never Said: The Narrative of Odette Harper Hines.* Philadelphia: Temple University Press, 1995.
Rouse, Jacqueline A. "'We Seek to Know . . . in Order to Speak the Truth': Nurturing the Seeds of Discontent—Septima P. Clark and Participatory Leadership." In *Sisters in the Struggle: African American Women in the Civil Rights–Black Power Movement,* edited by Bettye Collier-Thomas and V. P. Franklin, 95–120. New York: New York University Press, 2001.
Sanders, Charles L. "Barbara Jordan: Texan Is a New Power on Capitol Hill." *Ebony* 30 (February 1975): 136–42.
Sartain, Lee. *Invisible Activists: Women of the Louisiana NAACP and the Struggle for Civil Rights, 1915–1945.* Baton Rouge: Louisiana State University Press, 2007.
Scott, John H., and Cleo Scott Brown. *Witness to the Truth: My Struggle for Human Rights in Louisiana.* Columbia: University of South Carolina Press, 2003.
Silver, Christopher, and John V. Moeser. *The Separate City: Black Communities in the Urban South, 1940–1968.* Lexington: University Press of Kentucky, 1995.
Smith, Jessie Carney. *Notable Black American Women.* 3 vols. New York: Gale Research Group, 1992.
Spitzburg, Irving J. *Racial Politics in Little Rock, 1954–1964.* New York: Garland, 1987.
Spritzer, Lorraine, and Jean B. Bergmark. *Grace Towns Hamilton and the Politics of Southern Change.* Athens: University of Georgia Press, 1997.
Sproat, John G. "'Firm Flexibility': Perspectives on Desegregation in South Carolina." In

New Perspectives on Race and Slavery, edited by Stephen E. Maizlish and Robert H. Abzug, 25–47. Lexington: University Press of Kentucky, 1986.

Standley, Anne. "The Role of Black Women in the Civil Rights Movement." In *Women in the Civil Rights Movement: Trailblazers and Torchbearers, 1941–1965,* edited by Vicki L. Crawford, Jacqueline Anne Rouse, and Barbara Woods, 183–202. Bloomington: Indiana University Press, 1993.

Stoper, Emily. *The Student Nonviolent Coordinating Committee: The Growth of Radicalism in a Civil Rights Organization.* Brooklyn: Carlson Publishing Company, 1989.

Strain, Christopher B. "'We Walked Like Men:' The Deacons for Defense and Justice." *Louisiana History* 38 (Winter 1997): 43–62.

Taves, Isabella. "The Mother Who Stood Alone." *Good Housekeeping* (April 1961): 31.

Theoharis, Jeanne, and Komozi Woodard, eds. *Groundwork: Local Black Freedom Movements in America.* New York: New York University Press, 2005.

Thornton, J. Mills, III. "Challenge and Response in the Montgomery Bus Boycott of 1955–1956." *Alabama Review* (July 1980): 163–235.

Tuck, Stephen G. N. *Beyond Atlanta: The Struggle for Racial Equality in Georgia, 1940–1980.* Athens: University of Georgia Press, 2001.

Tyler, Pamela. *Silk Stockings and Ballot Boxes: Women and Politics in New Orleans, 1920–1963.* Athens: University of Georgia Press, 1996.

Umoja, Akinyele K. "Eye for an Eye: The Role of Armed Resistance in the Mississippi Freedom Movement." PhD diss., Emory University, 1996.

Walch, Barbara H. "Sallye B. Mathis and Mary L. Singleton: Black Pioneers on the Jacksonville, Florida City Council." Master's thesis, University of Florida, 1988.

Walker, Melissa. *Down from the Mountaintop: Black Women's Novels in the Wake of the Civil Rights Movement, 1966–1989.* New Haven: Yale University Press, 1991.

Waters, Roderick D. "Gwendolyn Cherry: Educator, Attorney and the First African American Female Legislator in the History of Florida." Master's thesis, Florida State University, 1990.

Webb, Clive. *Fight Against Fear: Southern Jews and the Black Civil Rights Movement.* Athens: University of Georgia Press, 2002.

Wehr, Paul Ernest. "The Sit Down Protest: A Study of a Passive Resistance Movement in North Carolina." Master's thesis, University of North Carolina, 1960.

White, Doris M. "The Louisiana Civil Rights Movement's Pre-Brown Period, 1936–1954." Master's thesis, University of Southwestern Louisiana, 1976.

Whitt, Margaret Earley, ed. *Short Stories of the Civil Rights Movement: An Anthology.* Athens: University of Georgia Press, 2006.

Wieder, Alan. "One Who Stayed: Margaret Conner and the New Orleans School Crisis." *Louisiana History* (Spring 1985): 194–201.

Williams, Cecil. *Out-of-the-Box in Dixie: Cecil Williams' Photography of the South Carolina Events That Changed America.* Orangeburg, S.C.: Cecil J. Williams, 2007.

Winegarten, Ruthe. *Black Texas Women: 150 Years of Trial and Triumph.* Austin: University of Texas Press, 1994.

———. *Black Texas Women: A Sourcebook: Documents, Biographies, Time Line.* Austin: University of Texas Press, 1996.

Woods, Barbara A. "Black Woman Activist in Twentieth Century South Carolina: Modjeska Monteith Simpkins." PhD diss., Emory University, 1978.

———. "Modjeska Simkins and the South Carolina Conference of the NAACP, 1939–1957." In *Women in the Civil Rights Movement: Trailblazers and Torchbearers, 1941–1965*, edited by Vicki L. Crawford, Jacqueline Anne Rouse, and Barbara Woods, 99–120. Bloomington: Indiana University Press, 1993.

Wynn, Linda T. "The Dawning of the Day: The Nashville Sit-Ins, February 13–May 10, 1960." *Tennessee Historical Quarterly* 50 (Spring 1991): 42–54.

———. "Toward a Perfect Democracy: The Struggle of African Americans in Fayette County, Tennessee, to fulfill the Unfulfilled Right of the Franchise." *Tennessee Historical Quarterly* 55 (Fall 1996): 202.

Contributors

Stefanie Decker received her PhD from Oklahoma State University; her dissertation topic was Alabama reformer and activist Virginia Durr. She has published articles on African Americans in the civil rights movement in *East Texas Historical Journal* and in *Black Women in Texas History,* edited by Bruce A. Glasrud and Merline Pitre. She teaches at Amarillo College.

W. Marvin Dulaney is an associate professor of history at the University of Texas at Arlington and former executive director of the Avery Research Center for African American History and Culture at the College of Charleston. He is a co-editor (with Kathleen Underwood) of *Essays on the American Civil Rights Movement* and the author of *Black Police in America.* He is completing a monograph on the history of African Americans in Dallas, Texas.

Caroline S. Emmons is an associate professor of history at Hampden-Sydney College in Hampden-Sydney, Virginia, where she teaches courses on American and African American history. She received her PhD from Florida State University. She has published essays and presented conference papers on Harry T. Moore, Ruby Hurley, and the NAACP in Florida. She is the editor of a collection of essays, forthcoming from ABC-CLIO Press, on the social history of the Cold War and McCarthy eras.

Yvonne Davis Frear is a professor of history at San Jacinto College Central, where she teaches African American history, United States history, and distance-learning classes. Her essays on African Americans in Texas have appeared regionally, nationally, and internationally in *Lone Star Pasts: Memory and History in Texas,* in *Major Problems in Texas History,* and in *Schriftenreihe des Fachberichs Betriebwirtschaft der HTW (Yearbook of the Department of Business Administra-*

tion). She has published several encyclopedia essays and book reviews regarding African American women and Texas history. Her current research examines African American youth and the sit-in movement in Texas.

Shannon L. Frystak is an assistant professor of African American history at East Stroudsburg University of Pennsylvania. She has published numerous essays on the role of women in the Louisiana civil rights movement. Her latest book is *Our Minds on Freedom: Women and the Struggle for Black Equality in Louisiana, 1924–1967.* Her current research looks at African-American women's participation in unions in Louisiana during the 1930s and 1940s. Presently she is serving as executive secretary for the Southern Association of Women Historians.

Bruce A. Glasrud is professor emeritus of history, California State University, East Bay, and retired dean of the School of Arts and Sciences, Sul Ross State University. He resides in San Antonio, Texas. A specialist in the history of blacks in the South and West, Glasrud lectures and writes on black Texans, buffalo soldiers, African Americans on the Great Plains, the civil rights era, and the Harlem Renaissance in the West. He is a Fellow of the Texas State Historical Association, which awarded his (and Merline Pitre's) *Black Women in Texas History* the 2008 Liz Carpenter Award for the best book on Texas women's history.

Dwonna Naomi Goldstone is an associate professor in the Department of Languages and Literature, coordinator of the African American Studies Minor, and associate dean in the College of Arts and Letters at Austin Peay State University in Clarksville, Tennessee. She is the author of *Integrating the Forty Acres: The Fifty-year Struggle for Racial Equality at the University of Texas,* which won the 2006 Coral H. Tullis Memorial Prize for best book on Texas history. She lives in Nashville, Tennessee, with her three dogs—Satchel Paige, Butterfly McQueen, and Charlie Parker.

Maxine D. Jones is professor of history at The Florida State University. She is coauthor (with Joe M. Richardson) of *Talladega College: The First Century* and (with Kevin McCarthy) of *African Americans in Florida.* Jones is also co-author (with Joe M. Richardson) of *Education for Liberation: The American Missionary Association and African Americans, 1890 to the Civil Rights Movement.* The recipient of several teaching awards, she received the Martin Luther King, Jr., Distinguished Scholar Award in 1989 and the Ross Oglesby Award in 1994, both from The Florida State University. The Black Alumni Association chose her as its "Outstanding Faculty Member" in 1994. She served as principal Investigator for the Rosewood Academic Study commissioned by the Florida Legislature and currently is researching blacks in twentieth-century Florida.

Bobby L. Lovett, a native of Memphis, Tennessee, is senior professor of history and former dean of the College of Arts and Sciences at Tennessee State University. He earned M.A. and PhD degrees at the University of Arkansas. Lovett's most recent books include *The African American History of Nashville, 1780–1930: Elites and Dilemmas; The Civil Rights Movement in Tennessee: A Narrative History,* which won the "Tennessee History Book Award"; and *How It Came to Be: The Boyd Family's Contribution to African American Publishing from the 19th to the 21st Century.* Among numerous contributions, he has served two terms on the Editorial Board of the *Arkansas Historical Quarterly.*

Tiyi M. Morris earned a PhD from Purdue University and is an assistant professor in the Department of African American and African Studies at Ohio State University, Newark. She specializes in black women's activism and women's contributions to the civil rights movement. She is the author of a chapter in *Groundwork: The Local Black Freedom Movement in America,* and she provided the foreword to *Black Power in the Belly of the Beast,* edited by Judson L. Jeffries.

Clarissa Myrick-Harris, PhD, is the co-founder of One World Archives, a public history and educational organization based in Atlanta, Georgia. She also is dean of the College of Humanities and Social Sciences and professor of African American studies at Morehouse College. An educator for more than twenty-five years, Myrick-Harris has been on the faculties of the University of Georgia, the University of Cincinnati, Morris Brown College, and Clark Atlanta University. More recently she was a Distinguished Research and Teaching Fellow in the Interdisciplinary Center for the Study of Global Change at the University of Minnesota, Twin Cities. Her research centers on the history of African American institution-building and leadership especially as relates to black women during the civil rights and black power eras. Her writings have appeared in scholarly and general-interest publications such as *Word: A Black Culture Journal* and *Smithsonian Magazine.* In addition she has written chapters for collected volumes such as Vicki Crawford et al., *Women of the Civil Rights Movement: Trailblazers and Torchbearers.* She is co-authoring a book on the history of the Atlanta Medical Association, an organization established in 1893 by African American medical professionals that played a role in the civil rights movement.

Merline Pitre is professor of history and former dean of the College of Liberal Arts and Behavioral Sciences, at Texas Southern University. She is the author of *Through Many Dangers, Toils and Snares: The Black Leadership of Texas, 1868–1900,* and *In Struggle against Jim Crow: Lulu B. White and the NAACP, 1900–1957.* A fellow of the Texas State Historical Association, Pitre also is president of that body, which awarded her (and Bruce Glasrud's) *Black Women in Texas History* the 2008 Liz Carpenter Award for the best book on Texas women's history.

Jeannie M. Whayne is professor of history at the University of Arkansas and adjunct curator of American history at the Crystal Bridges Museum in Rogers, Arkansas. She is author, editor, or co-author of eight books and of many articles in scholarly publications. Raised in northeastern Arkansas during the 1950s and 1960s, Whayne witnessed the transformation that prompted her lifelong absorption in the history of twentieth-century plantation agriculture and race relations. The Southern Tenant Farmers Union was founded near her hometown, and her first book placed the creation of that interracial union in the context of regional history. She is finishing a book on a sixty-thousand-acre Arkansas plantation, and she is initiating an environmental study of the lower Mississippi River Valley.

Index